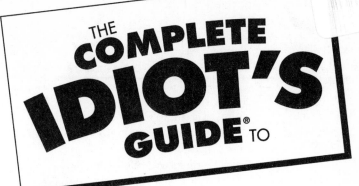

THE COMPLETE IDIOT'S GUIDE® TO

Ventriloquism

by Taylor Mason

ALPHA

A member of Penguin Group (USA) Inc.

ALPHA BOOKS

Published by the Penguin Group

Penguin Group (USA) Inc., 375 Hudson Street, New York, New York 10014, USA

Penguin Group (Canada), 90 Eglinton Avenue East, Suite 700, Toronto, Ontario M4P 2Y3, Canada (a division of Pearson Penguin Canada Inc.)

Penguin Books Ltd., 80 Strand, London WC2R 0RL, England

Penguin Ireland, 25 St. Stephen's Green, Dublin 2, Ireland (a division of Penguin Books Ltd.)

Penguin Group (Australia), 250 Camberwell Road, Camberwell, Victoria 3124, Australia (a division of Pearson Australia Group Pty. Ltd.)

Penguin Books India Pvt. Ltd., 11 Community Centre, Panchsheel Park, New Delhi—110 017, India

Penguin Group (NZ), 67 Apollo Drive, Rosedale, North Shore, Auckland 1311, New Zealand (a division of Pearson New Zealand Ltd.)

Penguin Books (South Africa) (Pty.) Ltd., 24 Sturdee Avenue, Rosebank, Johannesburg 2196, South Africa

Penguin Books Ltd., Registered Offices: 80 Strand, London WC2R 0RL, England

International Standard Book Number: 978-1-61564-000-3
Library of Congress Catalog Card Number: 2009938583

12   11   10   8   7   6   5   4   3   2   1

Interpretation of the printing code: The rightmost number of the first series of numbers is the year of the book's printing; the rightmost number of the second series of numbers is the number of the book's printing. For example, a printing code of 10-1 shows that the first printing occurred in 2010.

Printed in the United States of America

Publisher: *Marie Butler-Knight*
Editorial Director: *Mike Sanders*
Senior Managing Editor: *Billy Fields*
Executive Editor: *Randy Ladenheim-Gil*
Production Editor: *Kayla Dugger*
Copy Editor: *Christine Hackerd*

Cover Designer: *Kurt Owens*
Book Designer: *Trina Wurst*
Indexer: *Angie Bess Martin*
Layout: *Ayanna Lacey*
Proofreader: *John Etchison*

Contents at a Glance

Contents

Introduction

The book you hold in your hands is the most comprehensive, thorough, and complete how-to book ever written about ventriloquism, an art form that's made a significant comeback since the beginning of this century. In the following pages, I cover everything any fledgling ventriloquist—or "vent"—needs to learn the techniques and methods of this age-old art form. From talking without moving your lips, to creating interesting characters and voices, to writing the jokes and material that make up a solid performance, I cover it all here.

As you'll learn in this book, there are three keys to great ventriloquism:

1. A cleverly built figure

2. Great material, whether it's jokes or music

3. Brilliantly flawless technique

The Complete Idiot's Guide to Ventriloquism delves into each of these three categories with complete and comprehensive training exercises, coaching tips, and straightforward instruction. As you read, you're encouraged to enjoy the process, moving from how to pronounce words without any lip movement, to creating a character, to bringing it to life through a ventriloquist figure, to writing jokes for a comedy script.

Once you've accomplished those goals and reached the point where it's time to get onstage, I don't abandon you. In Part 5, I share insider information on getting an audition, finding all-important stage time, working with booking agents, and promoting your act. What's more, I give you some of the best advice and information on performing, finding a niche, and even working for children that I've learned along the way.

Ventriloquism is about having fun and making others enjoy themselves, too. If you follow the instructions I've given in this book and throw yourself into the practice methods and course work I suggest, I have no doubt you'll become a terrific ventriloquist. Good luck!

How to Use This Book

The Complete Idiot's Guide to Ventriloquism is divided into five parts:

Part 1, "Ventriloquism Basics," offers a brief history of the art to illustrate why it's so popular with so many people. Then we move on to what you need to think about before you get started.

Part 2, "Talking Without Lip Movement," dives into the nuts and bolts of the craft, including how the human voice is made and why this works for the ventriloquist. It also explains how to re-create those sounds that require lip movement and how to build a voice for your figure.

Part 3, "Working With the Ventriloquist Figure," starts with a discussion of the different kinds of figures and puppets available and helps you decide on the best one for you. Also included are suggestions for practicing body movement for the figure and creating a reality between you and the figure via simple things like eye contact and reactions, the same way an acting coach would teach fledgling thespians.

If you're going to work as a ventriloquist and get paid, you have to be a great comedian or a great singer or both. That's where **Part 4, "Creating Material,"** can help. Part 4 is a course in writing setups and punch lines for your act, complete with information on how to find the funny stuff and get it into dialogue format. There's even a short course on memorization and a final figure manipulation lesson.

Part 5, "Ready for Prime Time," closes the book with six chapters dedicated to the kinds of jobs and venues a ventriloquist might work, tips for working with agents and bookers, what a ventriloquist can expect to get (or *not* get) paid, and how to stage an act and interact with audiences of all kinds.

At the back of the book I've included a glossary to help you with unfamiliar terms and a resources section to help you further your ventriloquist pursuit.

Extras

Throughout the book you'll find extra bits of information in sidebars. Here's what to look for:

Pull Strings

Here you'll find tips that help you succeed in ventriloquism.

def•i•ni•tion

Check these boxes for terms and explanations related to ventriloquism.

Suitcases

These boxes contain fun facts and other bits of information you'll enjoy.

Hiccups

Don't skip these warning sidebars! You need to know this stuff to avoid falling flat on your face.

Acknowledgments

I've been writing and performing my version of comedy, music, and ventriloquism for my entire professional life, and I plan on continuing to do so until the day audiences stop laughing and enjoying what I do onstage. To have that kind of long career means I've had incredible support. My wife, Marsia, and my sons, Hank and Rett, have followed me across the country and around the world, and they've always given me grace and time to do this crazy business we call "show."

My parents, Bill and Patricia Mason, gave me their blessing to follow my dream while I was still in college. My Aunt Ardie, Uncle Gene Baroni, Uncle Art, Uncle Phil, brother Tony, many cousins, and brother Locke have all followed and rooted for me for many years.

Both the University of Illinois and Northwestern University, where I was taught how to work hard toward goals and write (somewhat) coherently, have my everlasting thanks.

Edgar Bergen and Shari Lewis were amazing ventriloquists who I tried, vainly, to follow. The Second City Theater and Zanies Comedy Club in Chicago were great places to learn the craft of making people laugh, and I thank Bernie, Rick, Bert, Brian, and everyone there for those wonderful years. Joey Edmonds is the best agent I could ever have. Bill Gaither is the best boss I will ever work for, as well as being one of the most brilliantly funny people on Earth (he's not a bad songwriter, either). I would not have had the opportunity to write this book without the efforts of Tim Grable and Jonathan Clements. Thank you.

Years ago I wrote down some 50 life goals. I've accomplished many (although not exactly as I pictured them). To Alpha Books, Randy Ladenheim-Gil, and Katelynn Lacopo, a sincere thanks for this amazing opportunity to cross off another of my life goals.

To you, the reader and future ventriloquist: I'd be honored to be your opening act someday down the road. Thank you for buying this book!

Trademarks

All terms mentioned in this book that are known to be or are suspected of being trademarks or service marks have been appropriately capitalized. Alpha Books and Penguin Group (USA) Inc. cannot attest to the accuracy of this information. Use of a term in this book should not be regarded as affecting the validity of any trademark or service mark.

Part 1

Ventriloquism Basics

Part 1 is an introduction to the ventriloquism profession. You'll discover how ventriloquism started as a spiritual/religious phenomenon and slowly worked its way into the mainstream as a performance art, similar to music or theater. Ventriloquism differs from puppetry in that ventriloquism, or "vent," depends on human interaction with the figure. A great ventriloquist routine requires an original and clever figure, great material, and the kind of flawless technique that makes it look effortless.

Part 1 outlines the tools you'll need to be successful and gives you a focused plan: how to handle practice sessions, what you need (a mirror, for example), and how to program yourself for success.

Chapter 1

Ventriloquism as Performing Art

In This Chapter

- ◆ Ventriloquism then and now
- ◆ How and why ventriloquism works as entertainment
- ◆ Some thoughts on how to practice
- ◆ Tips for setting your ventriloquism goals

Ventriloquism as a performing art dates back to the beginning of time, when man began using his voice to communicate. The first ventriloquists were deemed to have a special ability, and you will be using many of the same techniques today. Yes, it's almost like having your own superpower! Please use it for good, not evil!

This chapter gives you a look at ventriloquism's past, shows you why it still works as great entertainment, and clues you in to the things that make quality ventriloquists so sought after. I also share keys to success, tips on how to practice, and tools you need to become proficient as quickly as possible.

So relax and settle in—this is going to be fun!

A Brief History of Ventriloquism

Originally thought to be a divine power that was bequeathed to a select few, ventriloquism began as a part of religious and spiritual ceremonies. In a time before radio waves and loudspeakers and headphones, sound took on special meaning in all parts of life. The man or woman who could manipulate sound, or make it appear to come from someplace other than the speaker, was thought to have an extraordinary gift, and unexplained or mysterious sound took on deep meaning.

Ventriloquism in the Bible

Just how old is ventriloquism? Since the beginning of time people have used misdirection, deception, and hoaxes to trick others into giving up money and/or power. In the beginning, practitioners of ventriloquism were soothsayers and wizards or spiritual communicators. One career that relied heavily on ventriloquism was the necromancer.

Necromancy is divination through communication with the dead. From the practice of talking to the dead to tell the future came the art of ventriloquism. ("Talking to the dead" can sometimes refer to a late-night comedy club audience, but I digress.) The ancient ventriloquist often had no puppet to use, so he spoke with ghosts or the spirits of those who had died, evoking sounds from thin air, from nearby objects, or from the ground.

Ventriloquism is even mentioned in the Bible. The best biblical example comes from 1 Samuel 28:7, the story of a meeting between King Saul and the female necromancer at Endor. According to the legend, Saul was being threatened by Philistine armies, and his prayers for aid were not being answered. In desperation, he orders his servants to find a person who can talk to the dead (a necromancer) or foresee the future: "Then Saul said to his servants, 'Seek out for me a woman who is a medium, that I may go to her and inquire of her.' And his servants said to him, 'Behold, there is a medium at Endor.'" So Saul headed off to some small town and contacted the medium (a.k.a., "The Witch of Endor"), who panicked because at that time necromancy was punishable by death. Saul assured her he wouldn't kill her and commanded her to help him. The witch claimed to see a man down a hole, coming up out of the ground, and Saul believed it to be his deceased brother Samuel.

There's still ongoing debate as to whether the necromancer actually saw Samuel coming out of the ground, and if in fact Samuel made those predictions. Perhaps she was a great ventriloquist!

> **Suitcases**
>
> The word *ventriloquist* comes from the Latin *ventiloquus*, which means "belly speaker." Makes sense, because the skill of ventriloquism is not so much in throwing the voice, but rather in using the diaphragm and then *controlling* the voice. In the same vein, the ancient Greeks referred to ventriloquists as "engastrimanteis" (belly prophets), and the performers were called "eurycleides," named for the most celebrated of all Greek ventriloquists, Eurycles.

Ventriloquism Evolves

Throughout the Middle Ages, ventriloquism was considered part of the occult—something Satanic. Practitioners were often killed because they were considered witches. It wasn't until the late seventeenth and early eighteenth centuries that ventriloquism became an entertainment form, found in kings' courts and at rural fairs.

At music halls and theaters in London, performers began using ventriloquism as part of their music and magic acts. Sometime around the year 1750, Austrian ventriloquist Baron von Mengen began using a small doll that had a moving mouth, forever linking puppetry and ventriloquism.

In 1772, Abbe de la Chappelle wrote the first book dealing with ventriloquism as something other than a spiritual matter. Chappelle explained that the ventriloquist doesn't really "speak from the stomach," but rather mutes and diffuses sound. Although it was published at a time when ventriloquism wasn't yet considered an art, *Le Ventriloque ou L'Engastrymythe* (*The Ventriloquist or Belly Speaker*) was the ventriloquists' main reference for many years.

By the end of the 1800s, practitioners made dolls (or "automatons," as they were then called) the focus of their performances. Often the professional ventriloquist named his or her puppets as if they were actors in a play, touting the characters in the playbills or advertisements posted outside theaters, halls, and other establishments. By the turn of the century, money-making opportunities for ventriloquists existed all over Europe and the United States.

Ventriloquism in the Twentieth Century

When vaudeville became popular sometime in the 1920s, hundreds of professional ventriloquists were ready and waiting for their turn to perform on the circuit. When radio and motion pictures came along, sounding the death knell for vaudeville, it heralded the beginning of a career for the world's most famous ventriloquist team.

> **Suitcases**
>
> Every ventriloquist refers to his or her figure differently. Some use names; others use terms such as *character, dummy, puppet, prop, partner,* or *sidekick.* The universally accepted term is *character,* but for this book, I use *figure* to define your puppet or dummy. (I use *character* for a different function later in the book.)

Edgar Bergen and Charlie McCarthy are, to this day, iconic figures in American entertainment history. Born in Chicago in 1902, and inspired by *Hermann's Wizard Annual,* a publication that provided a crash course in "the arts" for 25 cents, Bergen decided to pursue ventriloquism as a vocation. In 1922, he sketched a figure modeled after an Irish schoolboy who sold newspapers near his school. He took the drawing to a Chicago woodcarver named Theodore Mack, who charged $35 to chisel out a mouth-moving head. Bergen made a body, attached the head, and christened the figure "Charlie Mack." (He later changed his last name to McCarthy.)

After playing successfully on vaudeville's Chautauqua Circuit, Bergen toured Europe, returned to the states, moved his act into nightclubs, and re-invented himself. Bergen and McCarthy both wore identical top hats and tails—Charlie with an ever-present monocle over one eye—and after wowing New York audiences for a couple months, the duo began performing weekly on national radio broadcasts. Their spitfire, joke-intensive dialogue was perfect for keeping listeners glued to the radio sets. Bergen's character and voice came across as wise, compassionate, and fatherly. Charlie cooed, whined, and made wisecracks (often improvised!), giving listeners the perception there were two distinct personalities on the air. Amazing that a ventriloquist was the most popular and most listened-to program on the radio. Did he move his lips? Could he make a *B* sound without using his lips? It didn't matter—*he was on the radio!*

The two of them had an almost magical career: movies, TV shows, a daughter who became a world-renowned comic actress (Candace Bergen), and the kind of legacy any celebrity would love. Edgar Bergen passed away in 1978 at the age of 75, after 56 years in show business.

As the 1950s and 1960s brought television into the American living room, ventriloquists followed suit. Paul Winchell was the first of the TV ventriloquists. His two figures, Jerry Mahoney and Knucklehead Smith, were household names in the early days of TV. Jimmy Nelson and his dog Farfel are still remembered for his popular Nestlé's TV commercial, in which Nelson sang, "N-E-S-T-L-É-S, Nestlé's makes the very best ..." and Farfel sang in a low, off-key voice: "Chocolate." Shari Lewis had one of the most popular children's TV shows in history with her sock characters, Lamb Chop, Charlie Horse, and Hush Puppy.

By the 1970s, ventriloquism had become a kind of parody, and the art was no longer considered hip or exciting. Bergen's quick-witted comedy had been on the cutting edge of show business 40 years earlier, but it paled in comparison to Richard Pryor's and George Carlin's comedy routines in the 1970s. By that time, ventriloquism appeared antiquated and old-fashioned, especially when compared to newer, sitcom-style comedies such as *All in the Family* and *Saturday Night Live*. The hit show *Soap*, for example, featured a talented young ventriloquist named Jay Johnson. The program had a healthy sense of irony about it, and the cast treated Jay and his wooden sidekick as if both were real. It made for great humor and memorable sketches, while branding ventriloquism a little weird and out of date.

> **Suitcases**
>
> The original Charlie McCarthy figure now sits prominently in the Smithsonian Institute in Washington, D.C.

Movies and TV programs often depicted the ventriloquist as somewhat crazy, if not psychotic, and there were fewer and fewer calls for vent acts to perform on TV and in major theatrical and showbiz venues. Coupled with the fact that the variety show—a perfect vehicle for ventriloquism—could no longer be found on TV, this decline in interest meant ventriloquism became that saddest of all entertainments: the lost art.

Things changed with the explosion of comedy clubs in the late 1980s. With the need for acts to fill stages and please ever-increasing audiences, ventriloquism began making a comeback. With cable-TV comedy shows and networks like Comedy Central on the rise, ventriloquists became more than children's birthday party acts.

Ventriloquism Today

Today you can find ventriloquists working cruise ships—not just as filler but as the most popular and sought-after performers. Showbiz meccas like Las Vegas and Atlantic City are home to some of the best in the business.

Ventriloquist and *polyphonist* Ronn Lucas (he can make anything talk!) has been wowing Vegas crowds for years. The aforementioned Jay Johnson has won awards in New York City and London for his brilliant theatrical show, *The Two and Only*. David Strassman, a popular Los Angeles act, hosted his own variety show in Australia, in which he featured his ventriloquist act. Terry Fator won the popular *America's Got Talent* TV program and now sells out his own theater in Las Vegas.

def•i•ni•tion

A **polyphonist** is someone who is proficient in the art of multiplying sounds or mimicking numerous sounds.

Suitcases

Vent Haven Museum is the only museum dedicated to the art of ventriloquism. Located in Fort Mitchell, Kentucky, Vent Haven also hosts the "ConVENTion," a yearly gathering of professional and amateur ventriloquists.

Perhaps the most popular ventriloquist of the day, Jeff Dunham, is a YouTube sensation with his "Achmed the Dead Terrorist" routine, which has been viewed more than 5 million times! Jeff can be seen regularly on Comedy Central, *The Tonight Show*, and his popular DVDs, and he sells out large arenas across the nation.

There are more puppet builders, more opportunities, more venues, and more ways for ventriloquists to find employment than ever before. This truly is a new golden age of ventriloquism. Clubs and organizations are dedicated to improvement and networking for ventriloquists. And whatever qualms agents and bookers had about using ventriloquists is now gone.

Why Ventriloquism Works

Ventriloquism is more than talking without moving your lips. It's more than having a figure on your knee who says funny things, sings a song, or insults audience members. Ventriloquism is fun, entertaining, and magical because of the relationship between the ventriloquist and his or her figure.

A really good ventriloquist forms a relationship with this inanimate object. It's much more than reeling off punch lines (although it's really good to have lots of punch lines). Ventriloquism is about the same things that make up good theater, situation comedies, and movies: relationships between the actors, story, and punch lines (or well-performed songs and music). I'm not just talking about the way the ventriloquist and his or her figure interact and work together. It's also about how the audience sees and perceives the ventriloquist and the figure onstage. How do each act and react to what the other is saying? And how do the performers interact with the audience?

The ventriloquist offers every audience, of every age and every kind of background, a peek into complete fantasy. This should be a magical event for the viewers because they're getting to see and experience something that just shouldn't be: a puppet that can talk, feel, and have opinions, reactions, and emotions. It's a total crossover into another world. Some of the most popular TV programs and movies deal with total fantasy, dependent upon special effects and staging to bring imagination to life. A ventriloquist taps into that same kind of dynamic with nothing but his figure and his skills. Not only do audiences appreciate the ventriloquist's abilities, but if it's performed with expertise and flair, they buy into it immediately.

There are, of course, those who will always maintain that ventriloquism is dead, that it has no place on the modern stage, and that it's kind of a sad stereotype. The truth is the exact opposite. People love to buy into the craft, talent, and cleverness that ventriloquism requires. The well-rehearsed and professionally executed ventriloquist act takes audiences on a trip into their imaginations. There's no other act like it, and when done well, there's no finer accomplishment than wowing a crowd with a perfectly performed vent routine.

The Keys to Ventriloquism

There are three basic requisites that make up a truly great ventriloquist act:

- A clever figure
- Flawless technique
- Great material

Having one of the three will probably get you a booking here and there, and might even get you some steady work. Having two would probably mean some kind of small-time career or at least regular employment as a ventriloquist. But if you take the time to perfect all three, and commit yourself to achieving all three keys to ventriloquism, you are destined to have a long, fruitful career as a professional.

Your Ventriloquist Figure

The figure is the least-important key. Many ventriloquists—particularly beginners—believe they need an expensive, hand-crafted, visually appealing figure to win over audiences and booking agents. The truth is that anything can work as a ventriloquist figure, as long as it's done with originality and some thought.

There are stereotyped figures, of course—the cheeky little boy, the crying baby, and the old man—but even these can be made unique and clever. One-of-a-kind puppets—a unicorn, a politician look-alike, or a larger-than-life polar bear puppet—will immediately grab the audience's attention.

But you need more than the visually striking figure to truly excel at ventriloquism.

Technique Is Everything

When I talk about technique, I'm first referring to lip control. But technique, and especially flawless technique, goes much further.

Technique refers to how the ventriloquist manipulates the figure. Technique is the reaction the figure has to audience laughter, the ventriloquist's set-up lines, and the moment at hand. Technique is a raised eyebrow, a turn of the head, a nod at the right time, or just the physical relationship between ventriloquist and character.

Make the Most of Your Material

What separates the good ventriloquist from the great ventriloquist comes down to this: writing and performing great comedy (or beautiful music). In the end, a ventriloquist can probably get away with a generic figure and average technique if his material is knock-down, drag-out funny (or if he performs inspiringly great music).

> **Hiccups**
>
> The audience won't recognize flawless technique (unless you want them to), but they will recognize *flawed* technique.

If you ever go to a ventriloquist convention, you'll find that comedy writers' seminars have the largest audiences. Comedy writers are also doing the most business. Proof that it really comes down to the writing.

Getting Started Practicing

You've heard it before: practice makes perfect. With ventriloquism, this is especially true. You're going to need some basics to start practicing your newfound art. Most of this stuff can be found in your home, and you shouldn't have to spend too much to get started.

First, you need a room with a mirror. If you have a floor-to-ceiling mirror, that's a big help, but it's not necessary. The mirror has to be big enough that you can clearly see both your face and your figure. You won't be practicing for long periods of time, especially at the beginning, so standing is fine if that's what your mirror requires you to do.

You'll also want a small recording device. It can be any kind of voice recorder, such as your cell phone's voice memo feature. You're going to want to hear the voice and sounds you come up with for your figure.

Your figure can be anything you'd like it to be. You can use a sock puppet—literally, you can make a puppet from an old sock if you like! You're not going to be performing for the public for a few weeks, so what you use to practice with in the beginning is inconsequential. Naturally, as we get further into the nuts and bolts of ventriloquism, you're going to want to make a commitment to some kind of figure you'll use for performance. If you already have your figure picked out and available, that's great! If not, don't worry. I talk about figures and where to get them later.

Have a glass of water in the practice area. No, we're not going to work on the "drinking a glass of water while the figure sings" bit. That's an advanced trick, and you're not there just yet. This water is for drinking. You'll get thirsty as you practice, so having a glass of water handy will save you an interruption that could cause you to lose momentum and concentration.

> ### Suitcases
>
> Not to burst your bubble, but the routine in which the ventriloquist drinks a glass of water while his or her figure talks or sings is a trick! The glass is actually two glasses—one within the other—and a small hole in one sucks in the water as the ventriloquist raises the glasses to his or her lips. The water goes into a chamber between the two glasses, from the inner glass to the outer. The vent only drinks a tiny bit, which he or she swallows at the end of the routine.

Plan on each practice session lasting about 12 to 15 minutes. That's a good practice time, and it's the goal we're going to set for your first audition or public performance. You need to get used to what 12 to 15 minutes feels like.

Try to pick a time and place where phone calls and interruptions won't happen. It's probably best to practice alone without anyone watching, at least for the first couple weeks.

Programming Yourself Into a Ventriloquist

Becoming a ventriloquist is going to take some realistic goal-setting on your part. It will seem daunting at first, and you're going to need to persevere through the rough spots. There will be times you feel awkward and creatively stifled. Everyone deals with that, and you have to fight through it.

It helps if your goals are realistic. There's really no timetable for becoming a great ventriloquist, but here's how I suggest you approach *programming* yourself into a ventriloquist:

- Work at your own speed, synchronizing words with your figure.

- Work on not moving your lips while working on certain sounds and letters, one at a time. You may get your *B* sound in a day or two. Or it might take a week. Or it might take longer! That's okay! Don't get dismayed. Remember to *persevere!*

- After you get the sounds and words down, begin a manipulation and technique program. Again, you set the timetable—you can work as quickly or slowly as you like.

- Spend some time in a joke-writing workshop. Again, no specific timetable is required. This is the hardest part of the program, because it is homework, but it will make you a solid performer.

- Finally: *be positive!* This is a great opportunity, and you're going to have a blast accomplishing your goals and doing your first show!

Program, persevere, positive—these are your three goals to get started.

What to Expect and When to Expect It

Excellence isn't going to happen overnight, so you need to be honest with yourself in all phases of ventriloquism. For stand-up comics who work every night, it takes 5 to 7 years to become "great." With this book, I hope to speed up that process for you, and it will take much less time than that to nail down hard-to-pronounce letters without moving your lips. You can expect that within 6 weeks you'll be making some sounds that are very close to *B*'s, *P*'s, *V*'s and so on.

Getting the technique part of moving and reacting to your character might take a couple weeks, but don't spend too long practicing manipulation techniques in front of a mirror. You're going to need to get in front of an audience after you've gotten your letters and substitute sounds in working order.

Hiccups

Don't rush yourself. And don't go out and perform until you're 100 percent ready.

Putting together your first 5-minute routine will take some time. You should be able to get onstage with a figure and perform a comedy routine within a few months of beginning your ventriloquism practice—and maybe less than that!

When that first performance does come along, it may go perfectly—but it probably won't. Don't be discouraged. Remember that important word: *perseverance.* It's not a race in showbiz; it's a marathon. Hang in there, and keep referring to this book as your guide and support system.

One final point in this section: don't even think about getting paid at first. You have to earn your wings. After you've had a few successful performances, you'll start to get paid for your work. But in the beginning, it's all about getting stage time and learning how to deal with audiences while perfecting your skills. I talk about money, agents, bookers, and personal managers in later chapters. Rest assured: if you want those things, you'll get them if you stick with me.

The Least You Need to Know

- Ventriloquism has roots as a spiritual/religious ceremony and, for hundreds of years, was thought to be satanic in nature before it became accepted as a performance art.

- Vaudeville was an early heyday for ventriloquism, and hundreds of professional ventriloquists—including Edgar Bergen and his wooden sidekick, Charlie McCarthy—worked in the first half of the twentieth century.

- The keys to ventriloquism are a clever figure, flawless technique (lip control, manipulation, acting, reacting and working with the audience), and great material.

- You don't need a lot to get started as a ventriloquist: a mirror, some kind of figure, a recording device, and at least 12 to 15 minutes every day to practice.

- To succeed as a ventriloquist, you need to persevere and be positive—no matter what happens!

Chapter 2

Before You Get Started

In This Chapter

- ◆ Ventriloquism tools of the trade
- ◆ Tips for storing and transporting your vent stuff
- ◆ A few words about time and timing
- ◆ Having fun talking to yourself
- ◆ Ventriloquism no-no's

Choosing the right partner is important for every relationship, and that's especially true for a ventriloquist. In this chapter, I help you decide how to start your training, and with what, including info on basic required ventriloquist props and what you need to store and transport your supplies. We also take a look at time in the following pages. Timing, as in most professions, is an essential part of show business—from dedicated practice time, to rehearsal before a performance, to getting on and off the stage at the right time, to delivering jokes with proper timing.

And before you know it, you'll be getting booked in paying venues, so I talk about how that will happen and how to make the most of it. Finally, we look at a couple things every beginner in the business should avoid.

Ventriloquist Figures and Other Props

During your first couple months of practice, it won't matter what you use for a figure. As you get started, you're going to be working on voice control and pronouncing words without moving your lips, not unlike a professional singer or voiceover specialist. You'll want to work on synchronizing words with a figure, of course, but this can be done with anything. An inexpensive puppet purchased at a toy store or garage sale will suffice. A puppet fashioned from a sock will work. Anything you can put on your hand and open and close (as a mouth) is perfect.

> **Suitcases**
>
> The term *dummy* was coined by a critic who watched a ventriloquist use a number of different figures during a performance. According to his review, the ventriloquist was "excellent," but when his figures weren't part of a dialogue, they sat around the stage like a bunch of "dummies."

Be aware, however, that whatever you start with could very well end up being the first figure you perform with in public. Most ventriloquists become attached to their first figures, as a guitarist might with his first or favorite six-string, or a photographer might with her first camera. It would naturally follow that a vent will have a certain predilection for the first figure he or she works with.

When you've reached the point where you're going to either purchase a used figure, or have one custom-built for you, or just continue with your practice figure, you'll have to start thinking about the character and personality your figure will become in your hands (if you don't already have something specific in mind). There are dozens of professional puppet-builders all over the world, and I share some with you in Appendix B.

But before all that, let's look at the basic styles of ventriloquist figure.

The Classic Figure

The classic ventriloquist figure has a wooden head—the most common and stereotypical of all. It's carved, usually from a soft wood (basswood, for example), and is shaped just like a human head. The head connects to the figure's body with a ball-and-socket joint, and a long stick protrudes from the bottom of the figure's neck into its body. On the stick are various levered controls—one that opens the mouth, one that raises the eyebrows, one that sticks out a tongue, one that closes the eyes, and one that moves the eyes back and forth. The ventriloquist grasps this stick and uses his fingers and thumb to depress the control levers operating various mechanisms for the figure's facial features.

The Modern Classic Figure

Looking just like his classic wooden-headed brother, the modern classic figure is built with updated materials such as fiberglass and plastics. These new-style ventriloquist figures have the classic features of old-time vent figures, but are often more durable and aesthetically perfect.

The controls are sometimes push-buttons instead of levers, and in some, electronics are now being used to create the illusion of life. Instead of being hand-carved, an artist molds and casts the figure.

Hiccups

Before you get your heart set on buying a hard figure, know that it can be expensive. Often these are custom-built figures, so even the used ones demand a hefty price. Expect to pay anywhere from $1,000 up for a hand-carved or molded figure. Older figures that can be found in secondhand stores, in magic shops, and online are often collectors' items that fetch high prices.

The Soft Figure

Soft figures are the Muppet-like figures you've probably seen. These figures are much cheaper than the classic and modern classic. Soft puppets are easily manipulated. While the materials used to build them vary from maker to maker, the buyer knows what he or she is getting.

Soft figures don't weigh anywhere near as much as the hard figures, so there are fewer problems transporting the soft puppet (more on transport later in this chapter) and there's less risk of damage. But they're not as durable and must be replaced or upgraded every few years.

Soft puppets are perfect for children's shows because kids have grown up watching *Sesame Street* and other TV shows that feature Muppet-like figures. And they're not nearly as frightening as some of the hard figures can appear.

Other Types of Figures

No ventriloquist should be hemmed in by what is acceptable or unacceptable. If you don't want to use a typical figure, that's fine. Use what you like, whether it's a boxing glove, a Halloween mask, a tennis ball that's been cut so it has a "mouth" when squeezed, or even a piece of tattered quilt. The sock-over-the-hand figure works very well and can be modified and easily changed. You can even use your bare hand as a puppet if you want to! Another choice is the plastic-molded ventriloquist figure found in novelty stores. This figure has a pull string located in the back of the head that, when pulled, opens the mouth.

It doesn't matter what you use. If you can make the figure come alive before an audience, then use it!

Adding In Props

After you've mastered your skills to the point where you're performing in front of audiences, you can use other props in your act. The glass of water trick, in which it appears the ventriloquist is drinking while the figure is talking or singing, is one example of a prop you can use. This prop, which is actually a glass within a glass, can be purchased at most magic shops or online. After a few hours of practice, you can probably master the trick.

def•i•ni•tion

Off arm is the ventriloquist's arm not being used to manipulate and hold the figure. You use the off arm to make gestures, push or pull your figure back and forth, or hold a prop. The off arm can be very helpful in creating the illusion of life.

Magic shops also sell stands. These fold and unfold and give you a place to put the figure so you don't have to hold it with your *off arm* while you're performing.

Specialty props are available, too, and will come in handy when you're ready for more advanced performances. These include talking chalkboards (you draw a face on a chalkboard and then make the mouth open and close so it becomes your figure), masks that fit over an audience member's face so the audience member (victim?) becomes your figure, talking books, and other items. (You can find these online. See Appendix B for some resources.)

I'm Gonna Need a Bigger Suitcase

Transporting and caring for your figure are almost as important as the figure itself. Just as you have choices for what to use as a figure, you also have options for storing and transporting it.

Custom Cases

A custom case is very expensive, but if you're going to use a classic or modern classic figure, you'll definitely want something that will hold your figure and keep it safely enclosed. Custom cases are made to form fit your figure's head (the most important and expensive part), with foam and padding that can withstand shocks and drops and wear and tear.

You can easily find custom case builders, but setting a price—within a budget—can be a struggle. These cases can be heavy, awkward, and large, which causes problems when traveling, especially if you're flying. Most major airlines charge a heavy baggage fee, which can reach into the hundreds of dollars. Add to that the difficulty of moving a bulky case (or more than one!), and air travel almost becomes cost-prohibitive.

Hiccups

No matter what type of case you use, wheels always come in handy, especially if travel is going to be a regular part of the performance schedule. On the downside, however, this can cause headaches because wheels, ball bearings, and other parts wear out and break down.

Standard Suitcases

Most ventriloquists use standard luggage and modify it to their needs. There are many ways to protectively pack your figures, especially those with delicate features and mechanisms, and you can do it yourself. For example, you can remove the head from the body, wrap it in a pillow or padded cloth bag, place it in the suitcase, and position it with more padding for stability.

Many ventriloquists pack the figures' heads separately from the bodies, going as far as having smaller carry-on suitcases for the most important part of the figure (especially for air travel). Bags get lost, sent to far-off locations by mistake, and are sometimes damaged. By taking the figure's head on the plane in a carry-on case, you're assured you have something to perform with when you land!

Hiccups

For the traveling ventriloquist, a new accessory that might come in handy is the GPS luggage tag. This tag attaches to the case like any nametag, but it is electronically outfitted with GPS software that allows the owner to track his case via computer or mobile phone.

Soft Bags

Suitcases and custom-made cases are better and offer more protection than soft canvas or cloth bags. However, especially for soft figures, the soft bags do a perfunctory job.

The soft bags offer major advantages, of course. They're lighter, more flexible, and easier to handle than suitcases and custom-made cases. As long as your figure is individually wrapped and the head is carefully wrapped, soft bags will transport your sidekick wherever you go in a safe and damage-free condition.

Suitcases
Whatever case you end up using, it will undoubtedly play into your act. If it's appropriate, you can even carry your figure in a backpack. For example, you're introduced, you walk onstage with your backpack, you take it off, and voilà! You've started your act!

When it comes to traveling with any kind of case, consider whether or not the case is stage ready. I get into this later in the book, but for now, be aware that having a case that doubles as a prop onstage is a good opportunity for humor in the stage act. With many ventriloquist performances, the case serves as the home, and pulling out and putting back the figure is great fodder for comedy material.

Be on Time

The cliché is true: timing is everything. This phrase applies to the way you approach your daily practice session and continues through showing up on time at the venue where you're booked and using your stage time efficiently and purposefully. Timing is everything to the way you deliver your jokes and hit the punch lines and words in the proper flow. It is key to getting off the stage, setting up the next booking, networking, and writing a new hunk of material.

Let me put it another way, using another cliché: time is money. Timing is just as important for the beginner as it is for the seasoned pro.

Be on Time for Practice

Let's start with practice time. The best way to practice is to set up a schedule and stick to it. Think of it as rehearsing with a band or scrimmaging with a team. People are creatures of habit; if you can manage to set aside certain time so your mind and body get accustomed to practice, it will quickly become routine.

Remember that these lessons and practices are supposed to be fun. You want to enjoy practicing your newfound craft, and you want to have tangible success you can see and build on, as quickly as possible. So limit your initial practices to short bursts of 15 to 20 minutes. Work at something specific, say pronouncing the letter *B* without moving your lips or learning simple manipulations with your figure. When the 15 minutes is up, *stop!*

Stop even if things are going well, and you think to yourself, *I can go all day today!* Why burn out all that enthusiasm in the first week? You want to not only enjoy the many new skills you have learned, but also carry that motivation over into your next practice, your next audition, and your next big engagement!

Stick to a schedule. If you can get two or three practices in a day, great! Once you've moved past the initial couple weeks of lessons, you'll have a good grasp of the practice time you can handle for each lesson and particular technique. From there, you can adjust your practice schedule accordingly.

Hiccups

Enjoy the process! Be aware that practice can become boring and redundant. Don't let that happen to you! Learn to really enjoy the process of becoming a great ventriloquist.

Be on Time for Performances

When it comes to getting a booking and performing your first sets, time is critical. You don't want to be late for a show or an audition. Check and re-check the performance time. Make the extra phone call just to be sure. It is unacceptable to miss an opportunity because you didn't know the time. This is show business, and the competition is fierce. As a ventriloquist, you're going to be vying for the same jobs as stand-up comedians, impressionists, magicians, jugglers, singers, and every other live entertainer. Losing out on bookings because you failed to show up on time defeats the whole purpose of what you're trying to accomplish. Opportunities often come down to who showed up on time.

Once you get booked, you'll be given a certain number of minutes to perform. It's always best to do *exactly* what the booker or emcee or client wants. If they say 3 minutes, do 3 minutes. If it's 10 minutes, do 10 minutes. Even if your set is rocking the free world and you could do another half-hour and blow the room away, discretion is the better part of valor, for a couple reasons:

◆ The showbiz adage "always leave 'em wanting more" is 100 percent true.

◆ There are other performers you will probably work with again on the same bill. Taking up some of their time to show everyone how talented you are is not only unfair, it's also unprofessional.

♦ One of the first questions people who book shows and hire acts ask is, "Can he take direction?" If the direction is to perform for 12 minutes and you do 25, the answer is pretty clear: "No. He cannot take direction. *Next!*"

Perhaps the most difficult aspect of time is going to be answering the question, "Have I put in enough practice and rehearsal time to perform for the public?" More to the point, the *really* hard question is, "Am I ready?" Only you can answer that one.

There's an old adage about learning ventriloquism: "Spend 6 months on each of the hardest letters to pronounce, and you're ready to perform." One of the purposes of this book is to make that statement obsolete. With diligence and constant practice, you should be ready to take the stage in much less time than that.

When you're performing regularly, in whatever venues you choose, it takes a few years to become a solid pro. For stand-up comics, the process takes 5 to 7 years. For singers and actors, it takes 4 to 10 years of classes and onstage experiences. For you, the key is *stage time.* When you start performing, the key to your success and how your career as a ventriloquist will unfold is all about getting onstage somewhere and making the best use of that time. Every performance, from the very first to the one on a national TV broadcast, is all about how you use stage time.

Hiccups

Most performances are obstacle courses. You cannot foresee what might happen in any given situation. Poor lighting, bad sound, belligerent audience members, having to follow an act that gets a standing ovation—these situations happen. As a working ventriloquist, using every opportunity you get on stage will give you the experience and the ability to handle yourself in any circumstance.

Talking to Yourself for Fun and Profit

There's that word again: *fun.* It's easy to get so caught up in the workings of ventriloquism that you forget what drew you to it in the first place. Ventriloquism is supposed to be fun, for you and for the audience. The intrinsic pleasure that ventriloquism offers is the relationship between a human being and something that isn't real—where real people and fantasy intersect.

This is where you come in as the director, head writer, and lead actor in a presentation that takes your viewers on a trip. The more you enjoy it, the more you apply your skills, and the more you keep improving, the more the audience will buy into your work.

People always want to know how much money they can earn performing ventriloquism, and it's true that the best in the business earn the kind of money movie stars and professional athletes make. But just like those other professions, 10 percent of the professional ventriloquists in the country earn 90 percent of the money. That's just the reality. (I talk more about the kinds of venues the working ventriloquist can use in Chapter 18.)

The best way to enjoy yourself as a ventriloquist is to do some very strong live shows. Your goal should be to work up to a 5-minute routine, then a 10-minute routine, then a 15-minute routine, and so on. It might sound easy at first to put together these short routines. But you'll find that it's a challenge and a constant work-in-progress to forge a solid comedy act, even if it's just a 5-minute spot.

What *Not* to Do

Before we get into the first ventriloquism lesson in Chapter 3, I need to point out some business, performance, and artistic taboos you'll want to avoid. Some of these are common sense, others are valuable bits of information, and all are good business.

Most ventriloquists use comedy as the main focus of their act. The easiest way to get laughs, especially when you're starting out and you don't have a lot of confidence, is to use comedy routines and jokes you've heard before. Actually, if you go to comedy clubs, you'll see many of the acts "borrow" material and jokes in almost every show.

Don't do this. You want to build your own act with your own material, in your own voice. The temptation will be strong to use what you know is going to work because it's been done by someone else. Fight that urge and stick to your guns. You'll be better off and have a better reputation if you're original. (I know, I know. This is much easier said than done.)

Ventriloquism, when done well, is an exciting performance piece that's often the highlight of a comedy show or TV program. At the same time, ventriloquism done poorly is an ugly stereotype that's reinforced by people who don't put in the time and effort necessary to become excellent. Put another way, if a booker hires a comic who doesn't do a good show or fares poorly, the club just won't book that comic again. The booker will, however, book another comic. If that same booker hires a ventriloquist who goes

Hiccups

Going up for an audition before you're ready will make it that much harder to get the booker to look at you again.

onstage and delivers an amateurish program, that booker might not use another ventriloquist for months or years! The connotation vents have with being "bad" is profound. Don't be that guy!

It's very hard to be honest with yourself. Answering the question "Am I ready to go onstage and try to entertain an audience?" is difficult. Keep this rule of thumb in mind:

> When you think you're ready, you probably still need another couple months to practice and rehearse and perfect what you have.

That rule holds true for your entire career as a ventriloquist. The biggest thing *not* to do is take your act onstage too early.

The Least You Need to Know

- Ventriloquist figures come in a few styles: classic, modern classic, soft (Muppet-like), and a host of others (including socks, molded plastic, and so on).

- You need a case to transport your figure, and your choices vary from high-end custom cases to standard suitcases to soft bags.

- Timing is everything. Be on time, set up and stick to a practice time, give yourself enough time to learn the ropes, and show up at your scheduled time!

- It's not about the money at first. Have fun, and enjoy the process!

Part 2

Talking Without Lip Movement

Part 2 starts off with a look at human anatomy, particularly the diaphragm and lungs, the larynx, and the voice box, and how these relate to and affect sounds. It's important for the ventriloquist-in-training to understand that ventriloquism isn't so much about re-creating sounds as it is replacing sounds with other similar sounds that the human ear has trouble deciphering.

The difficult letters to work with are *B, F, M, P, V, W,* and *Y* because those sounds depend on lip movement. But in Chapter 4, you learn how to trick the audience with replacement sounds. After that comes a study of the human voice, with info on how you can create entirely new voices by changing the register of your own voice and by using your nasal passages to speak—and create new characters.

Part 2 closes with a look at distant voice, which is difficult for even the most seasoned pro to pull off. As with most vent techniques, distant voice is as much about illusion, creating a diversion, and play-acting as it is about "throwing" your voice. (That's impossible, by the way!)

Chapter 3

How the Human Voice Works

In This Chapter

- How you produce sounds (a.k.a. how the voice box works)
- Getting your diaphragm in on the act
- A look at pronunciation
- The fine art of misdirection

The meaning of the word *ventriloquist* is "belly speaker," and that's confused people for years. Speaking from the belly? As you know, the ventriloquist does not actually create sound in his or her stomach (unless he or she is really hungry!). Rather, a ventriloquist uses the same vocal organs employed in daily conversation and communication.

Ventriloquism is really about how people hear what sounds are being made rather than where they're coming from. The human ear cannot always make out where a sound is coming from, where it was created, or even who or what made the sound. The ventriloquist makes use of this gray area, and "throws" his voice into the mix. By using his voice, his diaphragm, and a little theater, he tricks the listener.

Let's look at how this is done.

How Sound Is Made

The study of ventriloquism starts with how a normal speaking voice is made in the human body. Anyone who uses speech can be a ventriloquist; no special endowments or physical attributes are required.

Ventriloquism is more than not moving your lips and creating the illusion that a voice is coming from the ventriloquist's figure. Your diaphragm, lungs, vocal cords, larynx, soft and hard palates, nasal cavity, and tongue are all in on the act, too.

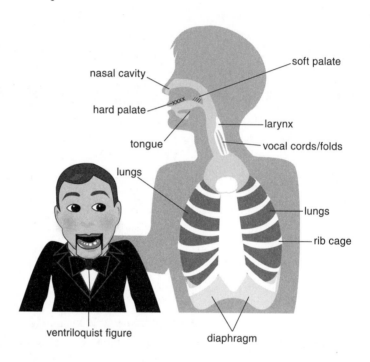

The Larynx and the Voice Box

Every time we speak, several elements work together to create our voice: a motivating push or force, our breath, and our vocal cords. The final result of this effort comes through our throat, mouth, and nasal cavities. That's how sound is made.

We take breath into our lungs, and it's then passed out through the larynx, which is sometimes called the voice box. This organ is located in the neck, and within it are folds of skin called the vocal cords. As air passes over these cords, it causes them to vibrate, which in turn produces a certain pitch or tone. This sound moves into the vocal cavities, the throat, the nose, and the mouth, where it gains power and amplification. Once this sound moves into the throat, nose, and mouth, it resounds as the tongue, teeth, and lips change fluctuation and articulation. This process is known as speech, and this is the point where the ventriloquist begins to play with the way the words and sounds are made and heard.

Obviously, these parts all need to work together to create the sounds that become the words we speak in daily conversation. But nothing can happen without breathing—it's the breath, and breath control, that's key to vocalizing.

Where Breath Comes Into Play

For the ventriloquist, nothing is as important as learning how to use and manage breathing. Sound and word production are closely associated with good breathing habits. A great ventriloquist is able to handle his or her breath with little effort. It becomes second nature.

For most people, breathing is second nature. You might be thinking, *Who needs training to breathe?* But breathing for ventriloquism is a completely different case. Similar to the way a singer manages his voice, the ventriloquist limits and restricts his breathing, sometimes employing a quick intake and retention of breath that's sufficient to support the voice during a speaking period. This gives the ventriloquist the ability to shade and bend sounds, confusing the listener.

Also involved in the process—obviously—are the lungs. Essential to respiration, the lungs draw in air, expanding the chest as we inhale. When that air is expelled, it rushes over the vocal mechanisms, and that stream allows for human speech.

> **Hiccups**
>
> Correct breathing for the ventriloquist is a natural by-product of the exact technique you're learning. You will not need breathing exercises or voice lessons if you follow the instructions in this chapter.

Getting Muscles Involved

The muscular motivation for all this work comes from the chest and the diaphragm, which work together to achieve inhalation and exhalation.

The diaphragm, muscle located between the lungs and abdomen, conforms to the concave base of the lungs. When you inhale, the diaphragm contracts as the abdominal muscles relax. When you exhale, the diaphragm is passive and returns to its arched position, assisting the lungs in exhaling air.

This action is automatic and almost involuntary on your part. Your body breathes in and out, the muscles do their respective jobs, mechanisms work in cohesion, and you speak. The ventriloquist governs the way this system works—in particular, he or she controls breath and the release of sounds. (More on using your diaphragm later in this chapter.)

Creating Voices

There are two distinct forms of ventriloquism:

- ◆ Near voice
- ◆ Distant voice

For now let's concentrate on near voice ventriloquism and how you produce it. (More on the distant voice in Chapter 7.)

When a vent performs with his or her figure, he or she is actually using two separate voices. The first is the ventriloquist's own natural voice, the one used in everyday conversation. The other is the figure's voice. These voices differ, and that's the classic definition of near voice ventriloquism. The differentiation between the two voices—the vent's and the figure's—is the first and most important step in creating the illusion that two separate beings are having a dialogue.

You need to become proficient in switching from your voice to your figure's voice. Don't worry—the following sections tell you how.

Speaking in Tongues

When speaking normally, your tongue lies flat and your voice passes over it, rushing out of your mouth and nasal cavities. Try speaking a phrase, and notice where your tongue is.

When speaking in the ventriloquist voice, your tongue arches in the back of your mouth, forcing the sound and tones to pass mostly through your nasal cavity and only slightly through your mouth. Experiment with this by gently touching your upper and lower teeth together, parting your lips, and reading this sentence out loud. Notice how your tongue naturally arches when your mouth is closed. Also notice that as you speak in this position, your voice becomes "nasal." That's because more sound is being pushed through your nose than through your mouth.

This is the same tongue position you use to make the *-ng* sound in words like *sing*, *ring*, and *bring*. The back of your tongue contacts the soft palate at the roof of your mouth, which changes your natural voice into something more nasal and different.

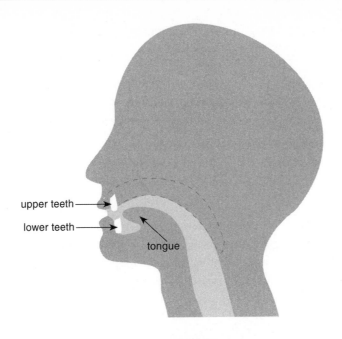

Normal voice position. Note that your teeth aren't touching and that your tongue either points straight ahead or lies across the bottom of your mouth.

upper teeth

lower teeth

tongue

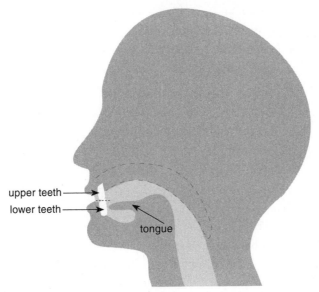

Vent position. Note that your tongue is slightly arched in your mouth and your teeth are lightly touching, not clenching, while your lips are parted naturally with no straining or tightening of the mouth muscles.

upper teeth

lower teeth

tongue

Here's a quick way to begin practicing initial ventriloquist technique:

1. Make the *AH* sound a doctor might ask you for at a routine checkup.

2. As you're droning your *AH*, change your tongue position from the natural way it is when you speak to the arched tongue position described earlier.

 Hiccups _____

You should not experience any pain during this simple exercise. If you feel any discomfort, particularly in your throat, you're doing something wrong. Don't hurt yourself!

Try this with your teeth gently clenched together: switch back and forth from your natural voice to your ventriloquial voice. The differences in pitch, tone, and clarity is how you will begin to create voices and sounds for your figures.

Finding a New Voice

You'll notice that it doesn't take much effort to create a second voice that sounds similar, but not the same as, your own voice. This is important. The slight change in tenor and tone, just from closing your mouth and arching your tongue, creates an entirely new sound—another voice! This may or may not be one you use with a figure in performance, but this should give you a basic understanding of the concept.

Finding a new voice or sound doesn't have to be something drastic. You're simply playing with sounds here. By using breath control and adding pressure from your tongue or nasal and mouth cavities, you can manipulate your voice. Be aware that a slight change in the way you release sound can alter your voice just enough that the listener can be misled. And that's just what you want!

This might seem like an overly intense look at the human voice, but it's important to know that ventriloquism depends on the vagaries of sound. By controlling your breath and strengthening your ability to hold it and release it, you can find ways to make sounds faint and difficult to perceive. The more you work at this, the easier it becomes.

Suitcases

There's no such thing as "throwing" your voice. It is humanly impossible to make your voice come from anyplace other than your body without using a device of some kind. With the ability to manipulate sound, however, and a little bit of acting, you can make it seem like there's a voice coming from someplace other than your mouth.

An Exercise in Creating a New Voice

Now that you know how to create sound and use your breath, let's really give it a try. Find a quiet spot where you won't feel self-conscious, and give your first exercise a go:

1. Clench your teeth, but don't bite down so hard that it's uncomfortable or painful. Part your lips enough so you can breathe in and out.

2. Say something in your normal voice. It could be this sentence or a comment on the room you're in or the weather. Listen to how it sounds and resonates in your head as you speak. Move your lips, and talk normally. Get a feel for your voice.

3. Now speak as a ventriloquist would. With your teeth lightly clenched, part your lips just enough to let air in and out. Feel where your tongue is, and put it in vent position—that is, arch the back of your tongue and speak mostly through your nose. You should hear a significant difference!

4. After getting used to how this new voice feels, try some different voices by letting small amounts of air out of your lungs as you speak in vent position. Try a variety of things. There is no wrong or right way to do this, so entertain yourself! Use your own voice, arch the back of your tongue, and get a feel for this new way of talking.

Remember, ventriloquism is about using diversion and misdirection. For most of this book, we're going to be concentrating on near voice ventriloquism with you and a figure. So the misdirection is already there. Focus on experimenting with sounds for right now.

Using Your Diaphragm

As I mentioned earlier in this chapter, your diaphragm is essential to your breathing and voice production.

Let's delve deeper into how your diaphragm affects how sounds are made. For this next lesson, …

1. Lie flat on your back and place your fingers lightly on the soft part of your abdomen just above your waist and between your ribs. This is where your diaphragm is located.

2. Breathe naturally and note the movement of your diaphragm, as your stomach muscles move outward when you inhale and move inward when exhaling. Don't raise your shoulders or rib cage as you do this; just breathe normally.

3. Try the same exercise while sitting in a chair.

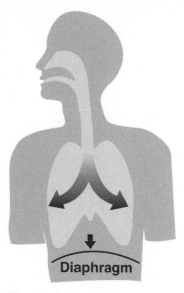 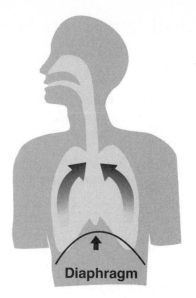

Your diaphragm is located beneath your lungs. As you inhale, your diaphragm contracts and flattens, your chest cavity expands, and air is drawn into your lungs.

As you exhale, your diaphragm relaxes, and air is forced out of your lungs.

Now let's take things a step further:

1. Inhale and fill your lungs.

2. Now try to let the air out by raising your diaphragm and then letting your ribs (and lungs) deflate. If this is difficult, try to breathe in and out using only your diaphragm.

Pull Strings

One way to listen to yourself practice sounds is to gently plug one ear with your finger as you're making sounds in the vent position. You'll hear yourself making sounds and words, and by blocking one ear, the sound will resonate right into your eardrum.

It isn't easy, and it might take some practice, but stick with it. With these exercises, you're learning to control your breath (and learning the extent of what your lungs can handle), and you're beginning to concentrate on *how* you inhale and exhale, and therefore how you make sound.

Take a couple practice sessions to work on both creating sounds in the vent position by arching your tongue and doing the diaphragm and breathing exercises.

Once you feel that you've got the gist of working with your diaphragm, you're on your way to becoming the master of your voice and the way sounds are made. This is a core skill of ventriloquism. In addition, you're building a foundation for future use. By controlling and working with your diaphragm, your lungs will always have a little air left in reserve—somewhat the way an athlete has an extra burst he or she can call upon. This will come in handy as you become an expert at working onstage and will make you a better ventriloquist.

This is a lot of information, and many of these nuances are things we take for granted. You're being compared to singers and athletes, who are in tune with their bodies and the muscles that make them successful. You'll need that same approach as you get better and better as a ventriloquist! You can strengthen your vocal cords, your lungs will gradually be able to take on more air and deeper breaths, and you'll build up a certain amount of stamina and power as a performer. When you start working with a microphone and the acoustics of different venues, you'll be mindful of how sound echoes throughout a building or a room. A ventriloquist must be aware of all this stuff, as it plays directly to his or her art.

How Words Are Pronounced

"Tongue tied." It's a phrase you've probably heard many times over, and it refers to a person trying to say something and stumbling over the words or even syllables as he or she tries to talk. For the successful ventriloquist, the tongue is going to be *untied* and doing a lot of work.

There are exercises for the tongue, like touching every tooth with the tip of your tongue while your mouth is slightly open, or licking your lips in single revolutions, changing direction every couple times you complete a circle. But as you begin to work in the vent position and make sounds and words, there's no reason to exercise your tongue. You're going to be working it like never before, and that will be exercise enough!

As a ventriloquist-in-practice, your tongue replaces your lips in making words and sounds. To be exact, your tongue will be doing the work of your lips to pronounce the letters *B*, *F*, *M*, *P*, and *V*, and it will stay out of the way to pronounce *W* and *Y*. (I cover all these techniques in Chapter 4.)

Suitcases
Some ventriloquists write entire routines that don't use any words with the letters *B, F, M, P, V, W,* and *Y*. You don't want to be that kind of act! With this book, you'll learn how to feel comfortable saying *any* word as a ventriloquist! Even the word *ventriloquist!*

Working in Vent Position

For now, let's consider the way words are pronounced. Put your mouth in vent position. That is, clench your teeth gently, arch your tongue, and part your lips slightly. You can do this in front of a mirror if you like, as you begin saying things with your mouth in vent position. Take a breath and say, "Hello." Say it a few times in vent position using your normal voice. Then say it normally, using your mouth and lips. Listen to the difference in timbre and quality. Say it slowly, both in vent position and normally. Say it quickly in both positions.

You're not changing anything about the word itself, its pronunciation, or the way you breathe and talk. You are changing the way sound comes out of your mouth and nasal cavities. The change might not be drastic, but it *is* significant, especially for the listener. It's almost as if you have split yourself into two different characters—and that's the whole point!

Try this with other one-syllable words that don't require the difficult *B, F, M, P, V, W,* and *Y* sounds. For example, try *did, done, good, joke, tight, sight,* and *clean.* When you say *clean,* break it down into two syllables: *kuh-leen.* Say them with your own natural way of speaking and then say them in vent position. Breaking down words like this is a technique you'll be using again, so follow the directions: say it slowly, say it quickly, and then say it normally.

Taking It a Step Further

You've now begun to think and act like a ventriloquist. You're paying attention to sounds, the way you make sounds, and how those sounds become words. You're noticing things like the resonance of your voice and how easily you can change your voice, and you're using the vent position. Let's go a step further.

In vent position, say the word *thought.* Gently put a finger in one ear and say it again. Say it again, only this time concentrate on the first sound you make: the soft *TH* sound. Try making just the soft *TH* sound, paying attention to your tongue pressing against your teeth to create the soft *TH* that leads the word. Got it? Good.

To the human ear, that soft *TH* sound is very similar to the *F* sound. Try it again, in vent position. Then say it as you would normally say it. In your normal voice, say the word *thought.* Now say, "I thought I fought, and it's done." Say it quickly, as fast as you can: "I-thought-I-fought-and-it's-done." You should notice something similar in the words *thought* and *fought.* Not only do they rhyme, but the words sound very similar, especially when you say them quickly.

Try it this way, using your normal voice and normal position: say, "I thought I thought and it's done." Try saying the same sentence both ways, back to back: "I thought I fought and it's done," followed quickly by "I thought I thought and it's done." Say it quickly enough, and you can see how the human ear, although it knows what each word is supposed to sound like, might not be able to tell that you're just repeating the word *thought* for *fought*. The way words are pronounced is a gray area the ventriloquist works with.

Tricking the Human Ear

You're probably catching on now. There are words and phrases and sounds that trick the human ear, especially if there's misdirection (as with a ventriloquist figure) and good technique on the ventriloquist's part. Tricking the human ear isn't hard, especially when you have visual props, flawless technique, and something entertaining and informative to say. It's almost as if the listener *wants* to be tricked. You, as a ventriloquist, are obliged to make that happen.

Practice saying simple words and phrases in vent position, and watch yourself in the mirror. Do the diaphragm exercise given earlier in this chapter while using vent position. Many words sound alike, or sound so similar that the listener won't be able to tell the difference, as you learned with *thought* and *fought* earlier. *Three* and *free* are another pair of words that can trick the human ear.

> ### Suitcases
>
> The way a room or any performance space is set up allows for certain acoustics a ventriloquist can use to great effect. We look into this in Chapter 7.

Sound is an inexact science. There are ways to manipulate it for your own gain as a ventriloquist. Here is one example you can use to trick someone:

The set-up: You need a "victim" (no, you're not going to hurt anyone; ventriloquism is not a contact sport!), an empty room like a bedroom or a hotel room that has a door, and your new voice that comes from vent position.

The trick: Open the door to the room before your victim does, which means you need to be about 5 or 6 feet in front of him or her, close enough so the victim has to be able to hear but not so close as to be able to tell *you* are doing all the talking! You open the door, act surprised, and say, loudly, "What are you doing here?" Now use your vent position voice—don't worry about moving your lips—and have your "other" voice say something unintelligible, for example, "I was wading for sunshine and I got into an argument with someone and …."

You need to really sell this. You can't turn and look at the victim. You have to act as if you really *are* talking with someone in the room, someone you know and someone you clearly didn't expect to see. Carry this on for a few seconds before opening the door completely.

The payoff: Invite the victim in with an "I don't know what's going on" kind of shrug. When your victim walks in and realizes you were only talking to yourself, you can say, "Sorry … I couldn't help it …."

Enjoy this trick the first time you do it because once you try it with someone, you will never be able to repeat it with that "victim." They'll remember you (fondly) for what you did.

There are lots of other ways to trick listeners and audience members, and you'll probably be able to think of a couple yourself. Be aware that part of ventriloquism is the ability to use and manipulate sound. The human ear can only disseminate so much information. Use that to your advantage as a ventriloquist!

The Least You Need to Know

- The human voice is created by pushing breath from the diaphragm through the larynx (or voice box) and out through the mouth and nose.

- Ventriloquism is not so much based on "throwing" one's voice, but rather is about disguising your voice and misdirecting a listener's attention.

- Learning how to control your breath and pronouncing words in vent position, which is to say without using your lips, are the first steps to becoming a successful ventriloquist.

- The human ear is not able to immediately differentiate where sound comes from or who and what made a sound, which works to the ventriloquist's favor.

Chapter 4

Don't Read My Lips!

In This Chapter

- The hard-to-make sounds: *B, F, M, P, V, W,* and *Y*
- Tips for cheating
- Tricks for tricking your audience's ears
- The nuts and bolts of practicing sounds with your figure

Ventriloquists will probably always be judged on their lip control and their ability to vocalize without opening their mouths. To the layman, this is the crux of the best ventriloquist acts, and all ventriloquists should master this talent. Fortunately, anyone who wants to can become a ventriloquist. With perseverance and concentration, a beginner can quickly see improvement in both areas.

Ventriloquists are judged on many things, including manipulation of the figure, showmanship, jokes, songs, and material, not to mention the venues they play and the careers they build. But the one universal judgment for ventriloquists comes down to the 7 letters that cannot be spoken without using your lips: *B, F, M, P, V, W,* and *Y.*

Welcome to the make-or-break point of your ventriloquist education.

The Labial Sounds: *B, F, M, P, V, W,* and *Y*

This is it! It's time to learn how to make sounds that mimic the real letters that are impossible to make without the lips. Once you master these sounds, your figure and routines will take on the exciting air of professionalism that wins over audiences and gets bookings.

To start, you need a mirror and a room where you have privacy because if someone hears you practicing all this, he or she will think you sound a little odd! Here we go!

The *B* Sound

As I discussed in Chapter 3, with ventriloquism, you're going to be using your tongue more than ever before. For starters, your tongue is responsible for making the *B* sound. The *B* is known as a *stop plosive*—that is, to create the *B* sound, the lips momentarily stop the airflow coming from the larynx up through the throat. Airflow is interrupted, your lips are pursed and then part, and as air is released, your voice pushes through your naval cavity as the *B* sound is made.

To make the *B* sound in ventriloquism, it's necessary to imitate the same quality as the consonant made with your lips. The word is *plosive*, as in *explosive*, and that's what you need to re-create with your tongue. Try this: place your fingers against your Adam's apple, or larynx. Make the *B* sound, and hold it for a few seconds. Feel your vocal cords vibrate? You'll want to duplicate as much of that vibration as possible when you make your ventriloquism *B* sound.

Let's look at how you do this: touch the tip of your tongue to your upper middle two front teeth. Now imagine your tongue as a pointer and touch the very tip—the "point"—of your tongue precisely behind your upper middle two front teeth. The tip of your tongue should be touching the gum behind your upper middle two front teeth.

Another way to approach this: say the sound *la* out loud. Now overenunciate the *la* sound and concentrate on where you put the tip of your tongue against the roof of your mouth. To make the *la* sound, the tip of your tongue presses against the hard palate directly behind your upper middle two front teeth.

You're going to use the same technique you used for the *la* sound by putting your mouth in good "vent position," gently touching all your teeth together, and parting your lips. Instead of putting the tip of your tongue against the hard palate behind your upper middle two front teeth as you did with the *la* sound, move the tip of your tongue forward to the point where your upper middle two front teeth meet the roof of your mouth. Touch the tip of your tongue to that point, a fulcrum where your upper middle two front teeth meet the gum line. (Get used to putting your tongue here because, as a ventriloquist, you'll use this position a lot!)

Now, just the way you make your regular *B* sound, try to get the same sort of explosion when you make your ventriloquist *B*. Remember, your tongue should be right at the point where your upper middle two front teeth meet your gum ridge. When you first try your ventriloquist *B*, it will probably sound more like your usual *D* sound. That's all right. You might have to practice this ventriloquist *B* sound a lot—it's very difficult to "get."

Try making the usual *D* sound in ventriloquist position. Your tongue presses against the hard palate behind your upper teeth, then pushes off the roof of your mouth, down and toward your teeth. Your ventriloquist *B* starts in the same position, but you'll jettison the tip of your tongue back toward your throat as you leave the hard palate.

Try pressing or flattening your tongue against the back of your upper teeth and make your usual *D* sound. Say "DUH" in this way. After a few times doing this, make that same sound, but instead of letting your tongue go straight down, pull it straight back as you make the *DUH* sound. Keep experimenting with different tongue positions and saying "DUH" until you come up with a different sound. You might not make the perfect *B* imitation, but that's okay! You want something that will fool the human ear: perhaps it's not a perfect *B* sound, but it isn't a *D* sound, either!

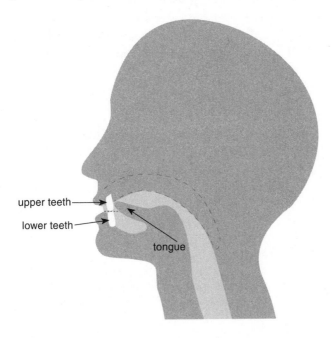

When making the ventriloquist B *sound (and also the* P *sound, coming up next), your tongue should rest against the point where your upper teeth meet your gum.*

upper teeth

lower teeth

tongue

> **Suitcases**
>
> With many ventriloquist acts, you can hear the B sound has not been fully completed. "Buddy boy" sounds like "duddy doy." Now you know why.

Take a break after a few tries, and rest your tongue. Then come back to it. Put your mouth in vent position, and try making a ventriloquist B sound again, watching yourself in the mirror. Your initial concentration will be on not moving your lips. Forget the sound itself, especially if it sounds like a D. For your first session or two, concentrate on where you put your tongue and not moving your lips while you practice.

The *P* Sound

The ventriloquist P sound is made the same way the B sound is made—with one exception.

As you did with the B sound, gently place your fingers on your Adam's apple and make the normal P sound. Hear the difference between P and B? The P is voiceless. Your vocal cords don't do anything. The plosive is the same—your lips interrupt the airflow—but instead of the nasally drone and BUH sound, there's no voice to accompany the P sound. You almost whisper the P sound. So to make the ventriloquist P sound, do the same thing you did with the B, but leave your voice out of it.

Practice both your P and B together. Your B sound, just like a D sound, is a hard and dry sound to the human ear. The P sound is softer and has a "wet" feel. (Sometimes when people make the P sound, they spit. Case in point: wet your lips and make a normal P sound. See how some saliva jumps off your mouth?) Try to think "wet sound" when making the P, then make both sounds individually (as in *buh!* and *pie!*). Then try words like *pub* and *burp* in vent position, and watch your lip movement in the mirror.

You won't be perfect in the beginning. Chances are your initial P's are going to sound like T's (and even when you hear vents perform, you'll notice "Peter Piper" sounds like "Teeter Titer"). But keep practicing. Don't move on until you feel you're getting very good at one of the two letters.

Pull Strings

Recording yourself while you practice, especially when you're just starting out, helps immeasurably. You can hear what your ventriloquist voice sounds like and make adjustments to the letters you're having trouble with. Everyone is different; edit and customize these instructions to your technique. The big thing is to get those sounds as close to B and P as possible!

The *F* Sound

F (and also *V,* which I discuss a little later in this chapter) is a *fricative*, or a sound you articulate by almost completely closing your mouth, leaving just enough of an opening to interrupt airflow.

The ventriloquist makes an *F* sound the same way he or she makes the soft *TH* sound. Think of the word *froth*. The ventriloquist pronounces this word *throth*—or, more accurately, the ventriloquist pronounces it *th-roth*. The small delay between the *TH* sound (the substitute for the *F* sound) and the rest of the word is to give the audience a base of reference. By that I mean that you cannot imitate the sounds perfectly unless you use your lips. But ventriloquism is not about perfect mimicry. Ventriloquism is offering the human ear a substitute sound, something so close to the "real" sound that the human ear cannot tell the difference. The listener makes a split-second acknowledgement subconsciously and decides what the sound is.

Let's practice it. Starting in vent position (lips parted in a natural way, teeth lightly touching, and tongue slightly arched), and watching yourself in a mirror, make the soft *TH* sound. By breaking *froth* into two distinct syllables—*th-roth*—you allow the audience to bridge the gap themselves. It might seem obvious to you, the ventriloquist, that you're saying *th-roth* and not *froth*, but they likely won't notice as they hear the pronunciation and the sounds. The human ear can't make that immediate judgment, particularly when the word is used in a sentence.

After you've practiced saying *th-roth* in vent position, and you can pronounce the word without moving your lips, try it in a sentence: "I like the *th-roth* in the ocean." See? The human ear makes the jump on its own. The sound might not be perfect, but it's close enough to fool your audience!

The *M* Sound

Because it's totally formed by the lips, the *M* sound is a tough one for ventriloquists. This consonant has a kind of singing quality (as in humming) that depends on the nasal cavity for its unique sound. You have two choices in forming your substitute *M* sound.

As with the *P* and *B* sounds, you make use of the hard palate located behind your upper teeth on the roof of your mouth to make the *M* sound. To do it, press not just the tip of your tongue but the entire front top one third of your tongue against your hard palate. Think of it as an exaggerated *N* sound. This is your first option, and the one many ventriloquists prefer. It will be difficult, and it's going to sound just like an *N* in the beginning. Don't get frustrated! Keep at it. And stick with your schedule time so you don't burn out by practicing too long!

You create the fricative F sound (and the V sound, discussed later in the chapter) by releasing your breath through a narrow opening between your front teeth.

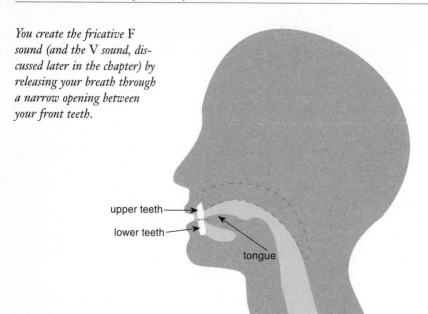

When making the ventriloquist M sound, the tongue lies across the hard palate, forcing sound into the nasal cavity.

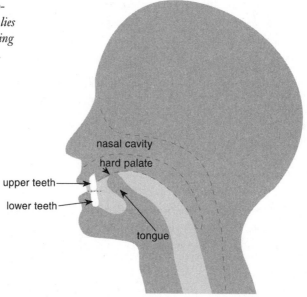

The second option is to use the back of your upper mouth, behind your hard palate, which is known as the *velum* or *soft palate*. Press the middle and back of the top of your tongue—the part of your tongue that's arched in vent position—against your soft palate. This diverts your voice and breath to your nasal cavity so when you part your tongue from your palate, you complete the sound.

The first option is the most accessible, while the second offers another way to create the substitute sound. Practice both styles, find the one that comes closest to what you hear as a real *M* sound, and stick with it. Remember, you can edit and experiment any way you like. Perhaps the first way comes naturally, or maybe you will use both techniques depending on the word you're pronouncing.

As with the earlier examples, try using your new *M* sound in vent position with words and phrases that incorporate all your newfound skills. Try *map, bumper, frumpy, bumble bee,* and *trumpet.* And try a sentence, too, such as "MapQuest trumps my GPS because it's perfectly framed in map form." Use your mirror, and be as honest with yourself as you can. Use your recorder. Persevere (a good word for practice: *persevere!*), and stick to your schedule times.

The *V* Sound

V is another fricative, like the *F* sound. Just as you made the *F* earlier by using the soft *TH* sound, substitute the hard *TH* sound (as in *those* or *them* or *bathing*) for the *V* sound. Starting in vent position, say the word *very* without moving your lips. Instead of touching your bottom teeth to your upper lip for the *V* sound, however, substitute the hard *TH* sound. Look in your mirror and say *thery.*

The *V* and *F* sounds are similar and shouldn't take a long time for you to master.

Pull Strings

At this point, you've learned five of the toughest substitute sounds. *B* and *P* are the hardest; *V* and *F* are the easiest. Start practicing short sentences in vent position using these sounds. For example: "Bathing is good for my personal hygiene." You're using all your newly learned substitute sounds in a sentence, and with practice you'll be able to make the sentence sound perfect!

The *W* Sound

We've learned the most difficult sounds for a ventriloquist to make (keep working on those!). Now let's take a look at *W*.

You say a normal *W* by forming your lips into an O-shape and parting them as the back of your tongue is slightly raised. Your vocal cords vibrate, your breath is forced through your mouth, and your lips part.

How do you mimic that as a ventriloquist? Simple! It's a case of breaking down *W* into syllables. The two sounds you'll be making are an *OOH* sound and an *AH* sound. Try it in your normal, nonvent position. Say "*Ooh.*" Say "*Ah.*" Now put them together, as in "*Ooh-ah.*" Got it? Now say "*Ooh-ah*" as fast as you can: "*Ooah!*" Can you hear the similarity between the regular *W* sound and this substitute? You're going to make that same sound without moving your lips in vent position.

Get your mirror, get into vent position, and softly say "*Ooh-ah*" without moving your lips. It will take a couple tries, but it shouldn't be hard for you, particularly because you're already getting more comfortable being in vent position and forming substitute sounds.

Now try saying some words with *W: wet, west, weird.* Put the substitute sound in a sentence with your other substitute sounds: "We flopped in our beds without purchasing much food." Make up your own sentences. Use combinations and multiple-syllable words that include everything you've learned, such as *multiple power fumble.*

The Y Sound

We've come to the easiest of the "hard" sounds, or labial sounds, that the speaker normally forms with his or her lips. *Y* is another nasal consonant, so the substitute sound is a combination of syllables.

The normal *Y* is formed by circling your lips into an O-shape, similar to the *W* sound. But instead of combining it with the *AH* sound, it comes out as *I,* as in *ooh* and *eye.* Just as you did with *W,* try to say the syllables *ooh* and *eye* in normal mouth position a couple times and then do it in vent position. Use your mirror. Say "*Ooh-eye*" as fast as you can, without moving your lips. It will come out "*Ooh-eye,*" but remember, you're breaking down the sound to fool your audiences' ears momentarily.

Pull Strings

Remember, ventriloquism is more than lip control. It's substituting sounds for the real thing! The listener won't be able to tell the difference because you're using perfect technique!

The easiest practice word for the *W* sound is *why.* Try it in a question: "Why pretend to make verbs for people when I practically fly away from bumble bees?" It doesn't make sense, but don't worry about it. You're practicing all your new sounds!

That's Cheating! (But That's Okay!)

You've learned the basic substitute sounds every professional ventriloquist uses to perform his craft. You're familiar with how to make sounds, how the human ear acknowledges sounds, and how you can fudge a little bit with the labials. Now it's time to learn the time-honored skill every conjurer uses: cheating!

Obviously you can't make exact replicas of B, M, and P sounds, but you can make the audience believe you made those sounds perfectly.

One way is to quickly gloss over one of those sounds during a sentence, as in "I want to pull that cord." The tough sound here is the P in "pull." The ventriloquist will, on occasion, skip over the sound so the sentence comes out like "I want to (t)ull that cord." The emphasis here is *not* on the silent T that's been substituted for the P in "pull." The emphasis is on "I want to" and "ull that cord." The P sound in "pull" has been replaced by a faint T sound.

But the human ear can't make out the difference between the P and T sounds. As listeners, we make the jump and give the benefit of the doubt to the speaker, or in this case a figure of some kind. So we believe we heard "I want to *pull* that cord." The ventriloquist knows that, and for this sentence, he cheated a little. So what? The listener couldn't tell the difference, and we're already on to the next sentence!

The problem inherent to cheating this way is that ventriloquists build their entire acts on cheating sounds. You can trick the audience once or twice or three times, but if every one of your labial substitutes is a cheating sound, the listener will eventually catch on. The cliché is true: you can fool some of the people some of the time, but not all the people all the time.

Suitcases
When it comes to ventriloquism, cheating is okay—as long as you don't get caught!

It's critical that you learn to make perfect-as-possible (there's a good phrase to practice in vent position!) substitute sounds. As you begin to practice and rehearse toward your first live performance, note places in your script where you might want to cheat a little bit. That's okay. Cheating is just another tool in your ventriloquist tool box. Don't overuse it, but don't ignore it!

Tricking Your Listener

Similar to cheating, you can trick your listener in a variety of ways using acoustics and sounds. Let's take a look at two examples.

One great way to set yourself up for success as a ventriloquist is to differentiate sounds so the human ear picks up exactly what you want it to. The ventriloquist B is similar to a D sound, but not quite a D or a B. It comes down somewhere in between, a kind of hybrid between D and B. Use this difference to your advantage! The best way is to "set up" your audience. Early in your performance, say a word with a regular D sound, such as *dud*. The audience hears it, understands it, recognizes the D sound, and knows what you're saying: *dud*.

Now comes the trick: say the words *but* and *bud*. Make your B sound in vent position and then say a regular D sound at the end of *bud*. The listener hears the words. They already heard the D sound in *dud*, but now they hear something different. It's not the D sound they just heard, but the way this new sound is used in a sentence (for example, "He's a dud, but he's my bud") is very clear. That sound at the beginning of *but* and *bud* is not a D, but their ears translate it immediately into a B sound. To trick your audience, you "set them up" with a sound similar to the one you want to substitute.

Let's look at another example with the words *tot* and *top*. The listener hears the perfect T sounds, followed by a sound that comes in somewhere between a T and a P. He makes the assessment on his own that it must be a P sound. So a sentence like "My tot is the tops!" will be very clearly understood.

Hiccups

Ventriloquists of the late 1800s and early 1900s grew long, bushy moustaches to hide their lack of lip control. In the 1980s and 1990s, ventriloquists in comedy clubs often hid their mouth behind the microphone! Neither trick worked for long, though, as audiences caught on. Be careful how and when you trick your listeners!

Obviously you're not going to use those silly sentences in performances. But you *will* be using something like that, and every time you use sounds that are close to your substitute sounds, you're going to trick your listeners. Remember, ventriloquism is more about playing with and manipulating sounds to your own benefit than it is about anything else.

A second trick you can use every once in a while is to turn your head away from the audience (or for right now your mirror) to say a particularly difficult word (like *particularly*). This has to be very well rehearsed and planned because if you pull this stunt in the middle of a sentence, it has to come off as natural and as part of the dialogue.

To do it, get into vent position and say something like, "I enjoyed our dinner, particularly the steak." As you did earlier, passing over the *P* sound in *pull*, you're going to trick the listener by slightly turning your head to make a perfect *P* sound as you normally would when you get to the word *particularly*. Then snap your head back to your audience and continue the sentence in vent position. This trick has been used by ventriloquists for decades, but use it *sparingly*.

Practicing Substitute Sounds with Your Figure

When you've reached the point where you feel you've got a good hold on your new sounds and how to make them in vent position, and your lip control is excellent, it's time to practice saying sentences and putting your skills to use.

Whatever figure you start with, a sock puppet or a full-fledged ventriloquist figure, use your dominant hand. If you're right-handed, put your right hand in the figure. Left-handed, same thing. You'll eventually want to work with both hands, but just use your dominant hand to start.

Begin by grabbing your figure—or making a simple sock puppet if you don't have your figure yet. You're going to start synchronizing the syllables and the words with your figure's mouth opening and closing. For example, when your figure says "Hello," that's a two-syllable word: *hell-oh*. So you will, naturally, open and close the figure's mouth two times, once for each syllable. The better you get at synchronizing the figure's mouth with the syllables, the more lifelike the figure will appear.

At the same time, you want to concentrate on saying the difficult words that contain the labial sounds: *B, F, M, P, V, W*, and *Y*. You can use the example sentences in this chapter, or you can make up your own. Be sure to use your mirror. Concentrate on not moving your lips, synchronizing the words with the figure's mouth, and using the occasional tricks and cheats you have learned here.

This is an exciting time! You are on your way to becoming a performer!

The Least You Need to Know

- Ventriloquists move their tongues in certain ways to make substitute sounds for *B, F, M, P, V, W*, and *Y*.

- There are some sentences that allow you to use the *B, F, M, P, V, W*, and *Y* sounds and practice substitute sounds without moving your lips.

- With his or her mouth in vent position, a ventriloquist can trick the audience into hearing what he or she wants them to hear.

- Ventriloquists use a couple good tricks of the trade to make their performances more believable to audiences.

Chapter 5

It's All in the Voice

In This Chapter

- ◆ Giving your voice different characteristics
- ◆ Working with pitches and tone
- ◆ Incorporating inflection, dialects, and accents
- ◆ Tips for protecting your voice and keeping it strong
- ◆ Learning to change your voice

We've reached the point where you're probably getting comfortable with vent position. You're able to do a very good job substituting sounds for the difficult letters that normally require the lips, and you're ready to do more with your voice. In this chapter, I teach you how to expand your voice to at least three more entirely different tones.

Regardless of your sex, vocal ability, and training, everyone has the ability to use different tones and pitches with their voice. You use some of these naturally, and you may not even know it! In the following pages, I show you how to create a couple characters with your voice.

Using All the Registers in Your Voice

Earlier in the book I recommended you cover one ear with a finger and listen to yourself speak. Let's do that again. With your forefinger, gently close off an ear so sound cannot get in, and listen to yourself speak. Say any phrase you like. The voice you hear now is your "real" voice. Now let's add certain characteristics.

Your First Character Voice

Get into vent position, and say any sentence you like using your real voice. Maybe try, for example, "I am going to be a great ventriloquist." Now say it as you move your lips and talk normally. Now go back to vent position and say your sentence again without moving your lips. Do you hear the difference? Without trying to add anything to the way you normally speak, your vent position voice is different from your normal voice. It's more nasal, is a little higher pitched, and has a slightly different tone. Try it again and listen to the difference.

Congratulations! You just created your first character voice! This is a great voice for practicing your technique with a figure. It might become a staple in your performance, or it might be something you never use again. But it will always be the first character voice in your arsenal.

Adding Highs and Lows

Let's take this a step further. Once again, gently block one ear with your forefinger. Put your lips together and hum, just making a normal "*Mmmmmmm*" or "*Hummmmmmm*" sound with your regular voice. Now try humming with your lips together in a high voice. It might sound good, it might sound funny, or it might sound obnoxious. All of that is good!

Now make yourself hum in as low a tone as you can.

You have four separate tones as of this moment: your own voice, the high and low voices you just hummed, and your vent position voice. Congratulations! You have three character voices!

Pull Strings

Another basic way to find a character voice is to imitate someone you're familiar with, such as a family member, a favorite actor or musician, or someone you work with. You don't have to do a perfect impression of that person, but just experimenting with those dynamics will eventually earn you a new voice character!

Putting Your New Voices to Work

Let's keep things simple and put two of your new voices to work, starting with the high voice you just came up with in the preceding humming exercise. You can use any figure you like for the following exercises and practices.

To start, hum in that high voice again. Gently block your ear hole and listen to yourself hum in this high voice, getting a feel for how it sounds and its timbre and resonance.

Now get into vent position. Hum in your new high voice again, this time using your ventriloquist *M* sound. Play with this for a while, maybe changing the tone. Try it in a whisper, try it as loud as you can, and try it with words. Try singing a song you like, or maybe something as simple as "Happy Birthday." If it sounds awkward or strange, that's okay. If it sounds funny, that's great! After all, what better way to start getting laughs than finding something in your voice you think is funny?

The next step is going to stretch you as a ventriloquist and as an actor or a comedian. You're going to begin having a conversation with your figure. It might feel odd because you're really talking to yourself, but give it a try. One way to get past this feeling is to try to think of improvising a theatrical scene or a sitcom scene. Don't try so much to be funny; just try to keep the conversation going with your figure. Ask the figure about the weather, about the room you're in, how it feels, and what it wants to do. Have it answer in the natural ventriloquist voice you started with, with your mouth and tongue in vent position and your normal ventriloquist voice. Don't worry about what the figure does right now. Just try to get some basic synchronization between the words you're saying via the figure and the figure's movements.

> **Pull Strings**
>
> Another way to find a new character voice using a high-pitched tone is to arch the back of your tongue underneath your soft palate, without touching your soft palate. This position restricts the flow of air from your larynx, forcing the tone and pitch of your voice to go up. Try it!

Now try the same thing, asking your figure basic questions it can answer with more than a "yes" or "no" answer—for example, "Where were you last night?" or "What's your favorite movie?" Have the figure answer using the high ventriloquist voice you practiced earlier. If you can record a short dialogue, do so and listen to the result. The figure's words have to be clear and well pronounced so the listener can hear everything perfectly. If the high voice you're using sounds muffled or unclear, try another voice. Make it just a little lower.

The most important thing about this exercise—and this part of ventriloquism—is that the figure has a distinctly different voice from yours (in this case, it's the high voice) and that the voice is easily understood. Words can't be slurred. The labial sounds have to come across as very good imitations of the real thing. Don't be afraid to work very slowly, getting every syllable and word correct. Use your mirror, and monitor your lip control as the figure speaks.

This is a lot of information, but this is why ventriloquism, when done well, is such a vibrant, entertaining, and fun art form. You are creating a character, much the way an actor creates a voice and character for a part he is playing. The difference is that you will be performing both parts at the same time!

When you've perfected this high voice, do the same for the low voice. Again, get into good vent position. You'll notice that it's easy to get a good low voice with the back of your tongue arched or lying across the bottom of your mouth. (The high voice usually requires the tongue to be arched toward the soft palate.) Find your comfort zone, using both the low voice and the placement of your tongue. The key is pronunciation and annunciation so the listener doesn't have to struggle to get the meaning of the words you make in vent position.

Pull Strings

Slow down! Most people have a tendency to get through things as quickly as possible, but this defeats the purpose of ventriloquism. Take things step by step and be deliberate. I discuss this in later chapters, as slowing down is a good rule of thumb in live performance as well, but for now, remember to take things slowly and get your technique, lip control, voices, and figure synching down pat.

You should now have three distinct character voices to use in addition to your own voice: the natural vent position voice where you don't change anything about the way you talk, other than the fact that you aren't moving your lips and you're using the figure. You also have the high voice and the low voice we just worked on. There is more to do, and you probably have ideas you'd like to try. That's coming!

Swallowing Your Voice

You've already learned that speaking in your natural voice sounds different from when you speak in vent position, even without any real attempt on your part to change it. Vent position forces more air into your nasal cavity, resulting in a voice that's similar but not quite the same. You can take that one step further by "swallowing" your voice.

To swallow your voice, first get into vent position and make an *AH* sound. Remember that this originates in your voice box/larynx. Now try to force that *AH* sound back down your throat. One way is to raise the back of your tongue that is under the soft palate and force all the sound to come out through your nose. This gives your natural vent position voice a different tone and pitch and sounds very different from your real voice, whereas the vent position voice might be too similar to your own.

And as easy as that, you have another voice to add to your ventriloquist tool kit!

Adding Character to Your Figure's Voice

You've probably heard boring, monotone speakers before, with flat, lifeless voices that made you want to stop listening or sent you off daydreaming. Don't do that to your audiences! The more engaging your voice is, the more your audience will be … well, *engaged* in your act!

Infusing Your Voice with Inflection

One way to make your routine more interesting is by using *inflection* in your or your figure's voice. We all use inflection, whether we know it or not, during even the shortest of conversations. Inflection can make a sentence direct, friendly, questioning, or factual, or express any range of emotions. Think of it this way: you come home to a seemingly empty house or apartment. You don't know if your spouse/roommates/children are there. You call out, "Anyone here?" It's an open-ended question, and the way you ask it tells the listener (if one is actually there) that you're home and you want to say "hi."

def•i•ni•tion

Inflection is the change or modification of the pitch and tone of your voice as you speak. It's the opposite of monotone. With inflection, you can give your figure his or her mood through his or her voice.

Same question, but now you're the actor in a horror movie. You come home to an empty house that's completely dark. A stark piano plays on the soundtrack. The door creaks as you open it. Something falls off a table and lands on the wooden floor with a *thwack*. You hit the light switch … but it doesn't work. You stand in the darkness. "Anyone home?" you ask. Same question, but your inflection is completely different. There's fear in those two words, and the audience feels it and knows what's coming. *Aaaahhh!*

Now consider how this applies to you and your ventriloquist figure. The figure is more dependent on vocal characteristics than body language, so every little variation you make with the figure's voice is exaggerated more than a real human being's voice. Using inflection and modulation of words is going to define your figure's character, make his emotions more accessible to the listeners and the audience, and most of all help you—the ventriloquist—get to the heart of just who your figure is.

To apply inflection to your figure, let's start with questions. Using questions is an easy way to apply a modulation to the voice because we do it anyway. When you ask a question, your voice naturally rises at the end, usually with the last word. Think, for example, of "How are you?" The inflection you give the word *you* indicates you're asking a question.

Okay, now grab your figure and get in front of your mirror. Have the figure ask "How are you?" in different ways by changing the inflection of its voice. Start with the emphasis on the last word, *you*. As you have the figure ask "How are you?" raise your voice suddenly and quickly when you get to *you*, as in "How are *you?*" The inflection offers a lot of images in the listener's mind. Try the same thing again, only this time drop your voice on *you* so it comes out lower and without much emotion: "*How are* you?" Same question, same words, but very different meaning all due to the vocal inflection you applied.

You can practice inflection with every rehearsal, with every script, and even in live performance. Think of the figure speaking in a sing-songy voice—that's a voice that uses lots of inflection. You'll find inflection easy to use with questions, but raising the pitch and modulating the sentences in a statement works just as well. You have practice time to find the kind of voice your figure will end up with.

Pull Strings

Think of your act and your skills as a ventriloquist as a work in progress. It's my sincere hope that you're going to have success with vent. And like a good musician, you'll keep growing and learning.

There are other ways to use inflection. Multisyllable words can have three different inflections. For example, let's look at *overstimulation*. Break down the word into six syllables—*o-ver-stim-u-lay-shun*—and have your figure say it slowly with the emphasis on the *U*, as in *o-ver-stim-U-lay-shun*. This gives the word a certain punch.

The idea is to use all the skills you have as a voice manipulator, and inflection is a valuable tool.

Doing Some Dialect

Inflection works closely with dialect. Every day, whenever you talk, you're speaking a dialect. Some dialects are well known and easily identifiable, and some are not. For example, in the Chicago area, there are numerous dialects spoken by people who have lived there for years, but the way they speak is a bit different county to county, town to town, and street to street. A suburban teen from a predominantly Caucasian suburb speaks differently than a retiree living on the near north side, who has a completely different dialect than a working African American mother on the south side, who speaks differently than a professor at the University of Chicago, also on the south side.

As a ventriloquist, you can't possibly pick up and imitate every American dialect. But it's important that you're aware of these different dialects. As you hear how people speak, you might come across a little nugget of inflection or vocal variation you can put to use with your current or a future figure.

Adding Accents

Dialects differ from accents, which are more general and can help establish your figure's character based solely on the accent of its voice.

For example, you're surely familiar with the accent that hails from the American South. There are even dialects within the southern accent. Don't believe me? Just listen to a native North Carolinian speaking to someone from the Louisiana Bayou. Accents aren't limited to the south. There's a New York City Jewish accent that's well known and identifiable. And if you're from New Jersey, your accent might give you away as a local.

Being able to imitate, mimic, and perform an accent or two with a figure adds yet another piece to your ventriloquist arsenal and enables you to create a character the audience can quickly and easily identify.

Although you can learn an accent by listening to videos and Internet downloads, imitating by listening to a native speaker is the fastest and most important way to learn an accent. When you do this, you're doing the same thing you did as a child: you listened to people speak, and you repeated what you heard. You may be older now, but you can still do the same thing you did then. Similar to what you've learned about ventriloquism

Hiccups

If you don't do an accent well, *don't take it onstage.* There's nothing worse than portraying a nationality or a culture in an insulting manner just because you didn't take the time to learn their accent properly.

so far, you're going to have to expand the abilities of your ear and your vocal cords by listening to examples of the accent you want to learn.

Changing Your Voice Quickly in Dialogue

Now that you've put together three new voices, it's time to practice some dialogue, get into a routine, and actually converse with your figure. To do this, you must "sell" your audience on the idea that two (or more) people are talking to one another, even though one of them isn't real.

This begins with you changing your voice—and doing it quickly in the routine, as two real people would sound when talking together. This isn't any different from all the other techniques you've learned to this point: you'll perfect it only through focused practice. While working with a figure, strive toward getting the synchronization of the figure's words and mouth movement as close to exact as possible.

Beginning the Conversation

The best place to start this exercise is in front of your mirror. You're going to have a "conversation" with your figure. As always, start slow and pick up the tempo as you become more familiar with the words and rhythm. To help you get started, I've given you a dialogue for you and your figure. You want this to flow evenly and purposefully, as in a normal conversation between two people. Ready?

YOU: Hello, figure, how are you?

FIGURE: I've been better.

YOU: What's wrong?

FIGURE: You can't tell?

YOU: No! You look fine. You sound fine.

FIGURE: Maybe I look fine. Maybe I sound fine. But I'm not fine! I'm in pain. Do you understand? *I am in pain!*

YOU: *Oh no!*

FIGURE: Oh, yes. I hurt.

YOU: Where?

FIGURE: I have a sore throat.

YOU: Really?

FIGURE: Yes. I have a sore throat, and apparently nobody is going to do anything about it.

YOU: What do you mean?

FIGURE: Well, I have a sore throat. Wouldn't it figure that someone else would have a sore throat? Someone like, oh, I don't know, someone like … *you?*

YOU: I don't have a sore throat!

FIGURE: Really? That's odd … now that I think about it, I don't have a sore throat, either! I guess I'm just fine!

This should give you an idea of how you should approach working with your figure, working with a script, and getting your voice changes down. Try this script in all three of your new voices, and use the one that feels the most natural (or fun!).

We'll spend some time working on figure manipulation and voice synchronization later in the book. For now, try to get the voice synch between the voice and the figure as close as possible: one open and shut of the figure's mouth should correspond with every syllable it speaks in your vent position voice.

Improving Your Technique with Wordplay

Tongue twisters and wordy songs are a great way to show off your technique and earn applause and appreciation for your performance skills.

The following tongue twister will make you focus on your technique and synching abilities. Start slowly and get every word and syllable down perfectly before moving on. And use your mirror so you can see as well as hear how you're doing. When you're comfortable, you can pick up the speed. You want to reach a point where you're saying this tongue twister so quickly that you do it better in vent position than most people say it when they use their lips!

Here we go:

A skunk sat on the stump and thunk the stump stunk.

But the stump thunk the skunk stunk.

Say this over and over in your regular voice, not using vent position. Just practice it yourself, without your figure. Get to the point where you've almost memorized the tongue twister and then try it with your figure. Start by trading the lines—the figure says the top line, you say the second. Then switch. Then switch back. And switch again. Get to the point where you can run both lines with your figure, lip-synching words in the vent position and getting all the substitute sounds down perfectly.

When you're doing this little tongue twister perfectly, break it up. Use it as a dialogue between you and your vent figure:

YOU: Did a skunk sit on that stump?

FIGURE: A skunk sat on the stump and thunk the stump stunk.

YOU: What did the stump think?

FIGURE: The stump thought the skunk stunk.

YOU: So let me get this straight. A skunk sat on the stump and thought the stump stunk?

FIGURE: Yes.

YOU: But the stump thought the skunk stunk?

FIGURE: That's right.

YOU: Okay. I think I get it, but could you just clarify it for me?

FIGURE: Sure. The skunk sat on a stump, but thunk the stump stunk. The stump thought the skunk stunk.

YOU: Who had it right?

FIGURE: Stump and the skunk both stunk, I thunk, so I put 'em in a trunk and sold 'em as junk.

Rehearse this. You want to get to the point where you've memorized every line and you don't need the script. And feel free to improvise, edit, and change it anyway you see fit. The idea is to get out and perform and have some material you can use. This is a place to start. If done well, in whatever voices you like, this will be an entertaining and fun routine. Good luck!

Staying Focused

Changing your voices back and forth is something that can only come with practice. This is not something that people do naturally, and three things will keep your mind occupied:

- ◆ Remember that you're trying to use flawless ventriloquist technique.

- ◆ Keep the voices straight. You are your own voice and the figure has its own voice. It will take practice to get them working in a natural flow.

◆ Really work on synchronizing the syllables with the figure's mouth opening and closing.

We work on that last one more in later chapters, but you get the idea. As a ventriloquist, there's more to it than just talking without moving your lips!

Stage Whisper

By now you have realized that ventriloquism incorporates many of the techniques and skills used in theater and acting. One of these is the "stage whisper." Mastering this ability will add believability and quality to your performance.

The stage whisper is something whispered by a performer onstage that's intended to be "private" and perhaps inaudible to the other actors onstage, but the audience can still hear it. In other words, the stage whisper is intended to be heard.

As a ventriloquist, you should practice whispering so that when you use the whisper in performance, it won't feel awkward or uncomfortable. Have your figure whisper a few lines of dialogue and get the feel of it. Record the figure in whisper mode so you can be sure the words are intelligible and clear.

A ventriloquist is inclined to whisper "loudly" so his or her voice can be heard. This is understandable because the sound is coming from a small opening between your non-moving lips, and you might think a certain volume is needed. But that's not the case. You'll be using a microphone to amplify your voice, so you can whisper in a normal tone and the audience will still hear you.

Remember that when people whisper something, they're doing it for a reason. Your figure will act the same way, so when it's whispering, you need to exaggerate the mouth opening and closing, the synchronization of words, and the figure's body movements.

Whispering is a wonderful tool. When your figure whispers during a live performance, the audience is drawn into the reality you're creating. Whispering *forces* the audience to strain a little bit to hear what's happening.

Don't Hurt Yourself!

Depending on your lifestyle and profession, and how you talk naturally, there's a chance all this vocalizing, arching your tongue, and using the diaphragm is taxing your voice. You may be experiencing a sore throat, some laryngitis or minor loss of voice, or some pain when you're working on your ventriloquist technique.

First and foremost, *if you're experiencing pain, something isn't right and you need to stop and examine what is happening and why.*

A sore throat and laryngitis probably aren't cause for concern, unless there are extenuating circumstances beyond ventriloquism. If you're not used to using your larynx and all these techniques, you might suffer some discomfort as your vocal cords try to keep up with your practice schedule and this new way of talking. When you start to feel taxed, take a break. You might even have to take a day or two off. Clearly, if sore throats and an overall weaker voice ensue from your ventriloquism practice, see a doctor.

Various homeopathic and medical cures and comforts for singers and people who strain their voices are available to you as a practicing ventriloquist. Hot tea (with or without honey), hot showers, and eucalyptus might all be helpful. You can find myriad "cures" online, and your doctor or family and friends will no doubt have some thoughts as well. Find what works for you.

Most importantly, and this is worth repeating: *if you're in pain, stop what you're doing and take the appropriate steps!*

Ventriloquism is supposed to be fun, and that means pain-free (at least physically!). It's an art form that has been practiced by hundreds of thousands of people over the past couple of centuries, and as far as I know, there have been no death-by-ventriloquism stories to date. If you're in pain, something's wrong and you need to figure out what that is.

The Least You Need to Know

- When you're using vent position, you speak in a different tone and voice than your natural voice. This happens without even making an effort because your mouth is in a different position!

- You have a wide range of voices you can call upon, and two of those are the high and low voices, which you can easily access.

- We all use dialects and accents every day. Giving a figure an accent is a great way to define who it is to an audience—but don't use a bad accent in performance!

- It will take some practice to switch quickly back and forth between voices (as in a real conversation) when using a figure. You *must* practice this.

- As with any exercise, you might feel some mild discomfort when practicing different voices and perfecting your technique, but you shouldn't feel pain. If you do, see your doctor.

Chapter 6

Putting Words in the Figure's Mouth

In This Chapter

- ◆ Analyzing the voice you'll use for your figure
- ◆ Tips for synching the figure's mouth movements with your voice
- ◆ The figure—what a character!

With flawless technique, the audience won't think twice about the ventriloquist figure "talking," moving its mouth in perfect synch with the syllables it's saying. But if the synchronization is off, they *will* notice. You can alleviate this issue through diligent practice and by employing some of the techniques in this chapter.

Finding the figure's voice, working it into dialogue, and performing flawlessly with your figure is perhaps the most challenging part of learning to be a ventriloquist. Combining vent position, change of voice, lip control, and mouth synchronization is the goal of this chapter.

Working on Synchronization

Well, you've been doing this for some time now, matching the syllables you make in vent position with the opening and closing of the figure's mouth. Easy, right? Not so fast. Let's dig a little deeper here. To add to the figure's overall personality and give the audience more information about who it is, you can combine some great inflection with your figure's mouth movement.

Synch Practice

Here we go again! Get your figure and your mirror, and get into vent position. You're going to have your figure say, "Oh no!" We'll do it a couple ways. First, say it just the way it's written here: "Oh no!" The figure's mouth opens and closes twice, and you say the words in vent position as two syllables, "Oh" and "No!" Easy enough—you've been doing this already.

Now elongate "Oh," as in "*Ooooooooooh* no!" As you speak the word in vent position, hold the figure's mouth open for the entire word. Maybe throw in some inflection, too, making the "Oh" rise and fall like a vocal roller coaster, up and down, "Oo-OO-oo-OO-OOOOOH No!" Do the same with the word "No." Start with the figure's mouth closed. When you begin the first sound of "Oh," open the figure's mouth and start speaking in vent position. Stretch out the word, using some inflection, and maybe even moving the figure's head up and down or back and forth with each inflection. Stop after a few seconds. When the word stops, snap shut the figure's mouth. Then start up again on "No!"

"No" has its own head movement everyone knows: the head shakes back and forth, as if it's on a swivel. So when you hold out the figure's "nooooooooooo!" and its mouth is wide open, maybe its head shakes back and forth, too—that is, your hand moves it back and forth. Again, close the mouth at the end of the word. If done perfectly, it could look like the figure is frightened or at least committed to *not* doing something. It could even be funny.

More Synch Tips

There are lots of ways to practice synchronizing your speaking voice in the vent position with the opening and closing of the figure's mouth. Have it count from 1 to 10, for example. Really overstate the mouth and head movements as you get to the 20s, 30s, and so on because these are multisyllable words that require the mouth to open and close in synch numerous times. The more you work at it, the better you'll get. Soon, synching your voice will become second nature.

Try breaking big words down into easy-to-hear syllables, which helps the audience understand what the figure is saying and helps the figure get its mouth opened and closed enough times to make it believable. *Uncomfortable* is a good word to try with *mouth synchronization,* and a good word to practice in the vent position. You're going to break it down into individual syllables the audience can hear:

YOU: Do you like the suitcase?

FIGURE: *Oooooooh noooooooooo!* How could you even ask me that? It's so *un-kum-fort-uh-bul.*

You can combine two exercises in one here. Practice mouth synching and inflection in the first part of the figure's line, where it says "Oh no!" Then, when you get to *uncomfortable,* break it down into five separate syllables.

Of course, bad mouth synchronization can be a joke for the ventriloquist and the figure, but it cannot be a recurring part of a performance. The better the synch, the more believable the figure is and the more convincing the relationship between figure and ventriloquist.

def•i•ni•tion

Mouth synchronization is similar to but not the same as lip synching. Mouth synchronization can be flexible and improvised on the spot because the ventriloquist is present in the moment. Lip synching is a recorded entertainment that has to follow a script A to Z.

Finding the Figure's Voice

You've put together at least three voices you can use for your figure. You've worked on your lip control and your mouth synchronization. You've thought about an accent, and you're feeling more and more in control of your ability. Let's nail down a voice for your figure once and for all.

The first rule of voices for ventriloquist figures: *there are no rules!* A female figure can have a dark, deep, low voice. A male figure can have a high-pitched, squeaky falsetto. The decision and the final product are totally up to you. Remember, you're the director and the lead actor in this show, so whatever you decide is the way it is!

Oftentimes voices work against character: a rough, tough-looking lion who speaks in a shy whisper, a lamb who talks like a thug from the streets, a teenage girl with a deep bass voice. The good thing about voice-against-character is that the audience gets the immediate joke—"Oh, the figure doesn't sound anything like what I thought it would!"—and you're off and running right from the first line.

Of course there are many figures whose voices will be marked by the way they look. For example, a celebrity or a politician look-alike figure is given to a vocal impression of that celebrity or politician. (And you better have that impression down perfectly, or you'll be in for a long night!) A figure that represents a cultural icon needs to sound like that culture—say a NASCAR driver figure or professional athlete. If your figure is a teacher or a professor, it needs to sound educated and intellectual, perhaps even haughty. Practice a couple different voices with your figure, and don't be afraid to experiment.

Pull Strings

Here's a hint you can use right now and should be kept as your modus operandi, especially as you get into live performance: don't be afraid to fail!

Once you've made a commitment to a particular voice for a figure, you are by no means compelled to stick to it. The best thing to do is let the audience tell you how the figure should sound! If you're getting big laughs or wonderful responses and applause from the audience with the voice you're using, why change? That's perfection!

But if the jokes are falling flat, or the voice doesn't seem to enthrall the crowd, try anything and everything to get the response you desire, including changing the figure's voice.

Which Came First, the Voice or the Figure?

Ventriloquists sometimes choose the voice and characteristics for a figure long before they actually have the figure in their hands. This is fine, and it actually plays into the way this book is set up. You'll have practiced your lip control and vocal technique in vent position for a few weeks before you actually start working with a figure on your hand to compliment your hard-earned skills. You very well may choose to keep that original voice you practiced with for the first figure you're going to use. That's a clear case of the voice coming before the figure.

Similarly, some figures will have voices defined by the way they look or what or who they're supposed to represent.

However, what ends up as your figure's voice may not be what you envisioned when you first saw the figure. And that's okay! It's always in your best interest, artistically, to see what happens with a different voice and different inflections.

Your assignment is to entertain and please audiences. You want to reach a point where you can take your ventriloquism skills out into the real world and share your craft with an audience. However you choose to give life and a voice to your figure should not be written in stone. You need to have the flexibility to adapt your style and, in turn, the voice, in any way you see fit. The answer to the question "Which came first, the voice or the figure?" is a trick question. The answer is "The enjoyment for the audience."

Voice = Personality

Ventriloquism is unique to show business because it incorporates so many different aspects into one skill. There's the technical aspect to ventriloquism, which is often the defining trait of a good or bad vent. There's the manipulation of the figure, the script, the performance style, the impressions, the jokes, and maybe the music. Often overlooked is the similarity between a ventriloquist and an actor.

Consider that you, as a ventriloquist, are splitting yourself into at least two if not more characters in any given performance. An actor in a play or film role takes months to do research to get into the head of the single role he's playing. You're doing the same thing, only you're remaining in character as yourself, while tackling additional roles (your figures) that you *also* voice.

Many people are defined by their voice. Famous singers and actors are immediately known by the way they sing. Think of your favorite musician or band or singer, and how their voice is instantly identifiable to you. Radio personalities are often no more than a voice to millions of their fans. Politicians, including the president of the United States, are known by their voices.

At the same time, those personalities can express who they are and what they believe with little more than a phrase or a couple words because we know their voices so well. Their voice *is* their *personality*, and we read into what we hear them say whatever emotion we feel is hidden in their words.

def•i•ni•tion

Personality is somebody's set of characteristics, including their manner, actions, reactions, and voice.

The same holds true for your figure. Once you've made a commitment to its voice, that voice will define for your audience—even in a short, 15-minute performance—what its character is. Does the figure whine? Yell? Is it ever remorseful or overjoyed? What do each of those emotions mean when it comes to the way the figure says something?

Whatever personality you give your figure, much of it will come through its voice, the way it says things, the words it uses, and the inflections you give it. It's hard to bring a figure completely to life—you only have two arms, and one controls the head and mouth of the figure. Your other arm can do some manipulation of the figure's arms or legs, but for the most part, your figure depends on its voice to define who and what it is. You have the power to make that happen—and happen well.

The Least You Need to Know

- Vocal inflections help give emotion to your figure's words, making it more "real."

- It's important to synch the figure's mouth perfectly with the words it's saying. This takes practice, but it gives your performance a professional look.

- Deciding on a voice for your figure is a personal decision, and being flexible and trying different voices will eventually lead to the perfect fit vocally.

- People's voices often tell us about their personality and who they are. Why wouldn't it be the same for vent figures?

Chapter 7

"Throwing" Your Voice with the Distant Voice

In This Chapter

- ◆ Putting your distant voice to work
- ◆ Using subterfuge and creating diversions
- ◆ Selling your distant voice
- ◆ Taking advantage of acoustics

Historically, the distant voice has created the most excitement about, and interest in, its ventriloquist practitioners. With this technique, the ventriloquist makes the audience believe voices are somewhere behind them, above them, under the floor, or down the street. It's where the phrase "throwing the voice" comes from. Hundreds of stories exist about ventriloquists stopping ferryboats with apparent cries for help from people "overboard," stopping elevators because there's "someone on the ceiling!" or just making it sound as if a man is underneath the stage, trying to get out.

The distant voice doesn't get much play anymore, mostly because sound has become such a different part of our lives. For a ventriloquist to make an audience believe a voice is coming from beneath the stage of a comedy club, he's not only fighting the skill it takes to pull that off, but also the cynicism that comes from audiences knowing that a recording device or some other kind of electronics can been used. So it's understandable that ventriloquism today is defined more by the ventriloquist figures and the material they execute during a performance than the distant voice.

But at the same time, this book wouldn't be complete without an explanation of the distant voice; a lesson in how to perform it, use it, and enthrall audiences with it; and some keys to the deception that it really is. The distant voice technique can be accomplished in a number of ways, and in this chapter, we zero in on two of them.

Who Said That?: The Distant Voice

As I've discussed in earlier chapters, we amplify normal speech with the mouth and nasal cavities, which also give our voice some depth, timbre, and resonance. The volume we use when we speak depends in large part on how close we are to the person we're talking to. We shout to the person down the street, and we talk in low, hushed tones in the library, putting our heads closer together to be heard.

So if someone's standing outside a closed apartment door, talking with someone who's standing inside the apartment door, there are parameters to the volume they use when talking. For one thing, they're not nose to nose or even close enough to touch one another. There's physical matter between them: drywall, paint, wood, a steel-reinforced door (I'm talking about an apartment in New York City, obviously), and so on. What these two people hear when they're conversing through the door and wall of the apartment is muffled and muted and absorbed by the stuff in between them—even if they're shouting!

That's the point of the distant voice. The ventriloquist tries to perfectly mimic the sound of the muffled voice through the wall. How does he do this? By using techniques similar to the ones already described in this book! The key here is to produce a sound without allowing it full access to your vocal system.

Breaking Down the Distant Voice

Here, in a nutshell, is how you speak in the distant voice: Draw in a big breath, filling your lungs with air. Partially close off your throat (remember how you raised the back of your tongue to almost touch the soft palate in vent position?) so your airway is tight. With your diaphragm, exert pressure, which constricts things in your airway to your mouth and nasal cavities. Slowly exhale your breath, exuding great control over your breath and voice. As the breath passes over your vocal cords, it's confined to an area close to your larynx. In other words, your voice is trapped down in your throat and has nowhere to go. It comes out faint and odd-sounding, which fools the audience and has them scratching their heads, trying to figure out where it came from.

To get the same result, you can modify the way you groan, believe it or not. When you groan, you tighten your stomach muscles, push the air from your lungs, and—as in the preceding example—squeeze out a voice that sounds a little strange and far-off.

More Distant Voice Tips

If you want to pick up the distant voice as part of your skill set, here are some suggestions to master the trick:

1. Start with the groaning sound. You're going to use the breathing system described earlier, whereby your tongue closes off your airway in your throat by 90 percent. Use your diaphragm to exert pressure, constricting things even more. Groan this way a couple times.

2. Now take a deep breath. Use your arched-tongue technique and slowly exhale, gradually exerting pressure with your diaphragm, and emit a long *AAAAAAAAAAAAAH* sound. It doesn't have to be loud.

3. Keep your voice in your throat. Literally hold it back! Don't let it out of your mouth or nasal cavities.

4. When you've mastered this technique, replace the *AH* sound with a couple words. Try "Help me!" Remember to hold your voice in your throat and push air up with your diaphragm.

As you get more comfortable with the concept and the execution, you'll notice that the more pressure applied on the vocal folds, the greater the illusion of distance. You'll no doubt also realize that, because your voice is so far down in your throat, it's impossible to say complete words with any clarity. Your voice never reaches your tongue, so how can you form any letters or sounds? This plays into the distant voice perfectly because a voice heard from somewhere else is often muffled beyond recognition.

It's very, very important that you don't practice the distant voice technique for long periods of time. Keep the session short and focused. You're going to be straining your larynx, vocal cords, and throat in ways you never have before, which could lead to problems. Be smart, and if something hurts, *stop*.

> **Suitcases**
>
> The distant voice is a very personal technique. Feel free to edit and make up your own ways of doing things. Many people modify sound for ventriloquism in different ways from what I discuss in this book, using their personal choices and alterations they discover through experience and trial and error. With the distant voice more than any other ventriloquial technique, you can find your own way of doing things.

Creating a Diversion

About 75 percent of the success of the distant voice trick depends on the ventriloquist acting as if the voice is coming from the focal point. If you're trying to make it appear that someone's under the floor, you have to set that up, make it real for the listener, and play along with the scam as long as you can.

Most distant voice performances are preceded by a prologue, during which you explain that someone is missing from the audience or that you heard something on the other side of the wall or on the roof. This leads to the question (the setup), "Who's there?" or "Are you trapped? Can you hear me?" The response comes back, muffled and muted, a faint "Yeah ... I'm here ...." The conversation doesn't last long for a variety of reasons: the distant voice taxes your throat, the novelty wears off, and the trick is quickly discovered.

But the voice alone doesn't complete the performance. First, you must set up and perform a diversion. The diversion might come as the prologue, with something as simple as, "Did you hear that?" Of course there was nothing to hear, but the inflection in your voice—the way you ask the audience or listener if they heard something—is often enough to make them listen for what you want them to hear. In this case, a voice or some sound to give credence and closure to the question you put out there.

For the distant voice to work, the diversion has to be as real as the voice you use. Putting a question in the audience's mind is a great place to start. "Has anyone seen my dog? He's been missing all day ..." is a nice setup. It's a complete diversion from what else is going on with your performance. Then, seconds later when you use the distant voice and imitate a dog barking faintly, the audience will put two and two together and hear your dog offstage.

Here's a simple diversion you can try: say you're working on a theater stage and you want to use your distant voice skills. Stuff a pair of pants with something that creates the illusion that they're being worn, sew a pair of old sneakers to the bottoms, and put the legs under the stage curtain, with the soles of the shoes facing the audience. The audience will see what appears to be a man sitting on the floor behind the curtain, his legs sticking out onto the stage. You can call to this "person" during your presentation whenever you like, asking him to come out and see everyone, to get you a drink, and why he's sitting there.

This is a classic ventriloquist diversion, and it always amazes an audience when you pick up the two legs and feet with no body. If you use your skills well, the audience will be surprised it's not a real man!

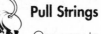

Pull Strings

One way to create a diversion is to have a live assistant working with you, unbeknownst to the audience. This stagehand can create the diversion with a muffled noise or voice. If you can carry out the trick, you will have your audience sitting in amazement.

Selling the Illusion

Perhaps more important than creating a diversion is selling the illusion. You have to convince your audience, through sheer acting (or is it conning?), that there really *is* a person under the stage, or down the street, or in the closet. There are lots of ways to do this. Let's look at a couple examples of how to sell an illusion.

The Heckler

Let's say you're going to be heckled onstage by someone sitting far off to your right, hidden from the audience by a curtain or a wall. To sell this illusion, you don't have to have your phony heckler say anything at first. It's up to you to sell the idea that someone truly is there. You have to see the individual, in your mind's eye, sitting there. You have to see what this person's wearing, what their hair color is—everything. You have to do this research well before show time.

Begin the setup for the illusion by acknowledging this imaginary friend. Allude to the person as you're performing by interrupting your act, looking straight at him or her, and asking, "Did you say something?" The audience sees you looking. They hear your words and the frustration or annoyance you feel toward this heckler thanks to the inflection in your voice. He or she gives some answer the audience cannot hear (neither can you, because he's not there!), and you go back to performing. A few minutes later you access the heckler again. "*What* is your problem?"

There are three things that will sell this bit to your audience:

- You set them up early by acknowledging this heckler.

- The audience is now ready for there to be another confrontation because the first one hasn't been resolved yet.

- You're selling by acting as if the imaginary person is really there.

You're using the distant voice to vocalize the heckler now, and he or she can say dumb stuff like "You stink!" or "I don't like you," or whatever you want the heckler to say. The audience isn't going to question anything—they've already bought your scam. So when you go over to the man or woman and pull back the curtain, revealing no one, or asking an audience member to deal with the heckler and they find no one, your talent and skill are immediately recognizable and you've pulled off a nice bit of business.

The Telephone Trick

Another great way to use the distant voice in performance is with a telephone. Especially with the popularity of cell phones, this seems like a natural for a ventriloquist.

You don't even need a prop phone to pull off the illusion; just hold an imaginary phone in your hand and tell the audience you want to make a call. Dial the pretend numbers on the pretend keypad on the pretend phone, and have the party answer using your distant voice. The phone—yes, the imaginary phone—sets the scene for the audience so they're expecting to hear another voice come through the phone, maybe a little muffled or static-y or far-off. But your skill as an improvisational actor helps sell the illusion.

Pull Strings

You can sell the illusion of the distant voice without perfect technique. If you're good at convincing your audience something is happening, they'll follow your performance until the end or until you break reality with bad technique, bad jokes, or poor execution. By mastering the distant voice, you make your presentation—and the illusion—that much stronger.

Acting Tips

Because acting is such a big part of ventriloquism as a whole, and the distant voice especially, let's go over some acting tips to help you sell the distant voice illusion.

If you have a voice call to you from someplace else—say behind a door, under the floor, or from the audience—be looking in the *opposite* direction from where you want the voice to appear to come from. This forces you to turn—preferably a quick rubberneck—to face the person who just shouted at you. Let's say in performance, you're walking across a stage or a room to your right. A voice comes from nowhere (your distant voice!) and says, "Hey! I have a question!" It's muted and hard to pin down where exactly it's coming from, but you stop in your tracks and spin around, looking into a far-off corner or putting your ear to a wall or the floor, and say, "Excuse me?" or "I'm sorry, you have a question?" It's the spin that gets the audience to focus and buy the fact that someone, somewhere, really did yell at you.

Another quick tip for selling the illusion is to have the imaginary person point something out about an audience member. It could be what they're wearing, where they're sitting, or what they're drinking. "I wish I had one of those little drinks with the umbrella in it," means there really is someone in the room, who can see everything, including what people are drinking.

And one last acting tip to help create the illusion of a person in a place where people can only hear him or her: set up the audience at the very beginning of your act with a short talk about how you might be interrupted by a plumber or maintenance workers as you perform. Explain that the audience might hear noises or talking during the show, but express that you hope everyone will just ignore the distraction and allow you to perform. This, of course, sets up a chain of events in the minds of your audience members, who hear the plumbers singing or shouting from behind the curtain or the wall. And you, frustrated and annoyed (of course), have to deal with the guys.

Much of a successful distant voice technique depends on your acting skills, as well as your ability to keep sounds deep down inside your throat. If you feel it's too much for you, or if you're still not confident in your technique, do what some ventriloquists have done: employ a helper to create the reality of a voice coming from beyond the wall or up on the ceiling.

Using Acoustics and Play-Acting

Every single place you work as a ventriloquist, whether a living room, a church basement, a comedy club, a Las Vegas casino, or a TV soundstage, will have its own acoustics. Because you're now in the business of how sound works and can be used for your own enjoyment, it makes sense that you start to pay attention to how sound travels and how it works in different settings.

For the distant voice, acoustics can play a very big role in creating the reality of the illusion. If there are echoes and natural reverb in a big theater or hall of some kind, your distant voice will come across well, even using the microphone. Everyone will be able to hear what you're trying to pull off, which is exactly what you want.

A comedy club's acoustics usually aren't as open or perfect, because the rooms are built to keep the laughter bouncing off the walls and back into the audience's laps. You won't need a microphone to sell the distant voice in a small comedy club. Even if much of the audience can't hear the muffled voice you're hiding in your throat, its all the better, because it adds to the reality of the situation. Some people heard it, some others didn't, but everyone wants to know what's going on.

The perfect acoustics you find in Las Vegas showrooms and major theaters can be used to complete the illusion you're selling to the audience. The microphones in these halls pick up everything, so you can use the distant voice to great effect, and the voices will be echoing throughout the building. You'll be able to ask people, "Where's that voice coming from?" and you'll get a bunch of different "Over there!" responses. Play it up, and you'll look like a genius in the end!

However, there's a payoff for the ventriloquist who perfects the distant voice. Within the small community of professional and great practitioners of the art, those who have achieved the perfectly executed distant voice are considered the top of the class. When done perfectly, the distant voice is a real crowd-pleaser and can be a fun feather in your cap.

The Least You Need to Know

- When using the distant voice, you keep your voice from escaping from your mouth or nasal cavities. The result is a muffled voice in your throat, and your audience can't tell where it came from.

- Pace yourself when doing the distant voice. Be careful—if something hurts, stop.

- To help sell the distant voice bit, you must also set up a diversion and the illusion that a voice really is coming from someplace else.

- Play-acting serves you well with the distant voice. It helps make the audience believe what you're telling them … from over there!

Part 3

Working With the Ventriloquist Figure

Part 3 discusses the ventriloquist figure and includes information on what kinds of figures there are, what figures are best to start with, and how to give the figure life as you perform. You're regularly instructed to see yourself as a director, an actor, and a writer in a movie or play, so the figure becomes an actor as well. This means there has to be give and take, and action and reaction during any performance. After you've chosen your figure, you're encouraged to work with it as an actor might work with a fellow actor.

There are many styles and types of figures to choose from, but beware of aiming too high: some fiberglass figures run into the tens of thousands of dollars! You probably don't need all that; you could use something as simple as a sock puppet!

Finally, Part 3 closes with a discussion on manipulation and giving the figure personality through movement and voice.

Chapter 8

The Figure

In This Chapter

- ◆ An in-depth look at the styles and variety of figures
- ◆ Tips for deciding what figure is best for you
- ◆ Help with how to avoid the mistakes first-time ventriloquists often make

Your figure is a big part of your ventriloquist act, and you have an incredible number of styles and kinds of figures to choose from. There's something for everyone, and it's worth it to take your time, decide what's best for you, and come to a decision that works not only with your pocketbook but also with the kind of act you want to be.

That's a lot to put on the figure's shoulders, which makes selecting the right one for you that much more important. So I've devoted this chapter to introducing you to the kinds of figures available and helping you find the one for you.

Before You Start ...

Before you look at or set your heart on a certain figure, stop and do a reality check. Ask yourself the following basic questions.

- Who is my audience?

- What's their age group, demographic, and location?

- What kind of venue do I want to establish for my act?

- How much can I afford to spend on a figure?

- What do I want to accomplish as a ventriloquist? (Am I a comedy ventriloquist? A musical ventriloquist? A combination of the two?)

Depending on how you answer these questions, the figure you choose dictates how you'll rehearse and practice. There's no urgency to this process, but it is important and should be taken seriously. More than anything, have fun with the evaluation and assessment of what will be the best figure for you right now! Let's take a look at your options ....

Simple Sock Puppets

The sock puppet. Even the words conjure up images of Shari Lewis and Lamb Chop, cheesy TV commercials, or even a rainy-day activity mom comes up with to pass the hours with her young children. But don't let that dissuade you from considering the sock puppet for performance. The positives far outweigh the negatives when working with this most basic figure. If you're doing close-up ventriloquism for a small group of relatives or friends, or if you're in a small venue working with children (for example, in a library room), a sock puppet is a great way to get into a vent act.

The biggest drawback to the sock puppet is its size, which is hard for audiences to see. But that almost doesn't matter in many venues these days, because big-screen video is often used. Other negatives to sock puppets include the prop itself, which can look kind of random and half-baked, and the association these kinds of puppets have with children's programs.

The machinations of the sock puppet are laughably easy: you put your hand in a sock. You stuff the toe of the sock down into the palm of your hand, and you open and close your hand to make it "talk." Voilà! Show business!

As you might guess, you can make a sock puppet pretty easily. Using rudimentary sewing skills, or just two-sided tape, you can come up with multiple characters using one sock on one hand! This makes it simple to show off your improvisation skills. And if you've developed more than one or two voices, you can quickly change the puppet's character and voice with a change of yarn for hair, or something draped over your hand as a dress or piece of clothing. The sock puppet offers you the chance to develop a wide range of individual or unusual characters that are voiced in different ways.

The best part? The sock puppet is a very inexpensive way to start your ventriloquist career! And if you're working or performing for small children, the sock puppet has exactly what you're looking for: it's nonthreatening and it won't scare toddlers (as the hard figures inevitably do). You can dress it up or make it up to look like a character in a fairy tale, or something out of a book your young audience is reading. The sock puppet is a great choice for work with children; a puppet-making workshop, during which you show children how you made your puppet and how they can make their own, will endear you to bookers and agents in lots of different markets.

Pull Strings

If you have a small hand, or you're helping a child learn ventriloquism, you might have trouble keeping the sock puppet mouth in place. To alleviate this problem, stretch a rubber band around the hand with the sock so it goes underneath the fingers and over the thumb. This will ensure that the mouth stays in working order.

But by no means is the sock puppet a children-only figure! It's the most cost-efficient and accessible figure there is, and it's ideal for someone just getting their feet wet in ventriloquism.

Soft, Lovable Foam Figures

Ventriloquism differs from puppetry, but the two arts have been closely associated for many years and the distinction is becoming more and more vague. No place is this more evident than with *The Muppets*, the lovable, soft-bodied creations of the late Jim Henson. The key to his performances, in many regards, owes much to ventriloquism, which is specifically based on the relationship between the human and his figure.

Soft figures offer many advantages. The soft figure is lighter and much more manageable. It offers the ventriloquist more range of movement, so it can exhibit more emotion, more expression, more lifelike qualities. It's easier to

Suitcases

Jim Henson coined the word *Muppet* by combining the words *marionette* and *puppet*. Unlike a ventriloquist figure, which the ventriloquist works alone, a single Muppet might require the aid of five puppeteers to make it work!

care for, and travel is much easier with a soft figure because it can be stored in a canvas or duffel bag. There's no doubt that soft figures appeal to children because they've grown up watching TV programming that features these kinds of figures.

Another huge advantage to the soft figure is its cost. A basic soft figure, which can be bought in-store or online from numerous sources, runs from $50 to $200—quite a savings from the higher-priced hard figures. A customized soft figure can be built within a couple weeks, and some are available via overnight mail, so you can have it in your hands and rehearsing within a few days of ordering.

Soft figures have moving eyes and eyebrows, winking eyes, tongues that stick out, hair that flips, and practically anything else you can think of. Every one of these extra features costs, of course, usually something like $100 per.

It's much easier to bring a soft figure to life than it is with a hard figure. The soft figure can bend and swivel and turn in any way you can think of. Working a soft figure is much the same as working a sock puppet: you open and close your hand to simulate the mouth opening and closing with each syllable. To work eyebrows, winkers, and other add-ons takes some practice and prestidigitation, but that comes with rehearsal and performing.

To give even more lifelike qualities to your soft figure, you could add a *rod-arm*, which enables you to move the figure's limbs. One word of warning: the rod-arm requires practice and rehearsal *in addition* to what you're already doing. But the payoff is greater illusion of life and bits of business that can get laughs and entertain audiences without you having to write a single line of dialogue!

def•i•ni•tion

A **rod-arm** is a thin metal or plastic rod you attach to your figure's hand or elbow. Usually it can be seen by the naked eye, but if performed well, the audience will happily suspend reality and allow the ventriloquist to help the figure make its arm motions. You use your "off" hand (the one not opening and closing the figure's mouth) to make the rod-arm move the figure's arm to point, scratch, rub, wave, and so on.

Soft figures come in a couple different styles:

◆ Those made with foam and terrycloth sewn and glued into position. These are the Muppet-like figures you're no doubt familiar with.

♦ The latex figure, which is made from a mold and painted. Often the body of the figure is built similarly to the hard or soft figure, with a latex head, and arms and feet attached with glue or thread. These are sometimes custom-built, but more often than not they're mass-produced from molds. Some of the most popular of these are animal figures because the colors can be so vibrant on latex material (although humanlike latex figures are popular, too).

Soft figures allow for a completely different range of motion than the hard figure. Because the head weighs so little and rests comfortably on your hand, you can pick up, put down, bend, slump, shake, and lift the soft figure with little effort. By putting shoes or something weighty on the feet or the bottom of the soft figure, you give it ballast, which enables the figure to stand or sit or take any position you like. Remember that much of ventriloquism is the illusion you create, beyond demonstrating your lip control and vocal technique. The soft figure has the ability to be lifelike in many ways.

There are drawbacks to these soft figures, of course. Wear and tear are part of the business for every working vent, and soft figures have a shelf-life of 3 to 5 years for the full-time performer. The paint and shading on the head fades after a while, due to bright stage lighting, constant packing and unpacking, and the general use in practice and performance. On the other hand, the soft figure is very easy to fix and update or overhaul because when something breaks down or rips, it can usually be sewn and repaired in a few minutes!

Hiccups

If you go the latex figure route, be aware of one big drawback: heat builds up inside the head. Whereas the regular soft figure, the hard figure, and even the sock puppet allow for some breathing room for your hand, latex does not allow for any airflow, and things can get very hot in there!

Classic Hard Figures

Now we come to the classic ventriloquist figure. The hard figure is the wooden-headed—or hard-headed, if you ask some ventriloquists!—slot-jawed character that's been carved or molded into shape. The hard figure is, most likely, what you picture when you think of ventriloquist figures.

Hard figures are icons of a different age, but they're still quite popular, and are used by the world's best ventriloquists today. For many vents, there's no replacing this style, because it speaks to the history of the art and a hard figure is a kind of collector's item for the future. Let's take a look.

Wood Figures

Hand-carved wood figures are the classic figures of ventriloquism. These are fashioned from all kinds of materials and made to represent any character you can name—animate or inanimate, human or animal, and everything in between. The wood figure relies on you opening and closing its mouth to create the illusion, and the ventriloquist completes the trick by giving the figure a voice. Over the years, these figures have become quite complex in what they're able to do, as creative builders have given them every imaginable human attribute, including the ability to stand, sit, cry tears, blush, smoke, bare their teeth, sleep, and even spit!

Now for the mechanics: most wood figures contain a post that extends from the head or neck, which rests ball-and-socket style on the figure's shoulders. The post is fitted with a series of levers connected to wires or strings that operate the mouth and all other movements in the head (eyes moving or blinking, eyebrows raising, eyelids shutting, and so on).

> **Suitcases**
>
> The mechanisms that work all the different features within the head are delicate and precision-made. It's a feat of engineering that the audience takes for granted when they see a performance, but the ventriloquist and the builder know there's nothing "easy" about what's going on.

The head is comprised of two pieces: the front half, which is the face, and the back half, which is fitted and either nailed or glued (or both) into place when the front is complete and the controls are finished. When the back of the head is attached, the builder paints the figure and attaches a wig or hair or some sort of covering that hides the seam where the two pieces come together. The body is form-fitted so the head can move back and forth to look left and right.

Unlike soft figures, where you put your hand right into the figure's mouth, the hard figure has a hole built in its back. To operate your hard figure sidekick, you reach into this hole and grab the post with the levers. Your thumb usually controls the opening and closing of the mouth, and your fingers generally operate the other levers or controls. But as with everything else I've taught you in this book, play with this area, too, and do whatever feels right to you.

Wooden figures are expensive, running into the thousands of dollars. Some of the famous figures of the past draw outrageous sums at auctions and sales, and some are considered priceless. You can find some of these in museums the world over. Some people who have no interest in ventriloquism have collected hundreds of wooden figures!

There are advantages to using wood figures. They have a retro feel that's kind of hip and contemporary, and audiences accept these throwbacks with no question. Plus, audiences expect a certain style from an act that uses a wood figure, which means no introduction is necessary. Everyone knows what's coming. You can always play on the word *dummy* with this kind of figure in your act, and you can make the case that "dummy jokes" are kind of expected.

Suitcases

Perhaps one of the biggest pluses to working with classic wood figures is the demand for them in the media. Often, when casting directors are looking for a ventriloquist for their program, TV special, advertising campaign, major motion picture, and so on, they have a specific style of ventriloquist-and-figure team in mind. If you're going to be auditioning for these kinds of opportunities, you *must* have a wood figure in your arsenal!

Finding a wood-figure builder is not a problem, but know that you'll have to decide what you want—and it won't be cheap. A custom-built wood figure runs into the thousands of dollars, particularly if you want add-ons like blinkers, a tongue, and so on. You might also have to be patient because there are waiting lists for the best and most expensive builders.

You'll have to shell out some dollars for a used figure as well, although it shouldn't be as costly as a custom-built job. Used figures should have a history you can trace from the seller, such as who built it and when, why the seller is parting with it, who used it last, and whether it's appeared on video or YouTube or TV. (Basically, you need to know what the figure's "credits" are, almost as if you're hiring an actor for a part in your show!) An important need-to-know is whether the figure has ever been modified and what exactly was changed. If a hard figure—and especially an older wood figure— has had work done, it might have been compromised. Red flags include multiple repairs to the mechanics (mouth, blinking eyes, teeth that bare, and so on). If possible, take the wig/hairpiece off the figure and check the skull for cracks and repairs. Does the wood or building material for the head match the body? If not, you have half the original figure.

Don't buy a figure without at least giving it a trial run-through, and don't pay for something you have to get in the mail because it could come to you in nonworking condition. Hand over your money only after you've looked over and tested the figure to your satisfaction. You want to be sure all the mechanisms are doing their job and the paint and aesthetics of your new partner are good.

Certain problems are par for the course with wood figures. You'll have to learn to deal with mechanical breakdowns (or find a good handyman or figure-maker nearby who can do last-second repairs), cracked wood, broken strings, and lots of other problems.

Hiccups

You fly to hot, humid Miami for a gig, glad to leave the cool weather at home. At the venue, you assemble your figure. You put your hand in the back, grab the post, and gently push on the mouth-lever. Nothing. You pull on the lever a few times, but still, nothing doing. Upon closer examination, you find all the mechanics in good working order. So why won't the mouth open? Humidity. The warm, damp Miami weather has caused the wood to swell, and the mouth is now stuck. If you know how to fix the problem—perhaps using a blow dryer or de-humidifier, or by carving out a little more space for the mouth to open—you're good. If not, you might have to improvise.

There's a certain prestige and immediate viability that comes from working with a classy wood figure. It's bulky, it has restricted movement, and there's always the possibility of a breakdown. But for many, the advantages—artistically and aesthetically—outweigh all that.

Fiberglass Figures

Fiberglass has quickly become the material of choice for many figure builders and ventriloquists. A fiberglass figure has classic looks and artistry. It can be molded into shapes and can have more intricacies than the classic wood figures. It has a clean, visibly pleasing, and close to perfect look the top acts in the world covet. So what's the drawback?

Fiberglass figures are some of the most expensive figures out there. You can find them used, but for the most part, these are one-of-a-kind custom jobs that command the highest prices—sometimes in the unbelievable range the most famous wood figures go for.

Most of the fiberglass figures built today still use the post in the neck, but the controls have been updated. Instead of the levers, pulleys, and strings of the older wood figures, these new fiberglass units have push-button controls. Some use minor electronics to move the eyes, bare the teeth, and so on. (These controls can even make the figure blush using small light bulbs in the cheeks! How much for that feature, you ask? A lot.)

There's a certain longevity to these hard figures that soft figures can't compete with, and ventriloquists value a well-made, perfectly proportioned figure and the viability and panache it adds to their performances. Naturally, there's always the chance that mechanics and technical workings will break down and have to be repaired. It's best to familiarize yourself with how these things work and what it takes to fix them. These figures can also be heavy, cumbersome, and hard to travel with, which is an important part of your decision-making process.

Plastic Figures

Especially when you're just starting out, you don't have to have a spectacular figure. You just need something you can turn into your muse or alter ego, and the cheapest figures are sometimes the best. Let's look at some of your options.

Lots of molded plastic–headed figures are available (often sold in magic shops) that have one moving part: a string in the back of the head that you pull to open the mouth. Easy enough, and very affordable at $30 or less!

Hand puppets are sold in nearly every children's store, especially designer kid's stores in larger cities.

If you keep your eyes open, you can find interesting puppets and figures made of all kinds of material, from papier-mâché to soft latex to hard plastic to terrycloth. These different kinds of puppets are available online and in novelty stores all over the country. There's no reason why these can't be part of a great ventriloquist act. The fact that you have never seen a vent use these onstage or on TV only means that it's a viable option: you would be the first!

These smaller, inexpensive figures can easily be personalized and made into something unique. Change the eyes, add a body, or put a hat and glasses on the figure. Add arms, take arms away, change the mouth, or make it bigger. There are no rules when it comes to making your own unique figure, and these inexpensive options are a great place to start.

Pull Strings

Other easy-to-use figures are the plastic and latex Halloween masks you see for sale every year in novelty and party shops. Modifying the mask to fit your hand with foam or cloth, you can build your own scary-looking monster that could sing or tell jokes or just freak out the audience!

Your First Figure

Now we come to the point where you have to decide: what are you going to do for a figure?

First and foremost, set a budget. There's no reason for you to go out and spend thousands of dollars on the best-looking, multi-featured, biggest, and most coveted figure on the planet. And this doesn't just apply to beginners; it's good advice for seasoned veterans who've been performing for years!

Now decide who you want to perform for. Will you be doing a nightclub act with bawdy jokes and cutting-edge humor? Maybe your goal is the college circuit, with students ranging in age from 18 to 25. What you're going to use as a vent partner is going to depend, in part, on who you're working for. At the same time, you need to be thinking about what kind of act you're focusing on: comedy, music, or both?

Hiccups

Don't go into this without a budget. Set a price you want to spend. That's going to dictate much of what you can and cannot work with.

The venues for ventriloquists are plentiful, but to get those cushy cruise-ship gigs or prestigious TV spots, you have to pay your dues. Your act is probably going to evolve and grow over time (another reason not to sink thousands of dollars into a figure at the start of your career), and your figures will probably do the same. So start out modestly, and try to pick your vent partner with a prospective audience in mind.

If you're doing church/synagogue/faith-based work in which the performance is more than just entertainment, consider using characters the folks who share that faith will recognize. Animal figures are great for this group. So are figures that represent humans from the workaday world.

If children's shows are your goal, animals and the typical human-looking kinds of figures will go over with this crowd as well. Children can be easily frightened by anything that looks remotely scary, so wood and fiberglass figures probably aren't good here. Anything from the soft figure world should be a hit.

Your choice of figure is up for grabs with colleges and comedy clubs. You can use just about whatever you want to use for this clientele and do anything you like with your act. Should you decide to go with an expensive figure for a nightclub act, you'll probably have some success with a well-built, one-of-a-kind figure. Be aware that it will take some time to pay for that top-of-the-line item, though, because it takes a while to put yourself in the money-making position that headlining acts enjoy.

Cruise ships and theme parks are similar to the children's and religious market in that you're dealing with a broad range of people from every walk of life; background; and race, creed, and lifestyle. Here, you need a figure that can speak to a broad base of reference. And it's important to remember that this crowd isn't necessarily as liberal-minded as the college-and-club group.

Vegas will accept just about anything onstage as long as it's entertaining. Branson, Missouri, has a ton of showrooms, and the audiences are very similar to the religious groups mentioned earlier.

To get a TV spot and/or a movie role, you're going to have to come up with something highly unique, very entertaining, and worthy of a network or studio hiring you. That usually doesn't happen overnight, and it does take a lot of practice, performance, and perseverance. Wherever and whatever you start with, your showcase act will improve and crystallize as you get more practice performing.

Take all this information into consideration. What got you interested in ventriloquism in the first place? How do you see yourself as a performer in 6 months? What are your initial goals as a vent, and how do you want to start? Who will your first few audiences be? The answers to these questions will guide your choice of first figure.

Be True to Yourself

It's very easy to want to imitate or copy what you've seen someone else do. Perhaps you were inspired by a ventriloquist you saw onstage or in a video, and thought, *I want to do that!* Imitation is the most sincere form of flattery, but it won't get you very far when you're trying to forge a career path. Most agents, bookers, and audiences want to see something original—something they haven't seen elsewhere. Sure, they probably like the same act you saw, but doing someone else's act with your figure isn't really flattering—it's plagiarizing. That doesn't just apply to material; don't buy a figure that will have you doing the exact same act someone else does, either.

You've come a long way, and you're going to continue to improve and become more and more professional. Don't take on more than you can handle, and that includes going out and performing before you're ready. Don't get a figure that requires lots of concentration and dexterity to operate, and don't work for an audience you really don't want to work for, whether that's children's shows or religious groups. You won't be happy, and it will show.

Most of all, don't sell yourself short. You've made huge strides. The next part of becoming a great ventriloquist (covered in Chapter 9) is fun and exciting, and you can put it to use right away!

The Least You Need to Know

- ◆ Sock puppets are a great way to get your feet wet with ventriloquism and can be used in a variety of ways.

- ◆ Soft, Muppet-like figures are very popular and generally accepted by audiences the world over. They aren't expensive, and they're easily manipulated and transported.

- ◆ Wood and fiberglass figures have a built-in audience response because they're universally recognized as vent figures. There are risks with these kinds of figures, however, including expense, breakdowns, and difficulty in transporting.

- ◆ Simple, cost-effective figures work just as well as the higher-priced models, and you can personalize them any way you like!

- ◆ Deciding who your ideal audience is helps you decide what figure you'll work with.

Chapter 9

"Say Hello to My Little Friend"

In This Chapter

- ◆ Bringing your figure to life
- ◆ Acting and reacting to your figure
- ◆ It's all in the eyes
- ◆ Tips and techniques for practice

As important as it is to perfect your mouth, voice, and lip control, as covered in previous chapters, manipulating your figure is, perhaps, equally important. In fact, there's a case to be made that if you do an incredible job of manipulating and bringing your figure to life through movement, it almost trumps lip control.

Much of what we look at in this chapter is acting. Just as you would in an acting class, I give you some exercises and concepts to rehearse and work on. It's time to start thinking of your work as more than being a ventriloquist. What you're doing is creating a little play, and the characters in the play are you and your ventriloquist figure(s). As such, you have to have some depth to your performance, some nuance to every line and song in your script. You're going to achieve that through many means, and one of those is the way you manipulate, or move, your partner in crime.

Moving Your Figure

It doesn't matter what your figure is—wood, foam, sock, plastic, or a piece of cloth dangling from your wrist. Giving that figure some life is your next goal.

Let's start with some basic moves. It might help to watch this rehearsal in your mirror, so you can get a feel for how each little movement and twitch you give your figure gives it life.

The Basic Setup

As I talked about in Chapter 4, you want to start by using your dominant hand to manipulate your figure. This will make things easier in the beginning. As you become more comfortable and more confident in your ability, switch your practice sessions between each hand. Eventually, there may be times when you'll want to use a figure on each hand. You might need your dominant hand to write your name as you're working with your figure (perhaps while doing a magic trick or producing something for video). Ideally, you should become adept at using either hand for a figure. At the same time, you should be comfortable using either hand as the *off hand*.

def•i•ni•tion

The **off hand** is the hand *not* being used to manipulate the figure during the performance. The ventriloquist can use his or her off hand to perform a magic trick, play an instrument, or make gestures.

You must also make a decision about your performance position. Will you stand? Sit on a stool? Hold your figure with your off arm or set it on a customized stand? These are personal choices you have to make. It comes down to this: whatever makes you comfortable, and whatever works for the audience. Experiment with different positions and staging. As you keep improving your technique, you'll find a position that suits you best.

Side to Side

It's time to get things moving! To begin, have your figure look side to side. Have it look slowly to the left, come slowly back to center, and turn slowly to the right. Do this a couple times.

Now, have the figure speak as you turn its head slowly to the right. Watch your lip control in the mirror, and keep the figure's head moving slowly to the right. Have it describe what it's doing: "I am moving my head to my right and then I'm coming to a complete stop." Good. Now do the same thing, moving its head back to center. As your figure narrates, watch your lip control and the movement of the figure's head in your mirror. Keep it talking, too: "Now I am moving my head back to center, and I'm going to stare straight ahead." Do the same thing, with the figure narrating a move to the left and then back to center again.

Repeat the movement—head to the right, to the center, to the left, and back to center—but without speaking. You want to give the impression that the figure is looking for someone. Maybe your vent buddy is on the run, hiding from the law; maybe there's someone out there it doesn't want to see; maybe it's looking both ways before crossing the street. Add to the impression by having the figure lean forward as it looks to the left and right. Have it lean slowly forward, look quickly to the right, look left, and finally look center at the same time it leans back to being straight up and down, still looking forward.

I've Got My Eye on You ...

In this exercise, the idea is to have the figure watch someone. For this one, use your imagination (or as they say in showbiz, "improvise"). Pretend someone walks into your practice room and drops his or her keys, wallet, or purse. Then they pick it up, examine it, look up at you and your figure, and walk away. You and your figure will have to mime your reactions to this sequence of events.

First, just look in the mirror and watch your figure follow the person into the room. No need to voice anything in this exercise. The person drops his or her wallet or purse. He or she bends down to pick it up. Your figure watches the wallet fall out (perhaps it looks at you as if to say, "Did you see that?!"), watches this imaginary person pick up the wallet, and then reacts when the person looks directly at the two of you. Then the person leaves.

After you've practiced this a couple times, have both you and your figure watch the sequence unfold *together*. Don't go fast. Take your time. Use every moment and interact with your figure. The imaginary person walks into the room. Perhaps you and your figure exchange a glance, a shrug of the shoulders, or a nervous smile and a silent laugh. The person drops his or her wallet or purse, and you and your figure look at one another—should we pick that up? Should we say something? Should we just sit here? Before you say anything, the imaginary person realizes his or her belongings have fallen down, so they bend down and pick it up. You and your buddy watch. You bend down and watch them pick it up *together*, both your heads slowly following the imaginary person's hand grabbing the wallet or purse from the ground. Then the person stands up as the two of you lean back and watch.

When this person looks at the two of you, it's a shock! You recoil! You look at each other and then look at the person. He or she turns and walks away, and both of you watch until the person is out of sight. Then you look at each other and shrug, laugh, sigh, or shake your heads.

Pull Strings

Don't constantly stare at your figure when you're rehearsing. The reason you use the mirror, even when the figure isn't talking, is so you can get accustomed to not looking at the figure when it's doing something. You need to reach a point where there's a natural give-and-take between you and your figure so it doesn't look like you're moving it. If you stare at the figure when it's moving, the audience will recognize that you're doing all the controlling. However, if you occasionally look the other way as the figure is moving, talking, or following something with its eyes, the figure will appear to be moving on its own.

You can run these exercises in a variety of ways, however you see fit, but you need to focus on the figure making exact, concise moves. It doesn't matter what kind of figure you're working with, but do come as close as you can to following the direction. Use the mirror to work the figure at first; then, work with the figure without the mirror. You should appear to be acting and reacting together to the situations at hand.

It's a Bird! It's a Plane! ... Nope, It's a Bird

For this exercise, watch in your mirror as a bird flies overhead. Have your figure pretend to watch a bird circling in the sky, too. The bird does a figure 8, and the figure's eyes and head follow it. The bird spells out H-E-L-L-O in the sky, like skywriting, and the figure follows the moves. The bird nosedives to the ground, but at the last second makes a pinpoint landing on both feet. The figure watches, swooping its eyes and head—and body?—along with the bird's movement, and then stops when the bird does. Do this a few times until you get comfortable.

Next, do the same movements with your figure. You *both* watch the lazy circles in the sky, the figure 8, the H-E-L-L-O in skywriting, and the nosedive to the perfect landing.

After you've worked together in silence, narrate the sequence together, occasionally looking at each other. "Wow!" says your figure, "that bird is way up there!" You nod and say, "He sure is." You look at each other when the bird skywrites H-E-L-L-O. Maybe the figure asks, "Is he talking to you or to me?" You look at each other and then both turn to watch the bird nosedive. You're both scared—"*It's gonna crash!*" But in the end, everything is okay. "Crazy bird," says your figure. You nod, and as your figure looks the other way, you watch the bird take off again, or vice versa.

This kind of manipulation helps prepare you for working in front of a real audience. Your figure will look out at the crowd as you introduce it: "Here is my pal, [*insert name here*]!" Perhaps it will be startled by what you've just said, or perhaps it will have a line of its own, but the two of you will be working *together* but acting *separately!*

Follow a Script

Let's try an exercise following a script. Read this simple script, and follow the directions. After you've run through it a couple times, stop watching yourself and your lip control in the mirror and work to make figure manipulation a part of your daily rehearsal routine.

YOU: Hello.

FIGURE: [*the figure is looking away from you—toward the wall or the door or something else*] Hi.

YOU: Are you okay?

FIGURE: [*still looking away from you*] Yes. Fine.

YOU: [*moving your head a little closer to the figure's head—as if you're concerned about him/her*] You seem upset ....

FIGURE: [*turns quickly and dramatically, so that the two of you come face to face, and the figure speaks loudly and looks directly at you, clearly agitated*] I said I'm *fine!* [*after it says this, the figure shakes violently, as if it's really upset*]

YOU: [*taken aback, you pull away*] Something is wrong, I can tell!

FIGURE: [*leaning into you and getting close to your face*] Duh! I'm hungry!

YOU: [*hitting your head with your off hand*] Oh, you're right! I forgot to make lunch! I am so sorry!

Lots of vent techniques and skills are at work here. You want to react to what the figure is saying to you, and you want to have the figure react as well. You want to look at the figure but not stare at it—you're trying to emulate a real conversation. And you're working with a script, which is what you'll be doing soon anyway.

On top of all this, you're managing perfect lip control in vent position while the figure speaks! This is a lot of stuff to do, and you might have to rehearse it a few times. Hang in there and keep working at it, and I know you'll get it!

Getting Emotion from Movement

Let's slow things down and backtrack a little bit. You've begun to work with actions and reactions your figure can make to different situations. Let's nail down some specific movements that relate directly to how your figure feels or how it exhibits feeling.

Get your mirror and get in good vent position. Start these exercises by watching the figure—and your technique—in the mirror. Gradually move to where you're not looking in the mirror, but rather looking at the figure and reacting to what it's doing. Maybe you mimic it, scold it, or roll your eyes at it—whatever. Just don't stare and focus so much on the figure that it gives the audience the obvious clue that you're the hand behind the figure!

Expressing Amusement

This is an easy one. Open the figure's mouth wide and move the head up and down. Do it quickly and add a little laughing sound, "Hahahahaha." Do it slowly and add the laughing sound, "Ha. Ha. Ha."

The same movement, but at two different speeds with two different emotions, produces two different results: the first is more like a real laugh while the second is sarcastic.

Expressing Agreement and Disagreement

You can make the figure's head move up and down in agreement in a couple ways: move your entire arm from your elbow up into the head straight up and down or just flick your wrist up and down. Experiment and see what you like!

To express disagreement, simply shake the figure's head no. Open the mouth and have it say "Nooooo" as it shakes its head defiantly. Then have it say "No. No. No. No. No." as it moves its head in herky-jerky motions, back and forth, one move for each time it says "No."

Expressing Surprise

Surprise is a great emotion to practice with your figure. Open its mouth wide. As its mouth opens, pull its head away from you. Have it say *"What?!"* as you do the move.

Try it facing you. And then try it facing away from you, reacting to someone else.

Expressing Embarrassment

Embarrassment is another good emotion to practice. Have the figure bury its head in your shoulder. You can console it, "There, there … it'll be okay." It can reject you or slobber all over you. Add some crying by putting the figure's head on your shoulder and shaking the body as if it's wracked with sobs.

Add sound effects in vent position. Try something like, "Wah, I'm a terrible actor!" Try to be supportive, "No, you're really doing well!"

Spend some time just moving the figure around—moving its head back and forth, watching things, looking at you, looking at itself in the mirror, and so on. All those little moves are important, and they help give the illusion the figure is a living, breathing entity.

Creating Character Through Body Language

Whoever and whatever your figure is, its voice is obviously a big part of its personality. But you can take that a step further and give your figure some depth through body language.

The more you work with your figure, the more you get to know its true personality— what it likes and dislikes, how it wants to be spoken to, and most of all how it likes to stand or sit when performing. Once you've established where the figure is going to be for a performance, you can begin to use reactions and actions in body language to "speak" for your partner.

Say your figure spends the performance being held by your off hand. Does it slump against your body, occasionally snuggling up against you? That's a certain personality. Let's say your figure is sitting on a stand, its legs dangling over the edge, and it kind of teeters in a circular motion during the performance. That's body language. Maybe it sits straight up and rarely looks side to side at all, very solid and staid, certain of itself and staring straight ahead much of the time. Maybe it leans forward and looks at the floor when it speaks. These are all examples of body language that help define exactly who your figure is and how the audience will perceive it. Practice all sorts of ways for the figure to act and use its body.

If you're using a hard figure, your options are somewhat limited because of the body style and composition of materials. But don't let that stop you from finding a good personality and body language for this figure. Practice all kinds of movements and performance positions for the figure. Eventually, you'll reach a point where, if you're doing it correctly, you'll get laughter and entertainment value just from the way your figure carries itself onstage!

The same goes for soft figures, which are more pliable and therefore offer a somewhat broader range of emotions. Use everything about the figure you can. It's made of lightweight foam and terrycloth, so you should be able to push and pull and swivel it around whenever you like. All those moves give your figure a certain body language that help define its character.

Let's look at a quick example: have your figure on your arm. Put it in a performance position (on a stand, in your off hand, however you will use it), facing forward. Now turn its head 45 degrees so it's facing you. Bend your wrist so your fingers, even though they're inside the figure, face directly toward you. This move should tilt the figure's head—no matter what kind of figure it is—toward you in a downward angle. For example, if this is a human-style figure, its chin should be resting on the shoulder that's closest to you. That gives a certain emotion to you partner, and the audience can feel it.

Another good way to learn some body language for your figure is to sit and watch people. Notice how folks carry themselves, engage in conversation, and try to convince someone else to do or not do things. TV commercials and programs are packed with body language. When you see something new, try to apply it to your figure.

Playing Your Part

As if we haven't given you enough to do as a ventriloquist, controlling your voice and lip movement and now controlling the figure's movements, I'm throwing one more thing at you: it's your turn to be manipulated. Not really *manipulated*, of course. But it's time to think about your role in the presentation and how you'll enhance every part of the set with the way you act and react to what's going on.

Acting is supposedly reaction. Because you're really the *only* actor onstage, playing different parts, you need to give the proper physical response to punch lines, songs, insults, and anything else that happens onstage.

Your role is pretty easy, actually. Much of what you need to do is going to be dictated by your script. One of your hands is inside your figure, so you can't do things like throw your arms up in the air, do the wave, or do anything that requires two hands. But facial expressions, turning your body to face toward or away from your figure, or using a finger to point—these are good movements you can use.

To practice your part, let's do a couple short exercises. Follow the directions in this script, and be careful to not stare at your figure.

YOU: *[looking straight ahead]* That was a great meal.

FIGURE: *[looks at your stomach, then your chest, then your face, in that order]* Yeah, I can tell.

YOU: *[staring straight ahead still]* I love Italian.

FIGURE: *[again looks at your stomach, then your chest, then your face, a little faster than the first time]* I can see that.

YOU: *[a bit confused but not worried—you move only your eyes to glance at your figure and then look straight ahead again]* And dessert was amazing!

FIGURE: *[gives a sweeping glance from your stomach to your chest to your face]* Yeah, it's obvious.

YOU: *[look right at the figure, and point at it]* How do you know? You weren't there!

FIGURE: *[looks right back at you]* No, I wasn't, but I know you had spaghetti, wine, and ice cream!

YOU: *[a little bit peeved]* And how would you know that?

FIGURE: *[laughs a little laugh before it says]* Because it's all over your shirt!

YOU: *[look at the mess on your shirt, then at your figure, and then try to find something to wipe the stains off with]* Help me will you? *[say this to the figure—without looking at it!—frazzled, trying to think of what to do, looking around for a cloth or napkin or towel]*

FIGURE: I bet you ruined that shirt! *[laughs]* Oh, you blew it! That is a $50 shirt! Oh, well, thank goodness tie-dye is back in style! *[laughs]*

YOU: Thanks for the help, *[insert name here]. [look at the stains, look at the figure, look at the stains, and then stare at the figure for at least one long beat]*

FIGURE: *[laughs ... then laughs slower ... then one little laugh movement ... then speaks]* What?

YOU: *[looking at figure]* I know how to remove this stain.

FIGURE: *[unsure of what's happening]* How? *[then realizes]* NO! You wouldn't! You wouldn't dare wipe that stuff on …

YOU: *[lean down and wipe your shirt on the figure, as it threatens to sue or something]*

Practice this scene slowly a couple times, reading from the script and getting your body movements down. Work on the reactions you need to pull off to make this work:

◆ Your sideways glance at the figure as you stare straight ahead

◆ Your reaction to the mess on your expensive shirt

◆ The reaction—a *double-take* really—when you realize you could just wipe your shirt on the figure

def•i•ni•tion

A **double-take** is a theatrical maneuver, often used as a comical reaction to a surprising sight in which someone casually sees something, briefly stops looking at it, realizes what it is, and snaps their attention back to the sight with an expression of surprise or disbelief. It's a time-honored and well-known comedy reaction, perfect for a ventriloquist!

Your part is more than just giving voice to your figure and manipulating its every motion. You have to be "in the moment" yourself, acting and reacting according to the script. Remember, you are the director, head writer, lead actor(s), and producer. You have a part to play onstage, just as your figure does. The better you can make yourself believable in your own role, the better your combined performance becomes.

Reality Through Reaction

Ventriloquism is an exaggerated art form, in which your figure has to become bigger than real life. It has to exhibit more personality than real people do because it can't get up and run around and do human things on its own. Therefore, "reaction" becomes an integral part of the ventriloquist performance, because it gives the figure—and you—the chance to imitate something truly human. You just have to embellish the figure's reactions and make them larger than life.

Here are a couple simple reaction exercises in which you can use some of the manipulation skills you've already worked on, in addition to learning a couple more.

Try this classic reaction to start: say something to your figure. "You look great today!" Have the figure slowly turn its head toward you and then ever so slowly have it open its mouth in disbelief. Try it with the figure staring straight ahead and opening its mouth slowly in disbelief. Then have it lean away from you as it opens its mouth (slowly) in disbelief.

Now have the figure laugh at something you say. "We got a gig in Atlantic City. Their motto should be, 'Your Last Resort!'" The figure begins laughing uncontrollably, buries its head in your shoulder, sticks the crown of its head in your side, looks at the ceiling, and laughs like crazy. As it's doing this, you should look away, toward the audience, as if to say, "It wasn't *that* funny."

Finally, have the figure faint. Practice having it fall into your arms or straight back off its stand or stool so you have to catch it. Maybe you could say something to cause the fainting spell, like, "The Cubs won the World Series!" Oops! There goes your figure!

Suitcases
You cannot overstate the figure's reactions enough. More is better. Bigger is best.

Making Eye Contact

This might seem very odd, and maybe a little creepy, but this is how you can make the audience believe that there's more going on onstage than just a person with a puppet. Making eye contact with your figure when you're in a dialogue absolutely sells the fact that, if nothing else, you believe your partner is real.

There are few exercises for this, other than what you have to do. Starting right now, during all rehearsals, practices, and performances, look directly into the figure's eyes when you're talking. This is the same direction you'd get if you were on the set of a TV sitcom and the scene called for a defining moment between you and another character in the show. Eye contact sells the relationship to the viewer at home. The same holds true for you and your figure in your performances, and the more you can nail down the bond you two have, the better your act will be.

There are ways to make this work and give the audience some insight. Have the figure looking away from you. Put your off hand on the figure's shoulder closest to you. When the figure feels your hand resting on its shoulder, have it slowly turn and look at you. Look directly into its eyes.

You can do the same thing in the opposite way. Look away from your figure. Have it lean toward the front, trying to get your attention. It says your name. You turn—nothing but your head turns—and look right back at the figure, making eye contact.

It seems like a strange little thing, but this simple technique defines the vent/figure relationship for the audience!

Practicing Your Reaction

There's a great way to work on your reaction and manipulation skills, and it can be a lot of fun: use real people as your practice session! You can do this in a variety of ways. Go to a park or mall or bustling street in town, sit on a bench or on the ground with your figure, and literally watch people. As you react, physically overexaggerate every response you have to what you're seeing.

The best way to do this is to keep up a running commentary of what you're seeing and improvise your conversation, doing all the physical reactions you'd be doing anyway. Remember that in practice and rehearsal, you should overdo everything. Every reaction and double-take should be done in an over-the-top style that borders on comical. You probably won't be so carefree onstage during your first performances due to nervousness. But if you do everything big in rehearsal, you'll probably do a good job of reacting in some way when the real performance comes along, just out of habit.

Once you have your first script down, practice your reactions to important lines, jokes, and all the other stuff. It's always a good idea to script exactly how you want a reaction to look, even if you end up not using that reaction in the final performance. The more you've scripted, the more freedom you'll have to improvise.

The Least You Need to Know

- Good manipulation makes your performance and your figure come to life.

- The illusion that your figure is real will be defeated if it doesn't have some kind of lifelike movements and reactions. The reality of it as a living entity depends on your work in manipulating and working with the figure as an "actor."

- Eye contact is essential to defining the relationship between ventriloquist and figure.

- There are lots of ways to practice manipulation and reaction, including watching real people!

Chapter 10

Bringing Your Figure to Life

In This Chapter

- ◆ It speaks! Working with dialogue
- ◆ Giving the figure personality
- ◆ Lip control + good dialogue + manipulation = success!
- ◆ What to do with yourself while the figure is talking

You've been practicing your ventriloquism technique, and it's now time to start putting things together—including an original script. You have your figure, and you've done some basic acting and reacting exercises. Now let's go through a script and block out how each of you will act.

As you practice your script, you have lots to keep in mind and work on. Obviously, you want to have flawless lip control. You want the synchronization between the figure's mouth and spoken words to be close to perfect. The two of you have to have excellent rapport, and your acting has to come through in both roles you play, vent and figure. Rolling all these skills and techniques into one package makes you a great ventriloquist—one well on his or her way to having a successful career.

Giving Life Through Dialogue

Let's run through a practice script. While working through this exercise, focus on the acting notes and adding reactions to the lines you and your figure are saying. This script is for rehearsal purposes only. It's not meant to be an example of how you should work, and it's not intended to represent the characters you or your figure should present in your performances. And there's no reason for you to memorize the script (unless you want to).

The best way to complete this exercise is to read through the script a couple times. Make notes if you want to, and feel free to edit it any way you see fit. You want to reach the point where you can anticipate your and your figure's next moves.

Have your figure in hand, on a stool, or on its performance stand. Have its head looking down, so the crown faces out and straight ahead. Try making a snoring noise if you like, and maybe raise and lower its body as if it's asleep. Look at it and shake your head, disbelieving.

YOU: *[shaking your figure]* Wake up! It's the middle of the day!

FIGURE: *[moves its head back and forth, unwilling to get up; it doesn't speak at first, it just mumbles something unintelligible]*

YOU: *[really shaking the figure now]* HEY! Come on! Wake up!

FIGURE: *[slowly raising its head]* Okay, okay, fine.

YOU: I can't believe you slept so late.

FIGURE: *[looks right into your eyes]* I can't believe you woke me up now.

YOU: *[still looking at your figure]* Haven't you ever heard the saying, "Early bird catches the worm"?

FIGURE: Haven't you ever heard the saying, "The worm that sleeps late doesn't get eaten"?

YOU: It's time to go. I have our itinerary around here somewhere. *[you begin to look around for your itinerary—on the floor, behind your figure, everywhere]*

FIGURE: Where are we going this time? *[looks up at the ceiling and shakes its head, obviously not wanting to go anywhere]*

YOU: Well, we start our tour in North Carolina. "First in Flight." *[maybe you make the "#1" sign with your off-hand index finger]*

FIGURE: We're flying? In first class? I don't like to fly …. *[looks down]*

YOU: Yes we're flying first class, but … "First in Flight" is what the state license plate in North Carolina says.

FIGURE: *[slowly looks up at you and then looks away]* Oh, right. 1901, Kitty Hawk, the Wright Brothers, man can fly …. *[he says this in a monotone, as if it's something boring and dumb]*

YOU: That's right! *[excited your figure actually knows this stuff]* The entire world was excited and happy because man had learned how to fly!

FIGURE: *[shaking its head no]* Not everyone was happy. The Chinese weren't happy.

YOU: *[whatever you were doing, you stop and look at the figure, as if it has a nugget of knowledge you've never heard]* How do you know? I bet the Chinese were just as happy as anyone else that man could fly.

FIGURE: *[slowly turns its head to you as it speaks]* I don't think so. See, the Chinese weren't happy that man could fly because they had just finished building this giant wall all the way around their country ….

YOU: *[a little bit testy]* Right, the Great Wall of China, to keep people out …

FIGURE: *[excited in a sarcastic way]* Right! So they've built this wall to keep people out, but now man can fly. I picture some poor worker putting the final brick in the wall. "Now we're all done!" he says … and then he looks up. *[figure looks up]* "OH NO! Now we have to build a dome!"

YOU: Ha ha. *[maybe you pretend to find your itinerary, and you begin to read where your next stop will be]* Okay. Then we go to Virginia.

FIGURE: I like Virginia. Virginia is for lovers.

YOU: Right! That's like their state motto or something! Then we go to Delaware.

FIGURE: Delaware. What does it say on their license plate?

YOU: *[looking up from the itinerary]* It says "The Constitution State." They were the first to ratify the Constitution of the United States! *[proud of yourself for knowing this and holding your chin high]*

FIGURE: Great. They were first to ratify the Constitution. What have they done since?

YOU: *[ignoring the sarcasm]* Then we go to New Jersey.

FIGURE: The only state in America where they use air freshener ... outdoors! *[the figure laughs at its own joke]*

YOU: Then Rhode Island.

FIGURE: Rhode Island? That little state? Three counties when the tide is out, two counties when the tide is in? *[it begins to bob up and down as if it's floating in the ocean]* Help! I'm floating away!

YOU: *[pushing down on the figure's shoulder to calm it down]* Then we hit New Hampshire. I bet you don't know what they're state motto is.

FIGURE: Sure I do. Everyone does. "Live Free or Die." They're very gung-ho in New Hampshire.

YOU: *[ignoring your figure and its smart-alecky replies]* Then we head over to Ohio.

FIGURE: *[looking up and thinking]* Ohio?

YOU: *[distracted from the itinerary, you look at your figure]* Yes. Ohio.

FIGURE: *[still looking up]* Ohio?

YOU: *[going back to your itinerary]* Yes, Ohio. I guess you can't think of something mean to say about Ohio, can you?

FIGURE: *[looks down and then at you]* Nope.

YOU: Good. *[you continue to look at itinerary]*

FIGURE: Ohio. Forty-eighth in tourism! *[it laughs]*

YOU: *[ignoring the figure]* Then we head over to the bluegrass state: Kentucky.

FIGURE: The grass is blue, but the sky is green. Poor guys. Have you ever flown through a green sky? *[looking at you]*

YOU: *[you look at the figure as if it has gone crazy]* Uh, no. But we will be flying on this trip.

FIGURE: *[buries its head in your shoulder]* That's right! Help! Don't make me fly! I hate flying! Can't we go by boat?

YOU: *[rolling your eyes]* Now how can you go by boat from Kentucky to ... we're going to Oklahoma. There are no rivers that go from Kentucky to Oklahoma!

FIGURE: Darn! *[gently pounds his head against your shoulder]* I don't like to fly, I don't like to fly, *[and then, louder]* I don't like to fly!

YOU: Why not?

FIGURE: *[pulls head up and looks at you]* The last time we flew I got to go first class.

YOU: Right. *[nodding]* We sat right behind the pilot.

FIGURE: We were so close I could hear him.

YOU: *[a little exasperated]* So?

FIGURE: *[head leaning in toward yours]* I thought he was calling the flight attendant. He kept saying, "Miss … Miss …" but then he said, "Near Miss!"

YOU: Oh, he did not!

FIGURE: *[shaking its head in disbelief]* But then we took off …

YOU: So why do you like going by boat so much?

FIGURE: Because … I float!

YOU: *[ignoring the figure, reading from the itinerary]* So we go west. Oklahoma.

FIGURE: *[tilts its head toward you]* I've never been able to figure out their license plate. It says, "Oklahoma is OK." *[you and the figure ponder this for a moment]* I mean, that's fine, Oklahoma is OK. But shouldn't it be a little more confident than that? *[repeats the license plate slogan in a defeated, reserved tone]* "Oklahoma is … Okay …"

YOU: *[Nodding]* Yeah, seems a little odd. Then we're off to Wyoming.

FIGURE: *[snaps its head toward you]* Wyoming? That's not a state! It's a question! *[looks straight ahead]* Why Oming? *[looks at you]* And do you know the answer?

YOU: *[exasperated]* No, I don't.

FIGURE: *[excited, wiggling for joy]* Go ahead, ask me! Ask me! I know the answer!

YOU: *[annoyed]* Fine! Why Oming?

FIGURE: I da ho! *[as in "I don't know"—the figure laughs; you put your face in your off hand]*

After you've read through the script a couple times, perform it with your figure. Use your mirror, and watch your technique. Try to follow the stage directions (those italic bits in brackets before or after almost every line) for interactions between you and your figure.

The purpose of this exercise isn't to give you a script to use (but you can if you want to). Rather, it's so you can practice the stage directions. To make your figure more life-like, you have to have constant motion and constant activity—and not just opening and closing its mouth. The figure has thoughts and emotions running through its head and dialogue all the time, just like you do! Putting both together with constant interaction and jokes, including the resulting head-in-your-hands closing action, defines who the two of you are.

Obviously your figure will have its own personality and its own style. The provided dialogue may have nothing to do with what you want to create. Run through it a few times anyway. See where the beats are for the jokes. Follow the stage directions for you and the figure. After working with this exercise for a while, you'll have a working knowledge of what's supposed to happen in the relationship between vent and figure when you're onstage doing your own thing—whatever direction you take it.

Establishing Personality in Under Sixty Seconds

In the big-time showbiz world of New York and Los Angeles, stand-up comics are paraded onstage one after the other, as bookers and managers and agents try to find the next big star. Comics have about 1 minute or less to get their persona and motivation across.

You, as a professional ventriloquist, will have the same challenge. You need to get your and your figure's personalities across to the audience in a minute or less. To do this, you must give the viewers a glimpse into relationship you and your figure have—and do it *right away!* You must also set up your figure for the rest of your set time, with its first words and what it does.

> **Pull Strings**
>
> When you take the stage, really *take the stage*. Own it. Make it yours. That space is your office, your field of play, and your own personal plot of land for however long you're there. Be confident, be sure of your ability, and *take it!*

First, *take the stage*. You're introduced, you walk onstage, and the applause stops. If you're starting out alone, without your figure on your knee or on its stand, immediately establish some sort of connection with the audience. You can do this with a smile and a gracious bow or nod of the head.

When you introduce your figure to the audience, they will make a decision about you and your act. Here's a great way to define yourself: you and your figure acknowledge one another, and you nod and laugh or smile. Then, introduce your figure to the audience: "Audience, this is my figure. Figure, this is our audience." Make immediate eye contact with the figure because this makes it apparent to the crowd that you have a working relationship.

Immediately give your figure life. Don't wait for the first punch line or even the first line of dialogue. Have it look around the room. Have it laugh, shake its head, and wiggle around trying to get comfortable. Those movements are human characteristics that, when applied to a vent figure, give the audience insight into your craft and a reason to pay attention.

Pull Strings

One way to bring your figure to life onstage is to start your act offstage. As you're waiting to be introduced or as you're walking onstage with your figure, have it start "performing" before you get to the microphone. It can check out the audience, whisper to you that it's nervous, laugh at people backstage, and so on.

What to Do When the Figure Talks

One problem for ventriloquists is what to do when the figure is talking. More to the point, many ventriloquists look at their figures way too much, particularly when the figure is doing the talking. This takes away from the reality of the moment, and it can take away from the illusion that the figure is real.

You have to find points in your rehearsals during which your figure speaks for long periods of time, and you don't look at it at all. Make the figure look away from you, and you look away from the figure. Then carry on a conversation, both of you looking in opposite directions.

Another way to practice not acknowledging your figure is to run through the dialogue in this chapter without looking at the figure. It is just as important, however, to have the figure do all the body and head movements dictated by the script. This way, you're manipulating and bringing reality to the figure, but you're not watching everything you're doing. From the audience's perspective, you are truly acting as two separate individuals.

You can also have the puppet follow an imaginary person walking into your practice room, except this time, don't pay any attention to either the figure or the imaginary person. For extra credit, have your figure look at you every once in a while just to see if you're aware of what's going on. When it realizes you aren't paying attention or don't care, it goes back to watching.

Avoiding looking at each other might seem trivial, but this technique adds to your skill set and will come in handy. You'll eventually be working in a club, theater, or large venue with a full audience. As you're working, someone is going to get up from their seat for any number of reasons and begin walking out of the performance space. To make this moment especially fun for the audience, have your figure follow the person who is leaving—just the same way your figure rehearsed following the imaginary person in your practice room. The illusion will be more complete if you, the ventriloquist, are oblivious to what's going on, looking away from your figure and the person leaving the room.

Pull Strings

Now that you're getting close to going onstage, there is an important practice lesson to remember: perform *exactly* the way you practiced, especially in the beginning. This will help you deal with any performance jitters.

Putting It All Together

With a ventriloquist act, there's always a lot going on. Lip control, manipulation, and dialogue (the script) are difficult in and of themselves. But putting all that together in a rehearsed performance is what gets you bookings and opportunities for career moves. And there's only one way to nail down those three systems.

As a ventriloquist, you have to rehearse on a regular basis, up until the time you're performing regularly—by that I mean more than twice a week. When you reach the point where you have three or more performances or bookings every week, you'll find that each time you're onstage is not only a presentation of your skill and your act, but it's also great rehearsal time. The only way to become a quality ventriloquist is to do it. The way to master lip control and manipulation, and to find the best material to use in your act, is to perform.

Your success and future as a vent will never be solely about your lip control, vent position, hilarious comedy material, or brilliantly played figure manipulation. Ventriloquism is just like every other art form: the prerequisite is not so much what you will learn here, but rather the indefinable talent of any individual to find new and entertaining ways to take audiences where they've never been or to treat them to something they haven't seen. When it comes to lip control, manipulation, and dialogue, you have two roles to play, and you cannot allow the audience to see inside that illusion.

Putting these skills together is not an easy task. Your abilities as a ventriloquist are not easily and quickly developed. The best "teacher"—even better than this book—is performing live in front of an audience. During a performance, you can begin figuring out exactly what you have to do to grow and succeed as a vent.

You need to apply yourself to the dialogue in this chapter and come as close as you can to perfecting all its parts. Use your mirror. Concentrate on what you do well. Find your weaknesses so you can work on them and hide them (if possible) in performance.

The Least You Need to Know

- When you start working with dialogue, you need to have the figure do more than just open and close its mouth. It needs to act and react as well.

- There's a lot going on onstage: flawless lip control, figure manipulation, and your conversation with the figure. To perfect all this, you have to practice!

- Don't stare at the figure while it's talking or moving. Keep your relationship as real as possible.

- The audience notices every move your figure—and you—make onstage. Use that to your advantage and own the space while you're there!

Part 4

Creating Material

Almost every ventriloquist act you will ever see, even the ones that refer to themselves as "musical ventriloquists," have lots of humor and comedy in their shows. There are three ways to get comedy material: steal it, buy it, or write it. Part 4 deals with learning how to write comedy, using exercises and assignments that will broaden your abilities and make you a good joke writer.

After learning how to write comedy, we move to putting those lines into context and creating a script for you and your figure. A well-written script won't mean much, of course, if you can't memorize the lines. So to help you learn, I have a whole chapter on preparing and committing everything to memory. With the chapters in Part 4, you're sure to develop material you can be proud of.

Chapter 11

What Do You Want to Do?

In This Chapter

- ◆ What kind of act do you want to be?
- ◆ Gathering your material
- ◆ A look at how your material defines your act
- ◆ Never-fail bits that can boost your performance
- ◆ Improving your comedy

It's the hardest question in show business to answer: "What do you want to do?" Headlining acts and well-known celebrities have never been able to answer that question after 20 years of performing, acting, singing, telling jokes, and working in "the biz." If they can't answer a question as simple as that, how can a beginner? This chapter is designed to alleviate that nagging doubt and set you on the path to excellence with focus and a plan.

There are three generally accepted ways for a ventriloquist to go with his or her act: comedy, musical, and a combination of the two. Clearly the best way to get yourself booked and please the broadest audiences is to use whatever you can to put on a solid show. Combining music and comedy with watertight technique is the best of all worlds. (Yes, you can use music in your act, even if you cannot sing a note!)

Your calling card will be whatever you decide to present—the words you use, the songs you sing, and the format you follow. In professional terms, you *are* your act, and what you do onstage is your own personal advertisement. As such, you need to be clear about every single thing you do from the moment you step into the spotlight.

Comedy, Music, or Both?

Many professional ventriloquists are comfortable doing what they do. They take their work seriously and approach their craft with sharp, concise decision-making and a long-term vision. But I bet most of them probably didn't start out that way. They no doubt went through a lot of trial and error as they worked to discover what they wanted to accomplish. Had you not picked up this book, perhaps you, too, would have gone down the same path. But you did pick up this book! And in this chapter, I help you define yourself as a ventriloquist.

Now it's time to determine who your audience is and speak directly to them. The first thing to do is get a good grasp of the style and approach you're going to take. Is your core audience high school kids and school programs? You're going to need to be well versed in pop music, the latest fashions, and the hottest TV shows. You're also going to need at least a few words from their lexicon because the slang in this group changes on a weekly basis. Knowing your audience is half the battle for live performers— especially those who depend on laughter, interaction, and response.

Pull Strings

The way you and your figure dress, the words you use, the songs you sing, and the material you choose define who you want to be on stage and who your core audience will be.

Comedy is a universal language, and it has become more so over the past couple decades. Music has become more stratified during the same time period. People who like hip hop music do not like classical music. Jazz lovers wouldn't be caught dead listening to pop. Adult contemporary fans don't go for R&B, and alternative country bands will not be found on Christian music radio stations. Music is personal, and each genre has a particular subculture that it caters to.

If you're going to work as a musical ventriloquist, you need to keep in mind a few things. First, you absolutely have to be a very, very good singer. (Audience members should be asking themselves, "If this guy is such a good singer, why does he need a ventriloquist dummy to do the singing for him?") Your vocal abilities also need to be as faultless as your ventriloquist technique.

Additionally, you need to be able to do some impressions of well-known superstar singers, preferably someone still alive and very vital to the music scene. If you follow this course, you should consider having a custom look-alike figure made so your impression will make a *big* impression on the audience!

Clearly, being able to read and write music is a plus because you will need to make your own recordings and have charts and sheets available for orchestras and bands when you're working casino and cruise ship shows. Yes, you can have these written and scored for you, but that's another expense (and you're already paying for that Kelly Clarkson look-alike figure, which is going to take a couple paychecks!).

Smaller venues don't generally have bands or orchestras, so you must have a transportable recording (digital or hard disc) you can plug into a sound system.

Your program as "The Singing Ventriloquist" or "The Musical Ventriloquist" has to be written out and planned. The set has to flow from one song to the next, and you'll need entertaining and informative "patter" (a.k.a. jokes!) between the songs. As a bonus, you'll always have to be prepared to go a cappella when the sound system breaks down.

Pull Strings

Before you say, "But I can't sing!" hold your tongue (with both hands—just kidding!). The fact that you can't sing doesn't mean your figure can't. Chances are, your figure thinks of itself as a world-class singer. Use your inability for comedy! Can't sing? Let your figure do an off-key rendition of "Happy Birthday," a current hit song, or a favorite tune. Take a negative, turn it into a positive, and find the humor in something that is not one of your strong points!

The great thing about a musical ventriloquist act is the sheer entertainment value it holds for the audience. The drawbacks are the dependence on superb talent and the dependence on others (a musical director, a band leader, a sound tech in the booth, and an audience that is prepared to sit and listen). The venues and opportunities for musical ventriloquists are few and far between, so you will find yourself moving to Las Vegas, Atlantic City, or perhaps Orlando to take advantage of the only real prospects there are for work.

Comedy is a more accessible way to go because it requires no singing talent. A ventriloquist who puts together a knock-down, drag-out funny 20-minute set can outshine an incredibly talented singing ventriloquist (and more often than not, any singer!)

because his or her four-punch-line-per-minute routine touches a larger percentage of the audience and has more variety and action.

The best of all worlds is a ventriloquist who does a very funny performance and adds some music or singing to his or her live act. As a diversion, a song or two adds to the overall breadth of any set for a vent, and the audience will enjoy the music as much as they enjoy the comedy.

Where to Get Material

As a ventriloquist, you must have perfect technique, you absolutely need a unique figure, and you cannot have enough jokes. With that in mind, much of the rest of this book is devoted to writing and performing comedy.

If you ever have the chance to attend a ventriloquist convention, look at the subject matter for the workshops and conferences. You'll likely find "Manipulation" classes, "Distant Voice" sessions, and even "What to Do When You Get There on Time but Your Figure Doesn't" discussions. But the best-attended and most-coveted workshops are the ones that deal with comedy writing, because comedy material and jokes are hard to come by. It's a difficult process and a skill that has to be learned, practiced, and constantly upgraded (sounds like another craft you've been working on … the one called "ventriloquism"). Writing fresh, original, and personalized comedy is as difficult as any of the techniques you've learned thus far—and it's the technique everybody takes for granted.

There are three ways to get comedy material: you can steal it, you can write it, and you can buy it. Let's take a peek at all three.

Steal It

Sadly, stealing is the most common form of finding comedy material. I'm not talking about taking jokes from a joke book or getting a bunch of one-liners from an e-mail forward from a friend. That's more like plagiarism. Stealing jokes is watching another act—perhaps a comic, a singer, or another ventriloquist—and then replicating something they did in your own act, verbatim. If you steal jokes from other ventriloquists or comedians, be prepared for a backlash. If bookers and agents catch wind of you doing this, they'll steer clear of booking you, mostly because their other comedy performers won't want to share a stage with you.

Naturally, stealing material is probably not something you want to do. It might get you laughs in the short term and maybe even a couple bookings, but once the pros catch on, your reputation is cemented as a thief and you will forever struggle to overcome the mistake.

Write It

By far the best possible way to come up with material for your act is to write it yourself. You know what makes you laugh, you know what you want to do when you get onstage, you know what kind of image you want to portray, and you know what you'd like to talk about. Coming up in Chapters 12 and 13, I give you the tools and the systems to create your own material in your own voice.

 Hiccups

If you use jokes from online joke files or old books, you run the risk of sounding redundant ("I've already heard that!") or being labeled that most insulting of all comedy nicknames: The Hack.

You've probably heard this saying: "Writers are born, not made." There may be some truth to those words, as some people clearly have a flair and a gift for putting words together, turning a phrase, and making a statement. Joke-writing is similar. Some people are given to seeing the way two divergent ideas can be brought together to create a punch line. Some people need a little help with this.

Most of us have a sense of humor. We "get" the jokes. We can sometimes see what's coming before a comic, ventriloquist, or talk show host gets to the punch line. We enjoy laughing, we enjoy good jokes, and we appreciate the talent it takes to perform comedy. We might like telling jokes, but actually writing them? It sounds difficult, and it is.

For some beginning ventriloquists and performers, the fallback position is "I don't write jokes down or anything; I just go out and wing it!" That improvisational style is fine, and many superstar entertainers do their entire live shows off the cuff.

Okay, not really.

The truth is, those improvisational entertainers appear to be making it up, but they're really not. They've spent years putting themselves out on a limb and working by the seat of their pants. They have accumulated a number of stock lines and short pieces they can always use to bail themselves out of a tight spot with a big laugh or applause break. And even though some of their act is extemporaneous in nature, they have cataloged ideas, premises, and material they can call upon at any time.

For the new ventriloquist, the temptation to go out and wing it will be strong. Occasionally, you might even succeed. But you should still script out at least a concept of how your set performance will run. It's one thing to entertain friends and relations at parties and social functions. Playing on professional stages where money and careers are at stake is a completely different experience. Oftentimes, winging it means finding the lowest common denominator for your laughs, and you end up writing an act without knowing it. What results is an act dependent on shocking audiences with insult jokes, dirty jokes, and sex jokes—all of which can be funny, by the way.

No rule says a ventriloquist has to work without any four-letter words, and no rule says he or she must be vulgar to be funny. Every person has his or her own tastes and opinions, which impacts what does and does not make him or her laugh. What kind of act and material you choose to take onstage is entirely up to you. But there are ramifications to every choice you make as a performer.

Working "blue" means you do a certain kind of act for a certain kind of audience. There is no doubt that casinos, comedy clubs, and TV programs use comedians and ventriloquists who are using "edgy" and "blue" material. However, with a blue act, you must cut off a lot of employment prospects just because you can't work "clean." One of the biggest problems entertainers have is getting booked to do a high-paying event and then being told they must keep it clean. If you've been working predominantly blue, you'll have a lot of trouble trying to clean up your act. You've likely become accustomed to saying things a certain way, getting laughs on a certain line that has a cadence that includes a four-letter word, and depending on big applause-and-laughter breaks with punch lines centered around something profane. When you change or edit the rhythm you're used to, even a little bit, your performance becomes awkward.

Hiccups

If you're planning on using "blue" material, or dirty jokes and profanity, be forewarned: there's only one way to go if you plan on doing a blue act. You will have to get more and more profane as your career goes on. Once you've crossed that line, it will be very difficult to go back.

Four-letter words are "comedy adjectives." If a joke isn't funny, just insert one of the comedy adjectives, and you have a good chance of getting a laugh. Everyone knows that this is a form of cheating, and that the performer didn't put much thought or effort into writing his or her act. It's just a case of spewing out vulgarities that still shock audiences and elicit laughs. And there's nothing wrong with that if you want that for your career.

But in this and the following chapters, I'll teach you how to write without using profanity or spending your set talking about activities in the bedroom or the bathroom. Of course, what you choose to do with your abilities after you've read this is 100 percent your call.

Once you start getting into the exercises and the writing programs discussed in the next few chapters, you might become frustrated (and maybe a little annoyed) with how hard it is to progress. Why do you think so many acts work dirty? When you're overwhelmed or you've hit a wall, take a break! You're going to be writing comedy for the rest of your life. No need to panic now!

Buy It

Easy. Expensive. Inefficient. Risky. Buying comedy material and jokes from writers is similar to what you have learned about ventriloquism. It's all about making fine distinctions. There are thousands of joke writers out there. Finding one or two who will work with you, who will get to know your act and your figures and their personalities, and who will understand the way you talk and how you like to perform is an arduous task. This search can be so time-consuming you may as well do it yourself!

> ### Suitcases
>
> Some of the best comics use writers, particularly those who host talk shows and variety programs and those who require fresh material on a daily or weekly basis. Another way to look at getting and using a writer: if you're talented and fortunate enough to earn a major career break after a couple years of putting together your own act, you'll need a writer. Your career will require an entirely new act, and you won't have the benefit of time to put it together. You'll need it right away. A writer can help.

If you feel that a joke writer is the best way to go for your act, let's look at some of the guidelines you will want to follow.

The standard rate for jokes is $50 per punch line, but that in and of itself is a joke. Joke writers will send you comedy material for a fee, usually in the hundreds of dollars range, and you have to make it work. Come to an agreement as to a price per joke, or a price per batch of jokes.

Here's how it breaks down: you contact a joke writer, receive a joke writer's card, or someone recommends a joke writer to you. After a short meeting, phone call, or e-mail trail, you purchase some jokes. You explain to the writer the "who, what, when, where, why, and how" of your act and send the writer some money. The writer sends you some lines—let's say 20 jokes. You pay the fee, and now you have to decide which ones are good for you and your figure and the kind of thing you're trying to do.

Let's say you decide 10 of the 20 are worth taking onstage. If you're lucky, three of the jokes will work and become part of your routine. It's similar to baseball. Even the best major leaguers hit only .350. And that's an all-star! It's the same with joke writers. If you can find someone who writes 3 jokes that get genuinely big laughs out of every 20 he or she writes, *hire them!*

Hiccups

Watch out! Scam artists and cheaters are just waiting to take your money without delivering what you pay for. Always ask for a writer's credits and do some follow-up before agreeing to anything. Beware of a comic who gives you 20 to 30 brilliantly funny lines that work the first time you try them. Something that seems too good to be true usually *is* too good to be true. One dishonest trick is to hand you 20 very funny lines that the "writer" has stolen from other comedians. With due diligence and some quick research, you can work with someone who is just as committed to excellence as you are.

As you work with a writer, your style and their style will begin to mesh. There will still be a hit-or-miss feel to what you're doing, but a rapport will soon develop and your combined work will become more proficient.

The best of all possible worlds is for a performer to work with a writer but do much of the writing on his or her own. This works on a number of levels. The performer clearly knows how to write jokes, and can write for his or her own act in a pinch (for a special client, party, or event). At the same time, a performer who can work with written material from another source has likely learned how to edit and tighten scripts, skills that will come in handy when working in media (especially film and/or TV, including commercials). And being able to work well with others, starting with writers, is an underrated skill every ventriloquist should have.

Defining Your Act

However you choose to garner the bits and pieces that go into your work, know that you'll be defined by what you talk about. Obviously, if you're doing topical and current events comedy, you will become known as a political comedy ventriloquist. If you spend much of your live performance interacting with the audience and using them for your comedy, you'll be known as an insult ventriloquist or an audience-participation act. This is all fine, of course, if that's what you want to do.

But it goes further than that. Any ventriloquist who spends his or her entire time on-stage talking about sex, the bedroom, and the bathroom is going to be seen as someone who talks about only those subjects. If you don't ever curse onstage, you'll be known as a clean ventriloquist. You'll be defined by whatever you talk about onstage. You might see yourself as a political comedy ventriloquist because you (or your figure) tell three jokes about the government. But in the course of your 20 minutes onstage, if those three political jokes are the only three in your act, you're not a political comedy ventriloquist—you're a ventriloquist who sometimes talks about politics.

The content of your presentation should be carefully thought out and rehearsed. Leave nothing to chance, including the way you walk onto the stage, the words you use to introduce yourself, and the demeanor with which you start your production. There should be a constant flow to your work, and the subject matter you choose is going to dictate who you are. It's always a good idea to write out your act, longhand, on a piece of paper. This forces you to examine what you're saying and how. What's the wording? What are the subjects you spend most of your time talking about? Think of the show as a story, and look at its beginning, middle, and end. How do you get from the opening line to the big closer at the end?

Using music defines you as well. The kinds of songs you sing tell the audience about you. If, for example, your figure and you sing all heavy metal power ballads, you'll be niched as a retro-1980s kinda act with a penchant for sappy lyrics. Singing Broadway show tunes positions you as a theatrical act. Obviously, the more variety you can display as a singer, the broader your audience can be. Try to be broad and use lots of genres of music. Most importantly, use songs you can sing well—or sing poorly—and get big laughs with! Don't waste your time or the audience's time by singing something that isn't particularly beautiful or hilarious!

Hiccups

It's become increasingly difficult for ventriloquists to use pop song parodies or spoofs in live acts because a residual fee is now due to the American Society of Composers, Authors and Publishers (ASCAP) every time you sing a popular song. Especially if you record video doing another artist's hit song, you absolutely need to clear up any and all copyright problems *before* you shoot!

You are in full control over the subject matter and content you put forth onstage. You decide how you want to be perceived and what kind of act you want to be. Your persona—the flavor of who you are as a ventriloquist—is in the subject matter, the observations and the information contained in your music, your dialogue, and your jokes. Immediately start making choices for these elements of your act, and stick to what you want audiences to know about your act.

Bits of Business

You're about to start writing comedy and preparing a script for your first performance, so let's take a look at some tried-and-true ventriloquist routines. These will give your act some punch and applause-getters, and you can build your routine of jokes and/or songs around them if you want to. These or something like these will give you a good place to start.

The Crying Baby Bit

This is a fun and inexpensive bit that's been performed by lots of very famous vents. From the audience's viewpoint, it appears the ventriloquist is holding a baby in his arms, wrapped in a blanket. The baby cries, and the ventriloquist calms the baby. Just when it appears the vent can place the baby down, the baby begins sobbing uncontrollably. The ventriloquist repeats this process at least once more. Finally, exasperated, the vent shakes out the blanket. As the audience lets out an "Oh no!" it becomes obvious the ventriloquist was doing the baby voice all along.

Simple enough, huh? You will have to work on a crying baby voice, and you'll need a blanket. Wrap something in the blanket that is approximately the size of a 6-week-old baby—maybe a bath towel, a large roll of paper towels, or a water jug. After wrapping up the item, take it out so you now have an empty blanket. Introduce the "baby" as your cousin's or your neighbor's (or the club/theater owner's), or your own, if you like. Tell the audience you're going to put the baby to sleep. You make the baby cry sound using a combination of a soft voice and a distant voice. You rock the baby to sleep and go to put down the baby in your bag, just offstage, maybe downstage, or wherever. As you do, the baby lets out a long wail.

You try to rock the crying baby back to sleep, gently cooing and coddling, until it finally quiets down. Again, as you try to put the baby to bed, it cries. For the third time, after you've calmed the baby and you're putting it to bed, it cries out loudly. Finally, you say to the audience, "I CAN'T TAKE IT!" and shake out the blanket. The audience realizes it was you all along, and they applaud wildly.

Rehearse this *well*. You need to perfect your baby voice before you attempt to take this onstage.

The Tongue Twister Bit

This next bit of business is even easier. Learn a tongue twister, any tongue twister, and memorize it. Rehearse it until you can't stand it. Then practice it with your figure. Practice until your figure and you can go back and forth, without stopping, for 45 seconds or so. Then put it in your act.

For a bonus, challenge someone in the audience to say the tongue twister back and forth with your figure. Obviously, you're figure will win because you've been rehearsing it forever!

The Drinking-While-Singing Bit

Finally, let's learn the crowd-pleasing "drinking-while-singing" routine that's a staple in many ventriloquists' acts. This isn't simple, and it takes some patience and rehearsal. One key to this famous bit is breath control.

Here's how it works: The audience sees the ventriloquist singing a song with his figure. At the very end of the tune, the figure hits a note. As the figure is singing, the ventriloquist takes a glass of juice or some other liquid and drinks as the figure completes the final note. Applause breaks out, and the vent and figure take a bow.

How does it work? Simple. You drink some liquid—usually just a couple ounces—and raise the back of your tongue against your soft palate. Think of closing off your throat during distant voice. This traps the liquid in your mouth. Don't swallow it. With the liquid in your mouth, maintain the single note the figure is singing in your nasal passages. Maintain vocal seamlessness until the figure finishes singing the final note. When the song comes to an end and the figure and you take a bow, you can swallow the liquid.

This bit has to be rehearsed to perfection. It helps if you bend your head back a little to drink some of the juice, and you must have total control of your respiratory system and voice during the entire process. In addition, you have to keep maintaining the figure, creating that important diversion as you appear to drink and sing at the same time.

Pull Strings

You can find a ventriloquist drinking glass at most magic shops. Also available are baby figures that come complete with a blanket and a crying face so the audience can actually see the baby you're working with.

As always, this must be practiced in front of your mirror and rehearsed until you can do it smoothly and without any urgency.

Enriching Your Sense of Humor

Not everyone can be a brilliant comedy writer, but everyone can be the best comedy writer they can be. The time has come for you to start thinking funny. We're going to start with what you think is funny. Chances are you were drawn to ventriloquism because you saw a vent or a comedian who made you laugh. That means you have a sense of humor, which means you know what makes *you* laugh. Let's start with that.

What Do You Like?

Get a piece of paper and a pencil and start writing down the best jokes you've ever heard. These are the kinds of things that you heard and said, "I wish I had written that!" or "That joke is so funny because it's so true" or "I feel the same way!" What you want are 20 to 25 funny lines you can look at and say, "This is the kind of act I want to do, and these are the kinds of jokes I want in my act."

If you can't think of 20, don't worry! Do a little searching. Google your favorite comedians. Watch some old reruns on cable. Watch the comedy cable channels. Try to remember the movie lines that caused you to laugh out loud. What was it that you read online that was so funny? If you're having trouble, ask others what their favorite jokes are. This is your first comedy writing assignment, and it should be fun.

Once you have 20 or 25 jokes on paper, look for similarities. Is there one subject you find funnier than others? Are they dirty jokes? Clean? Husband-and-wife related? Political? Puns? Maybe the content of your joke list is eclectic and all over the place. Whatever the subject is, you're going to want to hold on to it because it might come in handy later on.

For all these jokes, write down a couple things for each one. First, try to find out who told it, where you heard it, or what movie or sitcom it was from. Essentially, you want to find out the name of the person who performed or wrote these favorite punch lines. If you can't, don't worry about it too much and move on.

After that, take some time with each joke and write down exactly *why* you found it funny. What is it, specifically, that appeals to you about the joke? It can be anything: Maybe it's the subject matter. Maybe you like the wording. Could be that you love jokes about topical and current events. Or maybe you like sex or relationship jokes.

Write it all down. Don't overanalyze this; just look at the joke and decide what you like about it.

Now You're Ready to Start Writing

For the rest of your life, as a ventriloquist, you're going to be looking for what's funny and what makes you laugh. You're going to observe funny things in as many situations as possible, every day, everywhere you go. The world has changed for you. It is no longer just the place where you breathe and eat and go to work and live. You are now using the world and everything that happens as fodder for your performance.

Get a small notebook. Whenever you see something funny, or notice an opportunity for something funny, write it down. You're on the way to writing your own knock-out material, which is the subject of the next chapter.

The Least You Need to Know

- You don't have to be a great singer to perform music in your ventriloquist act. But if you're going to be a musical ventriloquist, you better be able to sing very well, and you better have your figure sing as well.

- There are three ways to get comedy material for your performance. The best way is to write it yourself. The next best is to buy it from a professional comedy writer. The worst thing to do is to steal it.

- Whatever you do and say onstage defines who you are with audiences and niches you as an entertainer.

- There are three really good tricks a beginning ventriloquist can put together to boost his live shows: the crying baby, the tongue twister, and the glass of water trick.

- You have a great sense of humor, and you know what you like. Use that to become a comedy writer!

Joke-Writing 101

In This Chapter

- The simplest and best-known form of joke-writing: the setup and the punch line
- Maximizing your punch words; maximizing your laughs
- Joke-writing formulas
- A close look at the theory of three

Jokes come in lots of forms. You can probably quote the best lines from your favorite comedians' routines. But all comedy and all comedians have one thing in common: they all work toward the punch word, the point where the subject matter comes together with the idea or concept that's funny. In this chapter, you learn how to write jokes—specifically, those all-important punch words.

Joke-writing is an acquired skill, something you'll improve at with each successful gag you write. Some of your stuff won't be funny, other stuff will give you a nice laugh, and some will have audiences bellowing and applauding your brilliance. To earn that reaction, you must build your act, get to your punch words as quickly as possible, and use everything you know together with the skills you learn in this chapter.

As a ventriloquist, your figure is your instrument, no different from a great jazz pianist or trumpet player. You've worked on all your techniques and become proficient with your craft. Just as every musician needs a hit song or a great album to promote his ability, you need a solid routine to move your expertise to the next level. Get your notebook and a pencil, and let's start writing!

The Setup and Punch Line

This is the perfect comedy style for ventriloquists because you're constantly in a dialogue with your figure. Much of the time, your figure is going to be delivering the line that gets the big laughs. So it would follow that you, the ventriloquist, deliver a setup line, so your figure can retort with the punch line. This setup line is often delivered in the form of a question. It can work the other way around, of course, but the audience response is much different when the vent gets the laugh as opposed to the figure.

Pull Strings

Scripting doesn't depend on you writing down everything. Lots of successful acts just rehearse and perform, never writing out their performances. Some only use recorded audio or video to build their set lists. Actually putting words on paper makes you aware of things that have to be cut and where another punch line (or word) might fit. Plus, it gives you another way of looking at what you've created. If you can't tell, I *highly* suggest you write out your act!

It's All in the Words

There are many keys to your setup lines. You want to use the right words so the audience knows exactly what you're talking about. If possible, you want to build a visual, or paint a picture with words, so it's very clear to your audience what you're talking about.

Let's start with a boring subject: driving a car. The word *driving* carries a lot of weight, because *driving* is a word that can mean more than one thing: driving an automobile, driving a ball down the fairway on the golf course, driving someone (like a reader trying to learn the art of joke-writing) crazy, driving to the hoop in a basketball game, and even having the drive to do something such as learning how to write comedy. You have to start looking at each word for all the possibilities it brings to the table.

Driving also entails something most everyone can relate to. All of us are driving, or we've driven to go to work; go to school; go to the store; go on vacation; or deliver goods, services, or people. *Driving* also relates to automobiles—all the makes and models and the ways people drive. It references the police, license plates, insurance companies, prestige cars and clunkers, tinted windows, and the elderly who drive slowly.

Driving is a great word because it means so much more than just someone sitting behind the wheel of a car and rolling down the road. As a joke writer, you need to start looking at each word for the connections it has with other words and subjects that aren't related to the first meaning.

Let's try a short exercise. Look at these five words:

◆ *Bear*

◆ *Ground*

◆ *Pole*

◆ *Plot*

◆ *Well*

Think of three different definitions for each word. For example, *bear* can be spelled *bare* and therefore have an entirely different definition. The word also can be found in the phrase "too much to *bear*" which is another acceptable definition. Now it's your turn.

Let's put this concept to the test. A fun way to get laughs and use words is to set up your figure with simple "definition" questions:

YOU: I'll bet you don't even know what "debunk" means.

FIGURE: Of course I do! Debunk! As in, "you better wake up and get outta bed before I *debunk* you!"

Let's break this down. The setup line is easy: "I bet you don't even know what _____ means!" It's simple and to the point. The punch line is "you better wake up and get out of bed before I *debunk* you!" The punch word is, obviously, *debunk*. Note that it's not the last word in the sentence. It is one the figure will enunciate and maybe say a little louder than the rest of the words in his line because that's where the laugh is.

Thousands of words have more than one meaning, and when taken literally, they can have an entirely new meaning. *Pasteurize* is a word that can also be heard as "past your eyes." Another good one is *euthanasia*, which, when taken in the wrong context, refers to young people in Asia. It's up to you to look for and find the double and hidden meanings in words and put them into question-answer or setup–punch line format.

Here's an example using another word you need to find three other definitions for: *ground*.

YOU: Thanks for making coffee this morning, but it tasted like mud.

FIGURE: Of course it did! It was fresh *ground* this morning!

This also works as a pun, which is a very simple joke form. Be forewarned that too many puns spoil the jokes, and audiences will not always (if ever) laugh. There's a reason why puns are often referred to as "groaners." You don't want an act filled with those! (Hey, it's all in good *pun*, right?)

Having a Little *Pun* with Words

Puns are close to *idioms*, which are similar to *clichés*, and these all work perfectly for the ventriloquist duo. You're always going to be setting up your sidekick, and plays on words get to the joke quickly because we've all heard such sayings many times in our lives.

def•i•ni•tion

An **idiom** is a fixed expression with a nonliteral meaning. A **cliché** is an overused expression or idea. These are similar terms, with only a shade of difference in meaning. For the joke writer? We don't care! To us they're just punch words waiting to happen.

Of course, there are some rules to using idioms and clichés in humor. You cannot make it so obvious that nobody finds it funny—it has to come as a surprise! At the same time, the cliché or idiom has to be recognizable to most of your audience. If they've never heard the phrase "finer than a frog hair," the line won't get a laugh even if you set it up perfectly. And there has to be something a little bit outrageous or shocking about the line, or it will pass the audience without them ever knowing it.

Here's an example of a pun/cliché that probably isn't going to elicit much response from an audience:

YOU: Did you drop your toothpaste this morning?

FIGURE: I did. And I was *crestfallen*.

There are a number of reasons this line won't work. The punch word isn't a word used much these days, so you lose audience members because they've never heard the word. Many people might not use or even know what Crest Toothpaste is, so you lose them. Even if people do know what the word means, and if they use Crest, they may not put two and two together because the word itself, *crestfallen*, is awkward and obscure. The line reads funny, but it won't get big laughs.

Pull Strings

Comedians often keep lines they like in their act even if those lines don't get big responses or resounding laughs. They fall in love with their own material. Try not to do this! It's better to shelve stuff that doesn't work and keep trying to add more lines that do. It will make your act tighter and funnier.

Let's use some clichés and idioms in our setup–punch line format, and see why these might work:

> YOU: Don't be so mad all the time! You know what they say: "Let a smile be your umbrella!"

> FIGURE: Right. Let a smile be your umbrella, and you'll be one wet loser.

Here's another one:

> YOU: "The early bird catches the worm!"

> FIGURE: Yes, but the worm that sleeps late doesn't get eaten!

And one more:

> YOU: We're together, just like a marriage: "For better or for worse!"

> FIGURE: More like "For better or … forget it!"

We've taken the question-answer out of the format, but the setup–punch line is still there. This is just another way to access humor quickly and easily with your figure. Now it's up to you to get a couple clichés and write some punch lines for each of them, noting the punch word in each.

So far, I've provided the jokes in which the cliché or idiom always comes first and the punch line plays on it. For this exercise, you can use that arrangement, or finish with the cliché if that's funnier. Here are three examples for you to write a joke with:

- ◆ Too many cooks spoil the broth.
- ◆ Money is the root of all evil.
- ◆ Easy as pie.

Finally, a quick line, just for fun, to close this section:

FIGURE: I use clichés, but none of them are original.

By now you're getting familiar with the design for successful ventriloquist joke-writing. You're expanding the use of your vocabulary to include double meanings, idioms, and punch words. As the guys working behind the counter at the Jewish deli in Brooklyn say, "Next!"

Working Toward the Punch Word

I've said it before, but it's worth repeating: one key with joke-writing is to try to get to the punch line and punch word as efficiently as possible. Put another way: don't waste time! How do you do this? You have to put in some time and effort.

Yes, you read that correctly! To save time and be fast, you have to take time and work slowly! Joke-writing is all about researching, thinking, analyzing, and putting words down on paper. Some beginners are inclined to go onstage and wing it. Some people are good at that; most aren't. Even the best are fully prepared, so that when they're improvising, they always have a fallback routine or joke they can use.

Looking for the Irony

To get to the punch word, you need a topic. It doesn't matter what the subject is. It might be good to start with things that irritate you or things you find hypocritical. This is also known as "looking for the irony," and it's been pillar for humor since … well, since man discovered iron.

Let's say you're looking for a parking space at the mall. A car with handicapped plates and a full load of people inside it pulls into a handicapped space, but all the passengers get out and sprint to the food court. One of them even has a skateboard!

Are you looking for a punch line to this setup yet? You should be! Here's one:

I was so upset when I saw that, I wrote the driver a long note, telling him how awful it is to take the space away from someone who needs it! How selfish! How rude! And let me tell you, my hand ached after scratching all that into the hood of his car with my keys!

The difference between this and what you've learned so far is that the setup is part of the entire line. There is no "figure" answering back. Let's fix that:

YOU: Did you go to the mall today?

FIGURE: Yes. And I'm still angry. This car with handicapped plates pulled into a handicapped spot.

YOU: So?

FIGURE: Well, the driver got out and skateboarded into the food court!

YOU: That's awful!

FIGURE: No kidding! I'M THE ONE WITH THE HANDICAP! I CAN'T WALK! *[figure tries to move its legs … nothing doing because they don't work]*

YOU: I'm sorry. That must be frustrating.

FIGURE: It is. So I wrote the guy a note. I told him how selfish he is, how mean-spirited and rude. Whew.

YOU: I'm sure that made you feel better.

FIGURE: Are you kidding? It hurt! It took every ounce of energy I had to scratch that note into the hood of his car … with my keys!

There are a couple jokes in this routine. First, the figure is upset it has the handicap but the skateboarder got the parking space. Second, it then scratched the note in the car's hood.

The setup–punch line format works very well here. This joke was written and then changed a bit when put into the ventriloquist/figure style you're going to use, and that added a punch line and punch word to an already-funny bit. Plus, the single punch line has now expanded to a short routine.

When you've written your punch line or punch word ("with my keys!"), the hardest part is done. The rest is using imagery and vocabulary to get to that line and those words in the strongest way you can.

> **Suitcases**
>
> As a ventriloquist, you have a great advantage in comedy, because the figure will allow for punch lines and laughs. As in the example here, the figure's legs "don't work," and therefore he's "handicapped."

Building Your Jokes

Back to the driving theme. You want to build a joke around the word *driving*, as in driving a golf ball. Let's say your figure is a golfer. But obviously, it can't move its arms and legs. It's tough to drive a golf ball without arms and legs. That's known as a "handicap," which is a word that has more than one meaning. *Handicap* might refer to someone who requires a wheelchair or cane to move around; it also refers to an aspect of the game of golf.

The punch word is almost set. We have worked backward, starting with the word *driving*. We applied it to golf, which naturally led us to the figure's inability to use its arms and legs and the word *handicap*. How do we make that into a punch word?

Simple! We set up the punch word as quickly and easily as possible: "What's your handicap?" The figure will look at you and say, "I can't move my arms and legs!" Great! Now let's build that into a good joke.

You're going to ask the figure about its golf game. The figure is happy to brag about its ability to play, and you'll ask it about the handicap. That will lead to the punch line. It will go something like this:

YOU: What did you do today?

FIGURE: I played golf.

YOU: Really? I didn't know you could play. What's your handicap?

FIGURE: *[turns very, very slowly toward you and finally speaks]* I can't move my arms and legs.

The long, slow turn toward you is almost its own little setup line, and it might even get some laughter before the figure hits the punch words ("move my arms and legs").

Premises, Premises

Another word for *topic* is *premise*, and a premise can go as far as defining what a single joke is about. It also might refer to an entire routine—say 8 to 12 jokes about one subject—in which you write jokes about it until you just can't think of any more. A premise might even refer to the overall theme of a 60-minute performance you put on.

For right now, let's concentrate on premise as the joke topic we're looking for. As stated in the previous section, a great place to look for comedy is in the stuff you find annoying in everyday life. Here is a list:

def•i•ni•tion

A **premise** is a basis or a proposition. For our purposes, premises are not only the subjects and topics you and your figure will discuss, but also the setup for your humor. Your personal premise is: a great ventriloquist with top-notch material!

- Things that happen that aren't fair.

- Things that shock you.

- Something really stupid done by a supposed genius or person of authority.

- Anything that makes you want to write a letter to politicians, big corporations, or media outlets.

- Rip-offs, lies, and hypocrites.

- Obvious discrepancies in the way people, including you, are treated. (This is really good for working with ventriloquist figures, who have the built-in advantage of victimhood!)

Premises can also be found by looking someplace new, going somewhere you haven't gone or had to go, and doing something you've never done before. At the same time, you never want to overlook the obvious, everyday stuff that happens, which can be funny just because everyone can relate to it (especially if it contains one of the places to look for comedy mentioned earlier). Finally, no matter what you decide you want to write jokes about, investigate the subject and get the whole story! The more info you have, the more words you have to work with, the more connections that can be made, and the greater the chance of finding the funny!

Whenever you get an idea, you need to write it down, record it, or catalog it in some way. *Don't lose ideas!* You can never have enough jokes, so you cannot have enough premises as a writer and performer.

Efficient Joke-Writing

Joke-writing is similar to studying a subject for a course in high school or college. You choose the topic and then you research and find as much information about it as you possibly can.

Time for Some Brainstorming

We started with driving, so let's stick with that. *Driving* entails so much more than just driving an automobile. Get your notebook and do some brainstorming. Come up with five or six different meanings for the word *driving*. They can be similar but not the same.

Next, break down *driving* into at least three categories, but more if you can think of them. Here are some examples:

- Roads
- Crazy drivers
- Police
- City driving

- Country driving
- NASCAR
- Foreign cars
- Domestic cars
- Mechanics
- People who leave their turn signals on
- People who don't signal

- Speeders
- Motorcycles
- Trucks
- Convoys
- Gas prices
- Night driving
- Parking

Lots of words are going to be related to driving, and the more information and the more words you have, the better chances you have of finding a joke or two inside the premise. Before you read any more in this section, add 20 more words that relate to driving.

Examining Your Premise

When I talk about efficient joke-writing, I am *not* talking about the process itself! You want to get to the punch words in an efficient manner. To do that, you have to research and study your premise and your topic until you have lots of words and phrases that relate to it. Only then can you successfully write an efficiently worded joke!

Pull Strings

An efficient joke writer organizes his or her thoughts, words, and ideas into columns. You can, too. Across the top of the page, list four general categories like Locations, Events, Clichés, and People. Then, list everything you can think of that relates to your subject (driving) that would fit under those headings. This will organize your thoughts and make things clearer.

We've already written one parking joke, so let's find another subject within the premise of driving. With the word *roads*, we can create an endless list of related ideas:

- Expressways
- Traffic jams
- Road construction
- Two-lane highways

- Toll roads
- Bridges
- White lines
- Etc., etc., etc.

Let's write about traffic jams. Everyone finds those frustrating and annoying. Within the traffic jams category is another list of related words and phrases:

- Time
- Sitting
- Being late
- Moving an inch at a time
- Accidents
- Nowhere to go
- Every lane is moving except the one you're in
- GPS
- Getting off the expressway and getting lost
- Realizing you are driving into a traffic jam as you go down the ramp

There are a lot more. Write down at least five more before you read on.

Let's go deeper. In a traffic jam, the cars inch along the freeway bumper-to-bumper. One efficient way to write jokes is using exaggeration, or sarcasm. Here's an example:

- The freeway was jammed. A Mini Cooper got caught in the windshield wipers of a Hummer and was thrown off the road.
- The freeway was jammed. My GPS just kept saying, *[in a monotone voice]* "We're doomed."
- The traffic jam was the longest I'd ever been in. The only way a car could enter the expressway was to hope someone died and then take their space.

Okay. We've written three punch lines for our traffic jam premise. All are in the setup–punch line format, perfect for you and your ventriloquist figure.

YOU: I heard you were in a traffic jam yesterday.

FIGURE: Yeah … the cars were packed so tightly together, a Mini Cooper got caught in a Hummer's windshield wipers and was thrown off the road!

Now it's up to you to write three more. You can either come up with three new jokes or add on to the three that have been written (more on that later in this chapter).

Here's another example:

> YOU: Yes, that Hummer is a big automobile.

> FIGURE: It seats eight. For dinner!

Basically, the more information you get about each of your topics and premises, the more opportunity you will have to find the funny. Efficiency comes with preparation and research, and you'll find that the ability to see punch lines and punch words will come to you faster the more you work at your writing.

Pull Strings

Some of the funniest jokes come when the punch line is, literally, one or two punch words. The more efficient you can be getting to the punch words, the bigger the laughs!

Formula Jokes and Joke-Writing

Many writers and comedians try to find a formula to write and/or tell jokes, which can work very well. One advantage to repeating a joke formula style during a live performance is that the audience knows when to laugh. But as a ventriloquist, you'll want to work with as many styles and formats as possible.

So far, we've covered setup–punch line and question-answer jokes. We've also looked at using puns, clichés, and idioms for comedy. Here are a couple more formulas to get you started as a joke writer.

"How" Jokes

We'll start with "how" jokes. These are based on theoretical concepts, and the punch lines come as a refutation of the setup. *How* is the operative word, and you can fit it to any issue or matter:

- ◆ "How messed up my family is."
- ◆ "How angry my boss is."
- ◆ "How bad my favorite team is."

The punch line comes in the answer. Question: "Just how bad is your favorite team?" Answer: "My favorite team is so bad, last year they didn't win a game. Which is how many games I won, and I didn't even play!"

There is an endless supply of how jokes because you can use them for any topic. These are perfect for ventriloquists because the joke can be set up with a question:

> YOU: Just how conservative is your hometown?

> FIGURE: It's so conservative, they can't say turkey breast! It's turkey boobs!

Take any premise you like: my education was so bad, my job is so boring, my house is so old, my dog is so flea-bitten, etc. Then write a punch line or two for each lead-in. If you don't like those, make up your own, "My _____ is so _____," and write two or three punch lines for each.

The Switch

The next style to look at is the switch. It can be done in two different ways, and both can be very funny. To switch requires a line of thinking that's thrown off by a comment or a word the audience can't foresee. For example:

> When I was a kid, I played little league. It wasn't a good experience. I was heckled unmercifully: "You stink!" "You always strike out!" "You can't catch the ball!" I finally stood up for myself. I said, "Hey! Stop heckling me … Dad!"

Here's a similar example:

> I want to tell you that I've always enjoyed performing, and I've always had a great time onstage because my audiences are always receptive, attentive, and intelligent—until now.

The switch can come differently, when the setup contains the joke, and the punch line reveals it:

> I was working as a lifeguard, and this little old lady came running up to me, screaming that her grandson was drowning. So I raced to the water and swam out. Sure enough, there was this little kid, barely treading water. I grabbed him, brought him to shore, and gave him mouth-to-mouth. I saved his life! The grandmother came over to me, and I was expecting a hug and a thank you, but she said, "He had a hat …."

One more example:

> There was a pro wrestler on TV the other day. He was shouting and screaming and flapping his mouth, and I couldn't stand it. I pushed the "mute" button on the remote and shut him up. He was still on TV, mouth going a mile a minute, no sound, and the word *MUTE* on the TV screen. Grandma walked in the room, saw the silent wrestler mouthing words, saw the word *MUTE*, and said, "Poor man. He's trying so hard!"

There are more formulas for joke-writing and setting up punch lines, but you have a lot to learn for now. Work on these formulas, and keep notes. There's more to come.

The Theory of Three (Taglines)

From now on, for every good joke you write, it is essential to your comedy education that you write at least three more lines for that joke. This is what I call the "theory of threes." Instead of writing one joke for a topic, premise, or idea, write the first one and then top it. And then try to top that one!

Often, the taglines—or the second and third lines—are funnier than the original punch line and punch words. This is more than an exercise. Look at it this way: instead of writing three jokes, you really should be writing nine. You should have three punch lines for each of the three joke ideas you have.

Let's write a joke. The premise is air travel, something everyone has strong feelings about. There are lots of ways to go:

- Bad food
- Late flights
- Bad weather
- Cranky flight attendants
- Obnoxious fellow passengers
- First class versus coach

First class is interesting because it's separated from the rest of the flight. The service is more personal, and you're sitting in bigger, more comfortable seats than those found in coach. The pilots are just a few feet in front of you, flying the plane to your destination. You're very close to the cockpit.

Let's use one of our formulas:

"How close to the cockpit are you?"

I'm so close I can call the pilot by his first name.

Or I'm so close I can flick the back of the pilot's head with my finger.

Or I'm so close I can hear the pilot talking to the flight attendants.

Those lines are all punch lines waiting for punch words. The first line about the name doesn't hold promise. The second line about flicking the pilot's head doesn't read well. The third line, about talking to the flight attendants, has promise. Let's go with that.

I'm so close I can hear the pilot calling the flight attendant: "Miss?"

Okay. *Miss* is a word with more than one meaning. In this case, it could mean "Miss" as in "Miss Jones" or it could mean "miss" as in, "Whew, I missed hitting that plane!" So we have a punch word. Now let's write a couple jokes.

I was sitting in first class. I was so close to the cockpit, I could hear the pilot. I thought he was calling the flight attendant: "Miss? Miss?" But then he said *"Near miss!"*

That's our first joke; now we need two more. Where is the plane? Has it taken off? It might be funny to say, "Then we took off!" as if there was so much congestion on the tarmac and at the gate that the pilot was maneuvering around. So now the joke reads:

I was sitting in first class. I was so close to the cockpit, I could hear the pilot. I thought he was calling the flight attendant: "Miss? Miss? Whoa! NEAR MISS!" But then we took off.

The wording has changed a little to accommodate the second punch line, which are really punch words, but we still need a third line to go in there. It could be something simple like "On the way up we hit a little birdie," which has double-meaning (golf and birds) or "Everything went perfect from that point on … until we landed and my bag was sent to Miss … Miss … Whoa! Mississippi!"

Instead of a 15- to 20-second joke, you now have a 45-second routine with three jokes. Add two or three more little routines like this about travel, and you have a nice hunk of comedy material that goes for 3 to 5 minutes.

Your turn! The premise is hotels, to go with our air travel bit. Write a good hotel joke and then add two taglines. Good luck!

The Least You Need to Know

- ◆ Setup–punch line is the best joke form for a ventriloquist. As a vent, you'll be setting up your figure for the punch line with almost every set you perform.

- ◆ The punch word is the word (or words) that makes the audience laugh. These do not always come at the end of the punch line, but often do.

- ◆ Premises are easy to come by. You can find them in everyday life.

- ◆ Efficient joke-writing takes time and effort, which isn't efficient, but that leads to tight, concise, perfect punch lines.

- ◆ There are a number of formulas, including the pun, the setup–punch line, the switch, and "how" jokes. More to come!

- ◆ A great way to build the act is to work on the theory of three, which requires you to write two additional punch lines for each original. Put five of those together, and you have 15 jokes. That's more than 3 minutes of comedy!

Chapter 13

More Joke-Writing Exercises

In This Chapter

- Writing your first routine
- Tips for coming up with punch lines and punch words
- All about cross-referencing and callbacks
- Keeping "boring" out of your routine
- A few words on shock humor and whether you should go there

Are you ready? It's time to write your first original comedy routine! Forget your fears and worries about writing jokes! It's time to take what you've learned so far and get some specific punch lines and punch words down on paper, scripted out, for all the world to see! Well, for you to see, anyway.

To help you get started as the head writer for your first gig, a few specific assignments will help you concentrate on getting some opening jokes in writing. This isn't beginner's stuff (that's what Chapter 12 was for), and many of these assignments are the kinds of things you'll be using for the rest of your career. As you write jokes, using some new instruction and some of the things you've already learned, a routine will begin to take shape. One example of what you'll learn is cross-referencing material, key words, and concepts so you can use an idea or a joke as a "callback" in your performance.

No entertainer wants to be boring and have people walk out on his or her program. This chapter looks at what the primary goal of your first few performances should be, as well as some words to help you stay on point as you write comedy. A couple tricks of the trade can save you from losing the crowd in a live setting, and you'll learn them here. Finally, we look at shock humor.

Start With What Works

To get you started on the right foot, let's look at some examples of tried and true material. These are jokes audiences of all ages, backgrounds, and demographics have been laughing at for years! These jokes were originally written for a figure that represented a white male between the ages of 19 and 25. As such, there's a particular tone and character to the relationship between the vent and figure, which evokes a certain personality.

Hiccups

If you bought this book, you can feel free to use the comedy material included here. However, you run the risk of being relegated to hackdom because you're clearly not using original, personal material. You're just using some stuff you got out of a book. You wouldn't be the first, nor would you be the last, to do that.

These are the figure's punch lines and punch words, written in the same style as previous dialogues in this book. You can practice if you'd like to, running through them a couple times to get the idea of flow and usage. Remember, these are just examples of jokes.

The first joke deals with the figure getting a job:

> YOU: You need a job.
>
> FIGURE: I've had jobs. I worked in Detroit.
>
> YOU: Really?
>
> FIGURE: Yes. I was a crash test dummy. And I failed the crash test.
>
> YOU: How could you fail a crash test?
>
> FIGURE: They tell you to sit in the car and "act naturally." So every time it looked like we were gonna crash into the wall, I would panic and do this. *[figure begins to shake in fear]*

As always, there are taglines that need to be written. Some might include the figure saying, "I couldn't get car insurance!" or "You can't imagine how hard it is for a crash test dummy to get health insurance!"

The first laugh comes on "failed the crash test." The second comes when the figure wiggles and writhes in fear, pretending to be headed into the wall. The third could be one of the two you just read, or another you make up on your own.

This is a very simple premise: jobs. You can choose any premise you like. I find it's best to write down 5 to 10 premises for routines, pick two of them—any two at all—and start! The more mundane it is, the better, because you're going to find funny stuff wherever you look.

Here's a joke about the figure having read (or not read) some literature:

YOU: What have you read lately?

FIGURE: Huh?

YOU: Books! Do you know any literature? Classics?

FIGURE: Oh! Right. Sure. *Huckleberry Finn, Native Son, Moby Dick ....*

YOU: Good for you. Mark Twain, Richard Wright, and Herman Melville. That's heavy reading!

FIGURE: Reading? Dude, I'm talking about videos! Fast-forward to the sexy parts!

YOU: There are no sexy parts in *Huckleberry Finn!*

FIGURE: There was in the one I watched!

The setup–punch lines are obvious. The three punch words are "videos," "sexy parts," and "I watched!" The last joke, "There was in the one I watched!" is a shock joke, something coming out of the blue. (See more on shock humor at the end of the chapter.)

The premise for this joke is "school." Of course, everyone in school must read books, and some of these are well-known pieces of Americana. Referencing things everyone knows makes the jokes universal. School is even more universal than books, so this routine will go toward subjects learned in school as opposed to more jokes about reading—which is a fine premise, but the jokes are already being written for school.

Now that you see some basic punch lines, punch words, and theory of threes at work, let's just put down some more setups and punch lines that stick with the jobs and school themes:

YOU: What are the first four words in the United States Constitution?

FIGURE: Show me the money?

That joke is simple enough and funny whether or not you recognize the "Show me the money!" line from the movie *Jerry Maguire*. But that's just one joke. Follow-ups might include these:

YOU: That's not what the Constitution says to America!

FIGURE: That's what it says to me!

YOU: That's just a quote from a movie. Now come on. What are the first words in the United States Constitution?

FIGURE: Greed is good? *[another movie quote—to go with the movie line used in the first part of the joke]* … May the force be with you?

Hiccups

References to pop culture and lines from famous movies, TV shows, and commercials are always funny when well placed in a routine. You have to be careful, though, because if you become dependent on those as big jokes in your set, you'll be in trouble when the lines eventually fade into obscurity. To get around this, you can simply think up some of your own! Note: the school jokes are kind of moving toward a college routine. So be it!

Ready for another example?

YOU: Where else have you worked?

FIGURE: I was a voodoo doll. Twist my arm around.

YOU: *[take the figure's arm closest to you and twist in around]* That doesn't hurt?

FIGURE: *[figure looks at you, laughs, and shakes its head]* Not me! But some guy in Texas is going nuts right now!

Another way to add a couple laughs to this voodoo bit would be to make yourself the victim of the voodoo gag. So when you twist the figure's arm, it hurts *you!* Like this:

FIGURE: Go ahead, twist my arm.

YOU: *[starting to twist the figure's arm]* Ow! Every time I start to twist it, a pain shoots up this arm.

FIGURE: Try giving it a really fast jerk and twist.

YOU: *[jerking and twisting]* OUCH! Oh my gosh, that hurt! Wait! Am I the person being voodoo'd?

FIGURE: I don't know. Pound a nail through my tongue and we'll find out!

Obviously this bit requires some acting on your part. Remember, ventriloquism offers the illusion that the figure is real, and you have to act and react the part! This is a perfect opportunity because you have to act as if you truly feel pain.

By this point, you should be thinking of your own lines. "Puppet jobs" your figure might have, regardless of its character, is a natural premise for a solid ventriloquist routine. What can you come up with?

Let's look at a hunk of material based around a simple premise, math:

YOU: Here's a simple math problem anyone can do. What comes between nine and eleven?

FIGURE: *Family Guy?*

YOU: No, I'm serious. Let's try again. Here's a simple math problem. X over Y equals ten. Solve for X and Y.

FIGURE: Here's an easier one. MTV over HBO equals CNN!

YOU: You're not even trying!

FIGURE: Yes, I am!

YOU: Okay, fine. Here's a really easy one. How many cents in a dollar?

FIGURE: Let me do this mathematically: one dollar equals one hundred cents, right?

YOU: Obviously.

FIGURE: Okay. Then one-tenth of one dollar times one-tenth of one dollar equals one-one-hundredth of a dollar, correct?

YOU: Uh, yes …. *[a little confused]*

FIGURE: Okay. So one-one-hundredth of a dollar equals one cent. Then it's obvious that one dollar equals one cent!

YOU: Wait. That makes no sense!

FIGURE: And that's what a dollar is worth these days!

YOU: This is scary. I'm starting to understand you …

In this bit, a popular TV show is used for punch words at the beginning, but the show can easily be replaced with a different one. Everything else comes directly from what you learned in Chapter 12. Some of the same formulas you learned in Chapter 12 are put to use here: the concept of letters as they relate to math problems and to television ID letters, the play on the word *sense* and its two meanings, and the theory-of-threes and/or the concept of taglines. You could make the case that some taglines are better than the first couple jokes!

The last joke, in which the figure ends up speaking gibberish in an attempt to throw the ventriloquist off-kilter, is an old joke form in which a deluge of information is thrown at the vent in an effort to throw him or her off the subject. Exaggeration jokes work the same way, in which the punch lines and punch words (in this case: "one dollar equals one cent") bring a close, hopefully with a laugh, to all the hyperbole.

Back to some job jokes:

YOU: Okay, where else have you worked?

FIGURE: Well, I worked in Orlando, Florida. I was at Disney World. The "It's a Small World After All" show.

YOU: That musta been fun!

FIGURE: Fun!? It was awful. I did this for six weeks! *[the figure moves its head back and forth, like one of the automatons at Disney World, and maybe sings a couple bars of "It's a Small World After All"]* It was awful. My brother and sister skated in a circle. Killed every brain cell in their heads. They were eventually fired.

YOU: What do they do now?

FIGURE: They're in Congress. *Or:* They teach at _____ University. *Or:* They're Hollywood screenwriters.

That last line, "They're in Congress" and the two alternatives, is a key concept I've not yet covered: some of joke-writing and much of comedy comes from the illusion that the performer telling the joke, and the audience, are superior to the subject at hand, be it politicians, celebrities, all authority, etc. After all, what better way to feel more intelligent and better than someone or something than to make fun of it? Comedy is social criticism in many ways, and you can use that to your advantage while writing jokes—especially for your figure!

Pull Strings

Your figure is a fictional character with its own personality and voice, so it can say the things you personally might never share with anyone, much less a bunch of strangers in a showroom. Now that you have your own personal "press secretary" of sorts, you can voice your opinions through it!

Some final jokes will help you see some setup–punch line structure and execution:

YOU: Wow, you have had some interesting jobs! Where were you last employed?

FIGURE: Sears. *[or any department store/children's clothing store]*

YOU: What did you do for them?

FIGURE: I did this .... *[you hold up one of the figure's legs as he strikes a pose like an in-store mannequin]*

YOU: You were a mannequin!

FIGURE: That's mannequin American to you!

YOU: What did you study in college?

FIGURE: I studied history. I know history like the back of my hand. *[you and figure look at the back of its hand, which is clearly just a piece of foam/wood/fiberglass]*

YOU: Okay, Mr. History. Tell me about the Ottoman Empire, how that affected Mesopotamia, and the ramifications that had on the Persian Gulf as we know it today.

FIGURE: *[long pause as figure stares at you]* I think I need to use the bathroom. *Or:* Can I Google that? *Or:* Can I call a lifeline?

And one more joke to finish off the joke-writing part of this chapter:

> YOU: Look, you can't read, you can't write, and you can't do math. What job could you possibly get?

> FIGURE: Vice president? *[or any person of authority]*

There are some 18 to 20 solid jokes here. The goal of any comedy routine is to pack your set with laughs and build it to a natural ending. One way to work is to put 3 or 4 jokes in every minute you're onstage. So 20 jokes, at 4 jokes a minute, comes to a 5-minute routine. That's a lot!

The time has come! You have the formulas, and you have the concepts and systems. You know what's funny, and you know how to write the punch words. Take a couple hours and write some jokes. Settle on two or three premises—it doesn't matter what they are. You can even use "jobs" and "school" and build from what's here, or you can write your own. Just go for it!

Some Joke-Writing Assignments

First let's "warm up" for your writing session. Find some cartoons, some photographs in magazines or newspapers, or some pictures online. If you have cartoons, do not look at the captions! As of now you are the world's best caption writer!

Using three to five of these pictures and/or cartoons, write three funny lines for each. Chances are you'll get a good punch line for your act. If not, it's still a great exercise to get your comedy brain functioning!

Now you need some topics. Choose three. As discussed before, you can go after things that annoy you or vent about something that happened. (Ooh! Double-meaning word for you there!) It's your choice. Feel free to use jobs or school for your topics. Make it whatever you like. Remember to list everything you can think of about your topic. Put it all down on a sheet of paper and organize the list into columns of your choosing, so you can cross-reference (more on that to come!) as need be.

Start using your comedy-writing techniques. You have the topic, the words, and the subjects that relate to the topics. Find a couple clichés that relate to your topic and write three jokes for each. Next go to your question-answer technique, and use these as introductory questions:

- "How did you ...?"
- "Why did you ...?"

- "When did you ...?"
- "Who did you do it with?"
- "What did you do?"

Next, use exaggeration, *hyperbole*, and all the words you've compiled. You want to let yourself go a little bit and relate all these words and write some punch lines and punch words. Use the "driving" example from the last chapter if you want. After you've written one joke, write two taglines.

def•i•ni•tion

Hyperbole is a figure of speech where exaggeration is used for effect. It is a staple of comedy writing. For example:

> YOU: I'm going to get some beauty sleep.

> FIGURE: Then I guess you'll be asleep for a million years!

Your last joke-writing assignment is to write a switch joke, based directly on the topics you've chosen. You only need to write one per topic. So if you have three total topics, you need 20 jokes for each, with one extra switch joke at the end.

Good luck, don't get frustrated, and have pun—er ... have *fun!*

Using Cross-References and Callbacks

Cross-referencing in this case means you're using topics and subjects in your performance to call back to something you said earlier in your routine. Let's look at the "mannequin" line from the example jokes at the beginning of this chapter. The joke reads this way:

> YOU: Wow, you have had some interesting jobs! Where were you last employed?

> FIGURE: Sears. *[or any department store/children's clothing store]*

> YOU: What did you do for them?

> FIGURE: I did this .... *[you hold up one of the figure's legs as it strikes a pose—like an in-store mannequin]*

> YOU: You were a mannequin!

> FIGURE: That's mannequin American to you!

The punch words are *mannequin American*, playing off the politically correct way people are identified with their personal culture. There's a joke waiting to happen with this, and you need to figure out the cross-reference and *callback* that might come from it.

def•i•ni•tion

A **callback** is a way to remind your audience of a joke you made earlier in your performance, usually in a different context, using the same words or phrases you used the first time.

It's a sign of respect to refer to someone as "Irish American" or "Asian American." It would then follow that to call an American citizen "Irish" when in fact he or she is a citizen of the United States could be taken as an insult. "I'm not Irish! I'm Irish American!" Apply the same thinking to your figure.

You can't refer to your figure as a "figure." It's a "mannequin American" or "figure American." So write the joke that makes that point:

YOU: I guess you can't walk because you're a figure.

FIGURE: I AM NOT A FIGURE!

YOU: Okay, fine. If you're not a figure, what are you?

FIGURE: I'm a mannequin American!

Great. You have the joke. Now find a place in your set to call back to it, cross-referencing one bit that mentions "mannequin American" with the other. This technique will get you solid laughs in many ways and can be used with live audiences to great effect.

Hiccups

A callback that comes as the closing line of a set or a long routine, referencing the word or phrase used earlier, can bring your set to a resounding close, as you might find with a musical play or book. Use your callbacks wisely! You don't want to inadvertently end your set before you're ready.

The most important lesson to learn here is that every reference to similar words and situations and observations is a possibility for humor and a punch line. Use it!

There are lots of ways to cross-reference material in your jokes. One of the best ways is to write out your script so you can actually see the punch words and lines written out in front of you. It's not a good idea to have an entire 5- or 10-minute routine based on cross-referencing, but used wisely, you'll find more jokes and taglines.

How Not to Be Boring

Comedians don't mind hearing an occasional audience member tell them, "I didn't find you funny." Hey, you can't please everyone, right? But no entertainer, especially those in the comedy business, wants to hear that their act and set routine is boring.

Letting the Figure Do Some of the Work

As with the advantage a ventriloquist has with his or her figure saying things he or she might otherwise not say, there's also a built-in advantage in a vent's relationship with the audience: a ventriloquist can have the figure "talk" to the audience.

The figure can stare at someone, come on to someone, or just come right out and ask someone, "Are you having a good time?" No matter the answer—"Yes I am" or "No, I'm really not"—the vent is in control, and the figure can get through anything by saying something that turns a negative into a positive. "You're not having a good time? Neither am I. What say you and I leave here and go bowling for an hour or so?" or "You're having fun? Good. Me, too! Hey, I think I'd rather just hang out with you! Can I sit at your table?"

No matter how the audience responds to your questions and your comebacks, there are some simple rules to follow:

- The figure gets to say the funny lines.

- When you have a choice, always take the "yes" or the positive choice. Saying "no" leaves no room for anything else—it's a scene-ender. Audiences can say "no," and it's up to you to make that positive. Whatever they say—and this is 100 percent of the time—you have to find a way to go with it that will eventually lead you to something funny. Negativity stops things. Positivity keeps things interesting.

> **Pull Strings**
>
> I don't recommend you build a routine around talking to audience members at the start of your career. But taking a minute or two during your first shows to have the figure pick someone out and say something—anything—will keep some freshness and vitality in your set.

- Before you "go to the crowd" and have your figure talk with audience members, know what your next joke or routine is going to be! There's nothing worse than doing a good job of improvising a short, funny conversation with the audience and then not knowing what to do next!

Talking to the audience can be a highly entertaining and fun way to do a set, and when done well, the exchange is a pleasure and a crowd pleaser. You could call this form of comedy "Where are you from and what do you do?" As you and your figure go around the audience, pick someone and "interview" them, asking where they're from, what their marital status is, how much they like their job, etc. With each answer, new avenues of humor open, and you have a couple choices: improvise comedy on the spot or work a routine or a joke or even a full set into the answer.

Be forewarned, though: an act like this has to be developed over time and requires more stage time than most other types of performances. The best way to become a "Where are you from and what do you do?" ventriloquist is to emcee at a comedy club for 6 months, spending part of each show talking with audiences.

Keeping Things Interesting

Here are some rules to help you avoid being boring:

First and foremost, have lots of jokes and do your best to be funny. This means lots of rehearsing and time spent working on your set, alone and in front of friends and family and anyone else who is willing to watch you get ready.

If you can't be funny, be entertaining. This can happen in different ways:

- Show off your vent technique by saying some very difficult words without moving your lips.

- Sing a song with your figure and have the figure do a big finale to finish the tune.

- Do the "drinking water" or "crying baby" routines (see Chapter 11). These fillers can get you to your next comedy set.

If you can't be funny or entertaining, be informative. Tell the audience how and why you started performing ventriloquism. Explain what you and your figure have been doing to get ready for this big performance.

If you can't be funny, entertaining, or informative, you can still have fun. Energy is a great equalizer, and an energetic act can usually get through a few minutes onstage if you're focused and able to maintain that energy throughout your set.

If you can't be funny, entertaining, or informative, and you don't have great energy, you need to start over at the beginning of this book and re-learn everything! (Just kidding!)

Perhaps the best way to be anything but boring is to know your audience. If you're doing a program for some senior citizens in a church basement, they won't understand references to hip-hop music and popular videos on YouTube. If you're working for teenagers, don't spend 15 minutes talking about marriage. One of the best ways to win over any audience is to tailor some of your jokes to them. Reference local towns, celebrities, and sports teams. Talk about the cultural differences between where you live and where your audience is. The more you endear yourself and your figure, the more the audience will be with you.

Pull Strings

By using local names and alluding to the customs of the audience, you'll gain attentiveness and responsiveness.

The best way to make your act solid and exciting is to write those punch lines and punch words and rehearse them until they're tight and perfectly carried out.

Simple Jokes vs. "Shock" Humor

Shock humor—it's not what you think (for this section, that should be written "it *snot* what you think!") it is. Shock humor could also be called unexpected humor because it differs so greatly from what the audience expects.

Radio shock-jocks make a living trying to top the latest scandalous thing they said or did on the air. That's one kind of shock humor, as is profane humor—the kind that's prevalent in comedy today. An entire subculture of comedians spend their careers trying to out-curse, out-vulgarize, and out-rage society. That's fine, but that's not what this book is about.

You're free to use your figure and get laughter any way you want to. You can take the joke-writing techniques learned here, add some "comedy adjectives" (a.k.a. profanities) that will tell the audience when to laugh, and go to work. Chances are you'll get bookings right away and have a long, successful career. Good for you!

If you're not going the vulgar punch line route, you'll be using shock humor in a different way, more like a surprise for your audience. And that's the difference to shoot for when it comes to shocking material. It should be a surprise, and the punch word shouldn't depend on the profanity itself for the joke. By working this way, in which four-letter words and deviance aren't the basis for your humor, you can always get risqué and create the kind of tension that leads to laughter, but do so without becoming vulgar. If you're an act built on shock, vulgarity, and that modus operandi, there's only one way to go: get dirtier and raunchier. Even that gets boring after a while.

Put another way, you want to write jokes that depend on real punch words used in clever, entertaining, and funny ways. Any joke in which the punch word is just a profanity or a vulgarity is not a joke. Its only purpose is to shock the audience into laughter.

The Least You Need to Know

- Part of becoming a good joke writer is writing lots of jokes. Some will be good; some won't.

- Cross-referencing is a great way to help you get some callbacks into your set.

- It's up to you to keep your live performance exciting and fresh.

- Shock humor can be merely profanity-laced tirades. But wouldn't it be better to have a punch-line-intensive routine that shocks the audience with surprising jokes based on cross-references and double meanings?

Chapter 14

Writing Dialogue

In This Chapter

- Maximizing laughs with a solid script
- Arranging your jokes in good order
- Get off on the right foot with outstanding opening lines
- Leaving 'em laughing all the way to the end

If you've followed along with the preceding chapters, you should now have 20 jokes on three different subjects. Pare those down to your top two subjects and then make a choice as to which you'd like to start with. (*But don't throw out the other two!* You're going to need jokes, remember? You can never have enough.)

The next task is to write a solid script, starting with the all-important opening line; followed by the meat of your routine, in which the audience gets to know you, your talent, and your figure; and the close, in which you get a big laugh and applause as you walk off the stage. Writing the script is going to be a great experience, as you will find more jokes and opportunities for humor you didn't see as you wrote your jokes and their taglines.

Closing a show is probably the most important part of your set. Your set might be so-so for the first 6 or 7 minutes, but if those last 3 to 5 are incredible, your routine is a home run.

Joke + Joke + Joke = Script

You did it! You wrote some 60 jokes and you've chosen 20 for your first big performance—that's a laudable achievement! Your work isn't done, but congratulations on coming this far!

Now it's time to put together your act. Remember, as a ventriloquist, you're the director, head writer, lead actor, and producer. Now it's time to be the director and take what your head writer has put together, look at your actors, and make decisions on how best to tell this story.

Do What Feels Right for You

Your first task is to get your jokes and punch words in an order that makes sense and works to a logical conclusion. Done well, your script is going to enhance your jokes and make them funnier. When one joke follows another, both come across stronger. Every punch word you've written is a joke unto itself, but each one can be a setup to the punch line that follows, requiring less time to set up your laughs and allowing you to get to the funny faster.

Hiccups

Reading your jokes off the page in a random order can't compare to the punch they pack when arranged in story-like fashion, creating a flow and rhythm.

You'll find that every script, and every live performance, has natural high points (hopefully one at the end) and low points. This isn't a negative because it only serves to make your entire performance stronger. Each of your jokes will suffer a little bit because they're now competing with one another. It's impossible for every joke to be a high point and get an explosive laugh. But you'll soon find that the softer laughs set up the bigger ones. It's quite a game, and you'll become acquainted with all the rules as you keep writing and performing.

There's one rule to writing a good script: *Do what feels right to you*. If you get a group of friends or family together to go over your script, every single one of them will have a different idea about which line to start with, what to close with, what goes where, and when you should do what. *You* are the director. *You* are in control. This is a low-tech operation, and the workings of a good script are easy to understand.

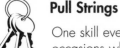

Pull Strings

One skill every ventriloquist needs to learn is "working with silence." There will be occasions when the audience isn't laughing or applauding your brilliance—when there is no response coming at all. The tendency to panic at this time is great, but you need to perform through that silence, stick with your script, and have confidence that what you've written is quality. There might be silence for the moment, but you know a laugh is coming. Hang in there, work to the punch words, and be secure in the knowledge that you have good jokes and a good script.

You're going to take your 20 jokes and arrange them by subtopics, cross-referencing as you go and sorting them by what you think are stronger or weaker—however you like. Maybe you'll find common words to guide you. There's no "correct" way to do this. Go with what feels right to you, and try to have the script logically flow from one subject and punch line to the next.

If you're working at a computer, cutting and pasting is a natural for the script-writing task! You can move jokes around, put them off to the side, make notes, and keep the subject matter interrelated in a variety of ways. It's a little harder with paper and pencil, but by using note cards and a blank piece of paper, you can arrange individual jokes on a desk or tabletop and then write out your script to match the order you've set up for your lines.

Getting Your Ducks in a Row

Let's take 10 or 12 of the jokes about school from Chapter 13 and begin to build a script. Here are the keys to script-writing:

◆ Get to the punch words as quickly as possible.

◆ Make sense. Your script cannot meander from subject to subject because you'll lose the audience's attention (unless, of course, the character of your figure is someone who cannot stay focused and on-point, but that's a different kind of act than we're working on here).

◆ Have a beginning, a middle, and an end.

For now, let's just focus on the school jokes:

YOU: What have you read lately?

FIGURE: Huh?

YOU: Books! Do you know any literature? Classics?

FIGURE: OH! Right. Sure. *Huckleberry Finn, Native Son, Moby Dick* ....

YOU: Good for you. Mark Twain, Richard Wright, and Herman Melville. That's heavy reading!

FIGURE: Reading? Dude, I'm talking about videos! Fast forward to the sexy parts!

YOU: There are no sexy parts in *Huckleberry Finn!*

FIGURE: There was in the one I watched!

YOU: Here's a simple math problem anyone can do. What comes between nine and eleven?

FIGURE: *Family Guy?*

YOU: No, I'm serious. Let's try again. Here's a simple math problem. X over Y equals ten. Solve for X and Y.

FIGURE: Here's an easier one. MTV over HBO equals CNN!

YOU: You're not even trying!

FIGURE: Yes, I am!

YOU: Okay, fine. Here's a really easy one. How many cents in a dollar?

FIGURE: Let me do this mathematically: one dollar equals one hundred cents, right?

YOU: Obviously.

FIGURE: Okay. Then one-tenth of one dollar times one-tenth of one dollar equals one-one-hundredth of a dollar, correct?

YOU: Uh, yes .... *[a little confused]*

FIGURE: Okay. So one-one-hundredth of a dollar equals one cent. Then it's obvious that one dollar equals one cent!

YOU: Wait. That makes no sense!

FIGURE: And that's what a dollar is worth these days!

YOU: This is scary. I'm starting to understand you .... What did you study in college?

FIGURE: I studied history. I know history like the back of my hand. *[you and figure look at the back of its hand, which is clearly just a piece of foam/wood/fiberglass]*

YOU: Okay, Mr. History. Tell me about the Ottoman Empire, how that affected Mesopotamia, and the ramifications that had on the Persian Gulf as we know it today.

FIGURE: *[long pause as figure stares at you]* I think I need to use the bathroom. *Or:* Can I Google that? *Or:* Can I call a lifeline?

YOU: Look, you can't read, you can't write, and you can't do math. What job could you possibly get?

FIGURE: Vice president? *[or any person of authority]*

Using the punch words in this script, we're going to tell a story, so we need a place to start. We want to open with a strong punch line that will get us out of the box, plus we have to keep in mind that the routine has to make sense.

Let's expand our school routine to focus on college. It works on a couple levels because people have a preconceived notion about what a college education means, and everyone has studied some of the subjects we make fun of in grade school and high school. Although we're using college as the focus, it's a universal comedy bit that lots of people of many ages can enjoy.

Pull Strings

Use your second-best line to open your set and your very best joke to close your set. You want to start and end with a bang and be funny and entertaining in between!

We will start with one of the two strongest lines. For this script, let's just say those are the history jokes and the reading jokes. We wrote the history joke with the word *college* in it already, and because both lines are funny, we'll open with the reference to college we've already made.

When writing your script, include *everything* you'll be doing, including stage directions:

♦ *Walk on to taped music.*

♦ *Walk on to applause, take center stage, and set figure on the preset stand.*

♦ *Walk on. Open stand, and face the audience.*

Leave no room for doubt. You're going to *take* the stage, set your figure, and begin.

First Things First

To get to that first line, you need a quick introduction. Tell the audience *exactly* what you're going to do. You can be literal, or you can allude to it:

> YOU: Good evening. This is my friend, [*insert figure's name*]. I hope you'll make him feel welcome, as this is his first time ….

> FIGURE: Whoa! Wait. You don't need to introduce me! I'm college educated! You're looking at four years and thousands of dollars of knowledge here!

This sets up everything. The figure is very proud of its education, it obviously has been to college, and it has a little attitude about itself. Perfect! The stage is set for joke #1!

> YOU: Really? What did you study?

> FIGURE: *[with pride]* History. I know all about history.

> YOU: Great! Tell us about the Ottoman Empire, how that affected Mesopotamia, and the ramifications that's had on the Persian Gulf as we know it today.

> FIGURE: *[long look at you]* Uh … can I call a lifeline? *[Remember, this might end up as "Can I Google that?" depending on audience response.]*

> YOU: No! You may not call a lifeline! Here's an easier one: what are the first four words in the United States Constitution?

> FIGURE: Show me the money!

> YOU: Come on, these are easy questions, and you don't know a thing about history!

> FIGURE: That's okay. History repeats itself. I'll watch the reruns!

Pull Strings

When in doubt, don't overanalyze your jokes and what you've written. Make an arbitrary choice, and just start. You'll edit your script and your jokes a hundred times before you have everything set in stone. And once it *is* set in stone, you'll edit it again!

So there's the first little hunk. We have our opening line, our first joke, two follow-up jokes, and (hopefully) the kicker joke at the end with the punch words "I'll watch the reruns!" That's the first minute or so of the comedy routine, and it's not too shabby. It's tightly worded, it moves toward a resolve, and it allows us to get to the next section of the routine about college with a joke.

That last joke, "I'll watch the reruns," comes directly from using cross-referencing and a cliché that applies to history: "history repeats itself." The audience might laugh at that line alone. If not, the kicker about reruns should do it. This is a simple joke-writing technique, and it's probably more obvious to you now: the cliché fits perfectly, and the joke almost writes itself.

Let's move on. Remember, we're just taking the jokes about school and putting them in an order that makes sense:

YOU: Read any books lately?

FIGURE: Huh?

YOU: Books! Literature! You know, the classics?

FIGURE: Oh! Right. Sure. *Huckleberry Finn, Native Son, Moby Dick ....*

YOU: Good for you! Mark Twain, Richard Wright, and Herman Melville. That's heavy reading!

FIGURE: Reading? Dude, I'm talking about videos! Fast forward to the sexy parts!

YOU: There are no sexy parts in *Huckleberry Finn!*

FIGURE: There was in the one I watched!

YOU: You don't know anything about literature!

FIGURE: I do, too! I know it like I know the back of my hand. *[you and figure look at the back of figure's hand—nothing there]*

YOU: Fine. Do you know any math?

FIGURE: I'm a mathematical genius.

YOU: Let's find out. I'll start with an easy one. What comes between nine and eleven?

FIGURE: *Family Guy!*

YOU: I'm not talking about TV! Math! X over Y equals ten. Solve for X and Y.

FIGURE: Here's an even easier one! MTV over HBO equals CNN!

YOU: Let's break this down to the simplest math example I can think of. How many cents in a dollar?

FIGURE: Hmmmm ... let me do that mathematically: one dollar equals one hundred cents, right?

YOU: Yes! Now we're getting somewhere!

FIGURE: Okay. Then one-tenth of a dollar times one-tenth of a dollar equals one-hundredth of a dollar, right?

YOU: Uh, yeah, I think so …. *[confused]*

FIGURE: Great. So one-one-hundredth of a dollar equals one cent, which means that, obviously, one dollar equals one cent! See? I'm college educated!

YOU: That makes no sense!

FIGURE: What did you say?

YOU: That makes no sense!

FIGURE: And that is what a dollar is worth these days! No cents!

YOU: You can't read, you can't write, and you can't do math! What job could you possibly get?

FIGURE: Vice president? *[or any public figure/celebrity you care to name]*

I changed and edited some of the jokes to make the opening few minutes work. For example, I moved the looking at the figure's hand bit from the history section (where it was first written) to the literature section. This change gives some balance to that part of our script, keeps us going in the theory of threes, and lends more punch words to that section. Editing is a never-ending process.

There are our first few minutes scripted out. Your job now is to use this as a guide, write your own jokes, put them in an order that makes sense, script them out, and edit as you go.

Preparing and Writing Your Script

Preparation is critical to any great comedy performance. That preparation began when you learned the tools and techniques required to be a ventriloquist with flawless technique. It continued through joke-writing exercises, and it goes on through writing your script.

Script-writing preparation boils down to three components I call the three P's of script-writing:

- Premise
- Progress
- Point (or finishing point)

Let's look at how each of these relate to script-writing.

Setting Up the Premise

To begin assembling your script, grab the original 20 jokes you wrote and choose your best lines to be in your first scripted act. Begin to put them in order based on any reference point you like. It doesn't have to be exact. For example, if you have a joke about how men often act like pirates and a joke about fashion or even just about women's clothing, you can make those work in the context of what people wear.

Use your imagination to find connections between your jokes, even if the connections seem far-fetched and somewhat iffy. You can make them work as you write the script! Make notes so you don't forget why a joke about ice cream and a joke about mountains might go together.

When you've loosely organized your jokes into categories that might reference one another, really focus in on how the jokes fit together, and lump them into one, two, or three groups. You're going to end up with two or three little hunks of comedy (the example in this chapter breaks down into two hunks: college and jobs). The fastest way to make everything flow and progress is to use your second-favorite joke or hunk as your first line. Close with what you feel are your strongest punch words.

This works whether you wrote a series of punch words about one subject or 2, 5, or 20 jokes that aren't related at all! Your job is to edit, re-edit, and find the commonalities!

The premise sets up your audience. You're going to tell the audience what the premise is near the beginning of your performance and then you'll spin your tale, working around and through this premise with punch lines and punch words. In the case of our chapter example, the premise started as school and narrowed a bit to college. As you work, you'll find that you may define your premise more and more, finding jokes related to and resulting from it. The obvious example in our joke-writing is school (or college) leading directly to jokes about jobs your figure has had.

Progress: Keep On Keepin' On

Once you've established your premise and you're writing your script, you want to develop a natural progression from the beginning to the end of the piece. In our example, the progress would start with a discussion of college education, which naturally leads to what jobs the figure has had since graduating, working to the point (a.k.a. finishing point) that will close the set to thunderous applause and laughter!

As you can see from our examples, some of the jokes have been rewritten, edited, shortened, or lengthened to make the punch words more effective. Words are added and taken out as the script-writing process evolves; the end result is a polished piece, ready for you to memorize and take onstage. As you're preparing and writing your script, you will be rewriting and editing your jokes.

Editing and Rewriting

Rewriting jokes is going to be a big part of your workload as a ventriloquist, especially as you work on your script. Let's take one of the jokes and do some rewriting. "MTV over HBO equals CNN!" are the punch words to the setup "X over Y equals ten, solve for X and Y." Let's come up with three different punch lines for that setup:

> YOU: X over Y equals ten, solve for X and Y.
>
> FIGURE: Sure, I can solve the problem for X and Y, but how does that make ten feel?

And another:

> YOU: X over Y equals ten, solve for X and Y.
>
> FIGURE: X equals forty-five, and Y equals five.
>
> YOU: Forty-five divided by five is nine!
>
> FIGURE: Hey, close enough! What do I get for second place?

And one more:

> YOU: X over Y equals ten. What are X and Y?
>
> FIGURE: The twenty-forth and twenty-fifth letters in the alphabet!

These might be funnier, or they might *not* be funnier, than the original jokes. That's not the point. As you're writing your script, take one or two jokes that you originally wrote and write three *different* punch lines, with all new punch words.

There are lots of ways to find the funny in your lines. As you're putting jokes into your script, adding more and different punch lines only makes your routine stronger. Plus, some of those "new" jokes might be funnier than the originals!

> ### Suitcases
>
> You can also rewrite punch words. Take some of your favorite comedian's jokes or those you've heard on sitcoms and *rewrite* them. You're not stealing another joke writer's joke; you're taking the premise and finishing it your own way, similar to a musician changing the melody progression of a song because he likes the way certain chords sound.

Part of script-writing is having a feel for what works best for you. Use a premise you feel comfortable with, something you know about. Taking on subject matter you have no interest in or experience with won't help you, especially as you're just starting out. The more you know about your premise, the better. You'll know the wordage and the concepts behind your jokes and your setups.

And always keep in mind that, even as you start out putting 20 jokes into context and an easy-to-follow order, you are working toward an ending.

Opening with a Bang!

Getting off to a good start is imperative. And to help with that, you need to script out the beginning of your set. You'll be nervous with your first few performances, so the sooner you can get a laugh, the better. You're also going to want to get to your figure and start sharing your talent as quickly as possible.

Taking the Stage

If you walk onstage with your figure and go straight to the microphone, the audience will know immediately what you are—a ventriloquist with his or her partner—and everyone will know you're going to tell jokes and/or sing songs. This is straightforward and easy to define.

But there are a few other ways to open your show:

◆ You can walk onstage with a suitcase or bag, set it down, and speak to the audience by yourself, without your figure.

- You can walk through the audience with your figure after you've been introduced and banter with audience members as you approach the stage/platform/microphone.

- You can have a figure set in the audience someplace and have him heckle you, so you have to go out and get him and take him to the stage. (This is a hard one to pull off because you'll have to be very, very adept at the distant voice.)

Those are just a few suggestions on how you might start your show, but the possibilities are endless, really. Think about how you want to get started, what the premise of your performance is, and what you can do to get going.

Script Out All the Details

Your script should begin with you introducing yourself (even if the emcee or the person who brought you onstage says your name during an introduction), introducing your figure, and then getting to your first joke. You might want to break the ice with the audience before you dig in to your prepared material, and that's fine, but script it out! Script what you're going to have your figure say in response to you, and script out anything that you're hoping might look "off the cuff."

Pull Strings

You'll have plenty of performances during which you can practice improvising and coming up with comedy on the spot. But to start, you want to be prepared. Script it out!

The best way to introduce yourself and what you do is with humor, so you should have three solid punch lines and punch words about yourself. This is more joke-writing work, but it will make your act better.

If you choose to walk on alone, you need to script that out, too.

Starting With or Without Your Figure?

By walking onstage without your figure on your arm, you have the advantage of setting yourself up as a character completely different from your figure. Getting your figure out of the bag or case and bringing it to the mic should also have a set of punch words so there's no wasted time as you get situated.

Walking through the audience is a fun way to start a ventriloquist show, particularly if you can have the figure converse with audience members. You don't have to be hysterically funny when you talk with folks, but laughter as you make your way to the stage and the microphone can only be a good thing. You can script out some lines before you go (good-natured jokes about people who are overdressed or underdressed or who walked in late can be fodder and are easy to write).

One way to become comfortable with the audience is to do a few shows during which you walk onstage with the figure in its bag or case. Begin your act by questioning people closest to the stage with simple-to-answer questions:

- ◆ Where are you from?

- ◆ What do you do for a living?

- ◆ Are you married? How long?

Your goal is to make people feel comfortable. You don't want to make fun of the way they look or who they're with. You're a kind of talk-show host, so let them guide you, and always take a positive approach: "I'm not here to make fun of you personally, but I have no problem making fun of your job, where you're from, what you drive, etc." Eventually, you might reach the point where your figure can do this for you, and that technique will come in handy as you're walking through the audience interacting with people.

If you have a strong distant voice technique, you can seat a figure in the audience before your set begins and have it heckle you as you take the stage. If done correctly, it will greatly surprise everyone as you reveal that it's your figure, not a human being, who has interrupted the show! But *only* attempt this if your distant voice is excellent!

Suitcases
You can also use a local flavor to start your show. Things like "It's great to be here during the humidity festival!" show that you're aware of where you are and give you an immediate bond with the audience, who probably feel the same way (unless, of course, you use that line in the middle of December in Buffalo, New York). Your opening line and/or joke will set the audience at ease and let them know they're in for some good laughter.

Closing Your Show

As you know by now, your original script should begin with your second-favorite or second-strongest joke and should close with what you perceive to be your best joke. That might change; if it does, don't hesitate to change your script to match. You want to end with a bang!

In a way, your entire performance is working to that closing line. One of the reasons you want to have a strong set closer is the security it will give you as a performer: "Well, I know I have a big laugh coming at the end of the set because that's my best joke." If nothing else, you know you will get offstage with a laugh.

As with the beginning of your act, if you walked on with your figure on your arm, you're going to leave that way. A bow by the both of you is a nice way to tip your hat to the audience. A well-worn closer premise for ventriloquists is to try to shut up the figure after that last joke, and the two of you struggle as you leave the stage.

Pull Strings

It's always a good idea to have a few "throw-away" jokes memorized in case you have the good fortune to get an encore. Also, because comedy is all about writing, editing, and re-editing, an encore is a great time to try out new material.

Putting the figure back in the case is a wonderful opportunity for humor. This is especially true if, as you try to maintain some control, the figure complains or berates you or becomes belligerent. Again, writing a series of jokes with the premise "putting away the figure at the end of the set" gives you a couple extra minutes and a natural way to finish things off.

If you've used or spoken to audience members during your set, give them an acknowledgement and an applause break as you finish off your performance.

The Least You Need to Know

♦ Start your set with your second-best joke, and finish with your very best one. Organize your jokes by referencing and cross-referencing subject matter.

♦ The three P's are your script-writing formula: premise, progress, and (finishing) point. You decide the premise or premises for your script, put the jokes in order so there's a flow and a rhythm to what you're talking about, and work to the big finish!

♦ The beginning and the end of your set are vital. There are different ways to walk on and walk off, but in the end, you need to decide what works best for you and your script.

Chapter 15

Rehearsing Your Script

In This Chapter

- ◆ Memorizing your script
- ◆ Rolling with the punch lines
- ◆ Finding the big laughs
- ◆ Tips to keep your act fresh
- ◆ Timing is everything

The hardest part is over: you've written jokes and picked the ones best suited to your style and what you want to do onstage. Memorizing those lines and punch words will take some effort, but committing your script to memory will make you feel much more comfortable and relaxed going into those first few performances. This chapter is going to help you learn how to memorize your scripts.

Each time you get onstage and perform will be a new situation. No matter how many times you rehearse and execute your routine in front of a live audience, it's going to be a little bit different each time. You, however, are in control. You will gain a working knowledge of the things you do the audience reacts to favorably and where the really big laughs are. Now you'll learn how to present those key moments in a natural, free-flowing way.

You probably already know that comedy routines depend on great timing. In this chapter, you'll learn how to perfect your timing onstage.

Finally, I share some tips on making each live presentation look as if it's brand new, as if the material is just "coming to you," and you and your vent partner are just a couple folks having a nice conversation with a couple hundred eavesdroppers.

WE ROBOT: Memorization Tips

Memorizing your first script might not be a chore for you. Writing and editing humor is new territory, and chances are you'll have a good working knowledge of your material before you begin your rehearsals. If not, it's time to start memorizing!

Remember, this is just your first script. There are many more to come, and thousands of new jokes to write. You will no doubt have to do some last-minute writing and memorizing as you become more accomplished and sought after, which means you'll need to commit lines and written material to memory in a short period of time.

I can help! In the following sections, I give you nine memorization tips that will help you quickly and efficiently commit words to memory. These nine directives are identified by the anagram *WE ROBOT*.

Pull Strings

Using anagrams and acronyms is a useful way to memorize lines, homework assignments, long speeches, and even comedy scripts.

(Yes, it's weird. Look at it this way: your figure is kind of a robot you control. You've joined an exclusive club, a club made up of folks who work with inanimate objects—robots, if you will—that are brought to life through skill and manipulation, almost as if the word *robot* can be made into a verb. As in "We *robot* our figures and make them come alive!" Thus, WE ROBOT!)

W = Write It Down

After you've written out your complete first set, read through it once or twice, without your figure, just kind of getting into the flow of the script. Next, get a pen (if you're brave and you absolutely know you will not make a mistake!) or a pencil and write out as much of the script as you remember, without looking at your original.

Writing down the words after a few rehearsals is going to help you immeasurably. Writing it down is one of the most helpful and organized ways to get all your lines learned. You'll find that writing out your script, longhand, during rehearsal time helps you with more than just committing it to memory. You'll find more jokes, you'll make more edits and make better vocabulary choices, and you'll get to those punch words faster and with more energy.

E = Emote

Part of your job as a ventriloquist is to act! Remember, you're not only the director and head writer, but also the key performer in your set. This requires you to act, react, roll your eyes, do double-takes, laugh, shout, shake your head, and do whatever else seems appropriate for you as the ventriloquist and (usually) the authority figure in the show.

Take this part of the learning process seriously. It would behoove you to make notes in the margins of your script about what you want to do as you carry on a dialogue with your figure. As you rehearse, and as you're concentrating on nailing down each line, try to picture yourself performing in a play or a movie.

Acting with your figure sells your routine and your jokes as much as the brilliant writing you've done. Give your jokes a chance to hit home the way they should by getting into your role as the vent.

> **Pull Strings**
>
> Consider taking an improvisational theater class or an introductory theater workshop. If there is a community theater in your neighborhood, that's a good (and cost-effective!) place to get some beginner lessons in how theater works. I bet you'll quickly see how that can apply to your ventriloquist career.

R = Read Out Loud

By now you should not hesitate to talk out loud to yourself as you practice ventriloquism and all its intricacies. That's good, because as you rehearse and memorize your script with your figure, you'll be doing it out loud. That's right. The best and fastest way to get things done is to practice your entire set out loud. This allows you to find some extra bits of business in your set and to work on reactions and your acting skills, and it helps define both your character and your figure's character.

You can memorize all you want by reading and saying the words over and over in your head, but that won't prepare you for the dialogue you'll be having onstage. Yes, you are technically talking to yourself. But from the audience point of view, there are two vital characters onstage, having a discussion in a performance piece that has a beginning, a middle, and an end. It is impossible to achieve the inflections and nuances of speech without saying and hearing the script out loud.

In addition, if you're using lots of music in your act, it's even more critical to rehearse and rehearse and rehearse those songs out loud.

Hiccups

You might try to memorize a script in your head and then execute the lines live onstage. Sure, you can probably memorize those lines, but having the figure respond and act and react silently while you practice won't do you any favors onstage. Those things have to be practiced out loud. Your performance hinges directly upon the amount of time and quality of effort you give to your rehearsals. You'll perform in the exact same manner in which you prepare!

O = Other Hand

You've probably already made a choice as to which hand you're going to use to manipulate your figure. Most right-handed vents put their figure on their right hand, and left-handers put theirs on their left hand. No problem; that's a great way to start. But now you're memorizing, so after you've rehearsed a while with the figure on your hand of choice, switch hands. This helps you concentrate even more on the words both you and your figure say.

You'll no doubt find some great new actions for the figure, and maybe for yourself, too, and you'll definitely see things in a new light. If you're recording video, take a look at the way you work with the figure on the off hand. There's a chance your act might work even better with your vent partner on your less-used hand.

If nothing else, you'll have prepared yourself for the day when you will have figures on both hands. And it's going to help you get things memorized as well.

B = Break It Down

A great way to learn anything is to break it down into manageable parts, and that works for your script, too. Divide your script into sections, even if the set is only going to last 5 or 6 minutes. One easy way to do this is by dividing the script into a certain number of pages to practice and remember. If your entire script is 6 to 8 pages long, you could divide it into three or four 2-page sessions you can work on individually, putting them all together after you've committed each to memory.

You can break it down into subjects as well. Using our college script example from earlier, you can start with the history part of the routine. When you have that down pat, move on to the literature or math part. Then put all of them together. After that, move on to the next part of the script, and so on.

Another way to use this method is to go line by line through your script, working on each individual setup, punch line, and punch word, until you have the entire thing set perfectly in your head. This is painstakingly time-consuming, and you'd probably be better off using one of the other techniques because you'll learn just as much, and just as quickly, by recording your performances.

O = Objective

When you're memorizing lines, you're not only committing a comedy routine to memory, you're also directing yourself as an actor. You're staging yourself. So you need to treat this script with the same dedication a head writer gives a screenplay. There's purpose and intent to the lines of your script. For example, using our college script from earlier, your objective might be something simple, say the frustration you have with your figure because it's kind of a slacker. It might be that you're annoyed with your figure, or that you find the figure kind of funny and whimsical.

Your objective is to use your script and jokes to convince the audience of the relationship you have with your figure and persuade them that you really are involved personally with the inanimate being on your arm. To do that, you have to make a commitment to the objectives you find in each line, each joke, and each premise within your performance. What is it, besides the punch words, that's being said? Did you include references to the local community, politicians, celebrities, current events, or someone in the audience? Be aware of those considerations as you're reading through and memorizing your script.

Having an objective—other than making people laugh—will bring to life both your figure and the jokes in your script.

T = Tape Your Act

There's probably no greater rehearsal component than the ability to tape or digitally record what you're doing so you can watch yourself on the playback. Investing in a small audio recorder pays you back tenfold in your career as a live performer. This might be *the* most important money you will spend—other than the purchase of this book, of course. It's even more important than the purchase of your figure. Having access to clear and well-lit video can help you see mistakes, new opportunities for humor, and where you need to improve. Either way, audio and video recording is a must for the modern-day ventriloquist, particularly an act that uses both audible jokes and visual gags.

Depending on where you're going to be working, some venues will offer (sometimes for a fee) to record your set. Some comedy clubs have this option. Churches and other religious facilities have state-of-the-art equipment and might be taping your act anyway. Corporate and industrial shows are usually video-ready as well. All it will take from you is a request to get a copy of the taping.

But you still need to purchase your own recording device, whether it's a small digital audio recorder or a video recorder. Venture into any comedy club in the United States, and you'll likely see a stand-up comic place a small recorder someplace near a speaker just as they walk onstage. You'll need that kind of diligence as well, especially when you first start out.

Some people enjoy listening to or seeing themselves onstage; others abhor it. But it's by far the fastest way to cut mistakes, make edits in your script, and find more opportunities for humor.

As a director, these taping sessions are just like the "dailies" of a major motion picture or hit TV show. And you will have to make tough choices and decisions about what you see, how it did or didn't work, and what changes have to be made. I recommend that you tape every single one of your performances for at least a couple years.

Suitcases
When you're memorizing your script, keep your practice time to about an hour. Work hard on your script for 60 minutes and then call it quits for at least a few hours if not for the rest of the day. An hour is about as long as a human being can spend memorizing anything. If that still seems too long to you, you could break your rehearsal time into short, 15- to 20-minute bursts.

A Few Final Memorization Tips

There you have it: WE ROBOT, your anagram for memorizing the first script you've written, and for those scripts coming in the future. Before we move on, I want to share a couple more quick notes on memorization.

You're going to be nervous for your first performance or two. That's to be expected. Nerves or stage fright can wreak havoc on a ventriloquist's performance as he or she concentrates on lip control, figure manipulation, and getting the jokes out with good timing. It stands to reason you might forget a line or two, or even every line, when you're introduced to go onstage the first time. The solution? Know what line you open with, and what line you close with. This way, you can try to improvise your way through the set and do your allotted time onstage because you know what your last joke is going to be.

If there's one section or a couple sections you just can't seem to nail down, or if there's a joke you keep forgetting, write it down. Highlight the words, lines, and punch words you can't seem to get. Then write out your script again, longhand, and again, highlight the lines you're having trouble with. (So you highlight those problem areas twice.) As you concentrate on not missing the highlighted words, your brain will pick them up.

Another memorization trick that might work for you: when you think you've memorized your act, try doing it double-time. That is, speed through your lines much faster than you would onstage. Go as fast as you can, using all your techniques and manipulations, acting and reacting the way you've rehearsed. After you've gone through it fast once or twice, go back and do your set in real, normal time.

Pull Strings

As you're going over the parts of your script you seem to keep stumbling over, ask yourself, *Why would I say this? Why would the figure answer me this way?* By adding those simple thoughts, you memorize the lines by answering questions, often-times learning the lines without even realizing it!

Finally, try not to just read through your lines, especially as a beginner. Go all out and use your acting ability from the get-go. Rehearse the way you want to perform onstage, and you'll perform the way you rehearse. That means you're in character, both you and your figure, in every rehearsal and memorization session. The pay-off? When you're onstage and fighting nerves, your brain and body will do what they've practiced over and over. You'll react to the stress and pressure of the situation by letting yourself do the things you've trained yourself to do. It will come off as a natural, organic, in-the-moment performance.

The Arc of the Script

As a comedy performer, your act is really just a series of jokes, punch words, and funny actions or reactions you and your figure make. It's up to you as the performer to transcend that and make your set into something more than a man or woman with a figure on his or her arm reciting lines from memory to an audience. To do this, you need to find the arc of your story, where the jokes and the scene you're presenting build to a finale that (hopefully) gets you offstage to applause and laughter.

In the end, you're going to make a point that the audience will be in on. Perhaps your point is that you're a very good ventriloquist, and your technique is second to none. That's a viable performance, no doubt. Or you might be making a point about current events, or that you're an amazing musician and your figures sing beautifully. You might be telling a story (this is especially true for children's entertainers) that resolves a mystery or a crisis at the very end of your show. Regardless of what it is, your script and your act must have an arc. How you want to present that and get from beginning to end is up to you. But you need to be aware of it and work toward that climax during your entire time onstage.

Defining Your Story

First, you have to find a theme or a story for your act. This will separate you from other ventriloquists. Like the jokes you've written, story is a highly structured mode of performance. At some point—probably not when you're starting out, but soon thereafter—you'll want to chart or write out the story arc you're presenting to your audience.

Basically, for the ventriloquist, the story arc will work something like this:

1. You and your figure will be introduced and you'll establish your personal relationship so the audience sees two different characters onstage.

2. A conflict comes up. For example, the figure claims he's articulate and well educated. You question his education, and the figure answers with punch lines instead of sincere responses.

3. The arc climbs higher and higher to the finale, which is usually a big laugh that sums up the attitude of the figure, or your inadequacy as a ventriloquist. Then you both walk offstage to applause.

Of course, there are other ways to resolve the set. But in the world of high-stakes ventriloquism, you'll find that your arc has to work to the punch lines and that you're obligated to close your show with a big laugh or an attention-grabbing, applause-inducing routine. This may be a difficult song, a well-worded fast-paced poem (à la hip-hop music), or something unexpected (for example, the figure's foot falls off, much to the surprise of everyone—including you!).

Learning by Example

One way to learn about character and story is to watch your favorite sitcoms. The arc in these TV shows is easy to follow: the lead characters are established at the beginning of the episode, a conflict is introduced, the characters work toward resolving that conflict, and at the end there is a resolve, whereby the characters have either learned something about each other or about themselves. Because you, as the ventriloquist, are doing a show with another character (your figure), sitcoms are good examples for you to follow.

Another reason sitcoms (and comedy movies, too) are good examples for ventriloquists to follow: sometimes there's more than one star of the show, so each actor must have a story line in each episode to keep the audience involved. In the case of your vent act, you and each of your figures is a star in your show, and so there will be conflicts and (funny) resolutions to those conflicts during your performance.

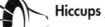

Hiccups

You can't afford the downward part of the arc that happens at the end of sitcoms because they don't depend on a huge laugh and big applause when their show ends. *You are!* So work to that.

The resolution could be as subtle as the figure saying "good night" at the end of your show, as it gets put back into its case. It could be a crowd-pleasing song at the end of your set. Or maybe you could close with a killer comedy routine that blows people away.

As the director, you need to be aware of the story arc and how it plays out in each of your live performances. One more reason you need to record every one of your sets!

Establishing Your Arc

Here's a quick way to establish a story arc for your act. This won't change the jokes you're going to use, and it won't alter the way you've been rehearsing.

Start with this: "My figure woke up this morning and it …." How you fill in the blank will launch your set with a defined story beginning. You can even use that as a starter for your set, before that first joke, by way of introducing your figure (and yourself) to the audience, like this:

> YOU: Hello, [*insert figure's name*], what did you do when you got out of bed to start the day?

FIGURE: I was answering e-mail from some old college buddies. I sure miss those days.

YOU: I never knew you went to college!

FIGURE: *[ever so slowly turns its head to face you]* Excuse me?

This is the beginning of a story that leads to your figure talking about what he studied and what he learned (or didn't learn!) in college, as in our example script. The audience gets a quick introduction to the relationship between you and your figure, there's a conflict ("I never knew you went to college!" and the obviously offended response from the figure as he slowly turns his head to meet your gaze), and it will work to a resolve (a final big laugh).

> ### Suitcases
>
> The starter line, "My figure woke up this morning and it …," does not have to be funny or even very interesting. It only has to establish a theme from which conflict can grow. You can write the starter line after you've written a script, you can base an entire script on that line, or you can enter it later in the set. It's simply a vehicle to draw the audience in, define your character and your figures, and help you work toward a big finish.

It helps to make an outline of your set. Do this even if your act is very short and you can't possibly see a need to make an outline for 15 or 20 jokes. This will get you into the habit of preparing your headliner set, a full-length performance that every audience will follow and enjoy because it works on three distinct levels:

- You're a great ventriloquist with flawless technique.

- You have very strong jokes in your set.

- You present a story that draws people in and resolves at the end with a huge finale.

Here's a quick five-point outline to get you into story arc mode as you work on and rehearse your script:

1. Setup—introduction for you and your figure, using a question or two to get into that first big joke.

2. Conflict—tension between you and the figure.

3. Things don't work the way you or your figure want them to.

4. You and/or your figure try to solve a problem.

5. The show works to big laughs and a finale.

You don't have to follow the five-point outline exactly, but being aware of these beats will help you move the show along. (It will help you memorize, too!)

Working to the Big Laughs

The concept of working to the big laughs will get easier once you've actually been onstage in front of people a couple times and you get an idea where the really good punch lines and punch words are in your act. This isn't something you have to watch for necessarily; the audience will tell you exactly how funny you are, what jokes work, and what jokes don't.

This makes things simple for you: throw out the things that don't get laughs, and keep the stuff that has people pounding the table because they're laughing so hard. Let's hope you have more funny lines than unfunny lines after a couple live performances. If you don't, it's not a big deal—you'll go home and write some more!

For our purposes, you're going to take it for granted that your strongest jokes are your first joke, your last joke, and the third joke of your theory of threes in your script.

Not every joke will be a powerful, applause-getting line, but some will. And every set you perform will be a little bit different. You have to allow yourself to work within those parameters and know what your best lines are.

Constantly work toward those big laughs. Often, those will be the third of the theory-of-three punch lines in your set. It's not always the third line, of course. So just let the audience's laughter guide you into those big laughs. Some comics have compared it to playing a jazz duet. The audience is your rhythm section, and you're a pianist riffing off their beats of laughter. When they explode with a huge hit, like a cymbal crash or a long bass line, you lay out and don't play until the moment dictates you come back in. It sounds sophisticated, but you'll get a better feel for this as you work and perform in different venues for different crowds.

> **Suitcases**
>
> There's only one way to get accustomed to working with laughter and playing to an audience, and that's to get onstage as much as possible. You can't become a solid performer and a great ventriloquist by doing your act alone in the mirror or once a month at the local coffee shop's open-mic night. You need stage time!

Watching other comedians live and/or on video will give you great examples of how professionals work to the big laughs. Some call it "riding the waves of laughs," or "playing to the crowd." Whatever you call it, you now have all the information you need to play to the laughter. Now get out there and do it!

Not Too Fast, Not Too Slow, but Just Right

This is another example of performance technique that is best learned by actually doing. And of course, I have some pointers that can help you hit your routine "just right."

As I mentioned earlier in this chapter, one way to rehearse your script and memorize it is to speed through it as fast as possible. That's only a technique for learning lines, however, and should not be done onstage—unless that's part of your act, of course.

Your job is to communicate ideas and jokes to the audience. To do that, you and your figure cannot speak so quickly that nobody can understand what you're saying. At the same time, if your cadence is too slow, you'll run the risk of boring and alienating your audience. There is a happy medium, and the way to find it is through rehearsing your script and memorizing it the way you would have a normal conversation. The human body is a creature of habit. You will perform the way you rehearse, so if you've been working and practicing in a manner that's just right, you'll perform that way, too.

There are numerous reasons for not talking too fast. You are making your figure talk by using a tiny opening between your lips, with your teeth together and your tongue, diaphragm, and nasal passages making the sounds that imitate human speech. Talking fast only makes it harder for the audience to hear what you and your figure are saying, regardless of how good your technique is. Going too slowly will bore an audience and open you and your figure up for some heckling and backtalk from the crowd. It's up to you to find that happy medium, where you're having a dialogue in real time that makes sense and keeps the audience's rapt attention.

The cadence and meter you use in performance will be dictated by your stage presence and the charisma you exude onstage. As a rule of thumb, work as slowly as you can without losing the crowd, but even that's up for debate because every person is different. The only way to truly find your best pace is to get onstage and do what you do.

Getting Into the Flow

The emcee introduces you to the comedy club crowd, and you take the stage, confidently breezing over to the microphone where you say, "Hello everyone. I'm here with my good friend, [*insert figure's name*]! Let me introduce him!" You set down your case, open it, and grab your figure. The crowd nods and smiles as you prop him up on the stool next to the mic, and somebody out there says, "Oh, no, not a puppet!" You're nonplussed so you smile and begin your routine smoothly and self-assuredly, just as you've practiced it a thousand times.

The first laugh comes when the figure slowly, slowly turns its head toward you after you ask it a simple question, as if you've insulted it. You hit your first joke perfectly, the audience laughs, and you maintain your flawless technique for the next 12 minutes, as you and your figure nail down a set of 36 well-paced jokes, including a gentle putdown of the heckler who said, "Oh, no, not a puppet!" (Your figure said, "Dude, it looks to me as if you have a girlfriend! Well, then, who's calling who a puppet?")

It all comes together beautifully because you are well prepared, you know your lines, you're comfortable with your act, and you're in the moment as you perform.

The more you work, the more you'll understand that each time you go onstage it's an obstacle course: one night the sound might go out; another evening you'll find that the audience is made up of mostly adults when you thought you'd been hired to do a children's program; you will, sooner or later, be heckled by an audience member, particularly if you play comedy clubs. Every situation is different, and every situation will call on you to be at the top of your game and fully engaged with what's going on—not to mention with the audience.

Every time you go onstage, you'll take control. You'll set the tempo. Sometimes you'll have to follow other acts that do really well, or you'll follow someone who doesn't do well. Neither case should matter to you, because you have your own mode, marching to the drum in your head, and the audience will follow your lead. In turn, you'll play to your audience, finding a rhythm and a course they can follow (for example, you'll probably go a little slower at the senior citizen's home than you will when you do the show at the local college), so everyone enjoys your set.

A Word on Hecklers

Every act has his or her own way to handle catcalls and jeers from an audience member. Some people memorize or write heckler lines they can use when the situation arises. Some just shout down hecklers with vulgarity and anger. There's no one best way to handle hecklers, but engaging them in a conversation usually works to your benefit because the figure is a sort of victim (it can't do much for itself) and it can usually win over the rest of the crowd.

Of course, there are only so many comebacks to "You suck!" But those experiences and situations are few and far between. Don't spend a lot of time working on or worrying about hecklers. Stay focused on what you're going to do with your act and the way you want to perform it!

A Word on Timing

There's an old joke that goes something like this: the comedian asks the audience, "What's the key to comedy?" Just as someone begins to give an answer, the comedian interrupts them and shouts out, "Timing!"

It's true. Timing is everything in comedy performance, and timing is one of those things that is, for all practical purposes, impossible to teach. The way to learn timing is to get onstage somewhere and start learning.

Your classroom is now going to move from the practice room in your house, apartment, basement, or wherever you've been rehearsing to the comedy clubs, kids' birthday parties, synagogues, Jaycees luncheons, and wherever else you can perform. You'll learn timing, but it can only be taught through experience. Timing is everything in life. This is particularly true in the world of ventriloquism and comedy, where being at the right place at the right time might get you the stage time you need to be seen by the producer of the next big show that needs a ventriloquist … who can do the time (30 minutes) they need.

The audience will teach you timing as you learn to communicate with them through your jokes and songs and techniques, never moving too quickly or too slowly along. Your timing is going to improve because each time onstage affords you another opportunity to hone your act and improve. You'll listen to or watch your recorded performances, edit your act, nail the story arc, and hit every joke with perfection. *This is your time!*

The Least You Need to Know

- A good technique to help you learn and memorize your script is WE ROBOT: W = write it out, E = emote, R = read out loud, O = other hand (use your off hand), B = break it down, O = objective, and T = tape it!

- Your script and your live performances will have an arc, from the opening line to the big finish, which you'll use to keep the audience involved and committed to your show.

- As you work with your figure, you'll be following the ebb and flow of your act, riding the audience laughter to the next big laugh.

- Go with the flow, and find a tempo that works for you and your act.

Chapter 16

Working for the Big Laughs

In This Chapter

- ◆ Bringing your figure to life
- ◆ Actions and reactions that get big laughs
- ◆ Every move or lack of movement onstage means something
- ◆ Wearing three hats: head writer, director, and performer

The complete ventriloquist act includes more than perfect lip control, replacement sounds imperceptible to the human ear, and hilarious comedy material. You have to make your figure appear to be a living, breathing three-dimensional character as well. Jokes help, but great figure manipulation brings your performance full circle. Your role as actor isn't just for you. You're acting for your figure as well.

In this chapter, you'll learn some great examples of figure movements with the head or body that have specific meanings for your audience. Remember that doing nothing—whether it's you or your figure—is going to be seen as *something* by the audience. Everything is connected to everything else in your ventriloquist presentation: technique, figure, and material. We've worked on material and technique, so now we're going to bring that figure to life!

One of the perks of being a ventriloquist is the multitasking you accomplish with every joke you write, every figure you use, and every show you put on. You truly are a one-man (or one-woman) show. To close out Part 4, we go over all the facets of your new chosen career and how you're going to make this come together in a great vent performance package!

Become the Figure!

"Become the figure"—it might sound weird to you at first. But it might be that learning how to make things that aren't real come to life *is* weird. If you can find a way to put yourself inside that figure's body, you'll be a better ventriloquist and make what you do onstage even more exciting for your audience.

Whatever your figure is—boy, girl, bird, sock puppet, etc.—you must put yourself in those shoes … or feet … or claws. You're no different from any actor getting into character. Similar to what you learned in Chapter 9, becoming the puppet is just another way to access emotions and reactions from your figure. What follows are some acting tips, systems, and ideas to get you into your figure's head. In acting terms, you're *method acting*.

def•i•ni•tion

Method acting is a technique wherein an actor tries to produce the thoughts, emotions, and physicality of the character they're playing to create a lifelike performance. It doesn't matter that the actor may not have had an experience with the character or any working knowledge of the character. Method acting is all about finding those thoughts and emotions within yourself.

Let's run through some acting exercises adapted to you as a ventriloquist.

Passing the Object

First, get an imaginary object in your mind. It could be anything: a coin, a dollar bill, a hamburger, a box, or a feather. You and your figure are going to pass this object back and forth between the two of you. *Hmm*, you might be thinking. *I can pass it to my figure, but my figure can't move its arms!* No, it probably can't. This is your first test: how are you—as the figure—going to pass this object to yourself as the ventriloquist? You could use your mouth. Maybe you'll push it with the figure's head. Maybe the figure will grab the ventriloquist's arm with its mouth and push the object to the vent. See?

Don't overanalyze this; just do it to the best of your ability for a few minutes. Make yourself work from the puppet's point of view. Look at what you're doing in the mirror. Work together, figure and ventriloquist, to make something happen. You're not only building up a reserve of actions you can use onstage in any number of ways, you are also forming a bond with the figure, and the payoff will come onstage when the audience sees a ventriloquist who effortlessly brings his or her partner to life.

For extra credit, try this: instead of some small object, pass a ball back and forth as if you're a father and son in the front yard playing a game of catch. Again, the problem: "But my figure can't move its arms!" Right! So you might have to throw the ball to the figure's mouth, and the figure might have to catch the imaginary ball and throw it back to you using just its head and mouth! You, the ventriloquist, might have to use your off hand to throw since your other hand is working your figure, and this might lead to the ball dropping and rolling away, the ball falling painfully on your foot, or anything that might come up during your improvisation. The ball can be heavy, like a bowling ball, or as light as a balloon.

The Mirror Game

In this acting exercise, two actors stand face-to-face and mirror one another's movements while making constant, never-ending eye contact. As a ventriloquist, you're going to look directly at your figure, and vice versa. Hold eye contact with your figure and imitate the movement of its head. For extra credit, take one arm or leg (or even tail!) and hold it in the hand that's not manipulating your figure. Now move everything you can (heads, arms, and tails!) together, in synch.

Do this very slowly at first, just getting into the flow of working with a figure. Then speed up your actions after a few minutes of work. (This is also a good warm-up exercise you can use before or during rehearsals and memorization sessions.)

Silent Conversations

Ventriloquism, like comedy and music, is all about communication. Living creatures communicate in many ways, and vocally is only one option among many. Body language is often as important, if not more so, than spoken words. An exercise in total silence forces you to concentrate on the things in your act the audience sees instead of hears.

For this next exercise, you and your figure are going to have some discussions in total silence. You, as the vent, will mouth the words you're saying to your figure. Your figure will then speak, silently, back to you. You're going to set yourself up with various situations and then carry on a silent dialogue. Here are some examples to get you started in your voiceless dialogue:

- One of you has a secret.

- You are teacher and student.

- You are boss and employee.

- Each of you has a secret.

- You are sworn enemies.

- You need to share good news.

- You are best friends.

- You are winner and loser.

- You are sitting together on a plane.

- You are stuck in an elevator.

As you silently relate your short story or incident, the two of you will interrupt each other on occasion, trying to communicate an idea or thought. Lots of good things can happen here, solidifying your manipulation technique and making the vent/figure relationship stronger.

The figure should try to read your lips while you're speaking silently. It can stare right at your lips as you try and pronounce the words slowly and perfectly, letting your partner see what you're saying. You both might have to "act out" the idea or concept. If you're keeping or sharing secrets, you might whisper something to one another, which gives you the opportunity to show the figure as a real person when you whisper something in its ear, it looks around, laughs, and then tries to shush you. Try it the other way around, in which the figure has a secret for you, makes you laugh, and then looks around to be sure nobody else was in on the secret.

The Five W's

Acting is about the five W's—who, what, when, where, and why—and these push along the narrative or story in every kind of performance. There's no reason you can't apply the five W's to what you're doing as a ventriloquist. If nothing else, it's incumbent upon you to answer the five W's as they relate to your figure because this will force you to come up with a history or background for your figure.

Can you answer these questions about your figure?

- Who is your figure? Not just its name or gender or animal or whatever it is; go deeper than that. Who is it?

- What is the history of the figure? What was it doing before the two of you got together? What are its goals? What does it want?

- Where is it from? Where does it want to go? Where will you go together?

- When was it conceived? When did you get together? When will it be leaving?

- Why are the two of you together?

It doesn't stop there. You need to imbue your figure with the five senses as well: sight, hearing, smell, taste, and touch. Giving these qualities to your vent partner brings it to life for the audience as much as your great jokes will.

Just as important as the words you deliver during a performance is the *behavior* both you and your figure exude. You could say that your behavior is going to make your jokes funnier, your technique better, and your performances stronger. It makes you a complete act.

Suitcases
Any journalism student will tell you that the five W's are the key to good reporting. That makes it even more important for you, the ventriloquist, to have them committed to memory because you'll be interviewed down the road, and those are the questions you'll be asked. Try to come up with answers to these questions not only for your figure, but also for yourself.

Behavior Exercises

Now let's look at a couple fun exercises that enable you to create a behavior for your figure. You, as the ventriloquist, are just as important in this exercise working for the two of you, so I've made the instructions detailed (just like you'll do with your first performance) so nothing is left to chance. You don't need anything but your mirror to make these short drills work.

You, the ventriloquist, are a boxing trainer. Your figure was just in a prizefight, and it won! *Wow!* You and your figure are in the corner, by the ropes, and there's pandemonium all around you. Go through all the actions a trainer and his world-champion fighter would at the end of a heavyweight match. Hear the crowd chanting the figure's name. Wipe the sweat off its brow. It's exhausted after going 15 rounds with the former champ, so see how it slouches and catches its breath. Maybe wipe the sweat off your own brow, too. Help your figure get its gloves off and give it the kind of congratulations only a trainer can give to the boxer he trained just for this moment. An interviewer sticks a microphone in the figure's face, and it answers a couple questions. Lightbulbs are flashing everywhere.

Got the idea? You're the figure *and* the ventriloquist. Let's try another one.

You and the figure are in the cellar. No lights. It's cold, damp, and uncomfortable. You're hiding in the corner, trying to hide from the evil monster upstairs. A spider crawls across the figure's face, but it can't make a sound because the monster might hear. Then the spider crawls across *your* face. You want to scream, but you can't. The figure tries to say something, but you cover its mouth with your hand. Maybe the figure starts to cry, and you have to comfort it. Or vice versa! Maybe you're both trembling in fear. Maybe you're so cold you have to hold on to one another.

The more you can get into the character and the figure's behavior, the more defined your performance will be. Don't forget that you have to define your own character and behavior as well.

You probably can already see yourself walking into various venues where you'll be working and going through the checklist of behaviors you and your figure will exhibit onstage (looking at the people, the ceiling, the lights, each other, the curtains behind the stage, etc.). That's exactly what you need to do when "becoming the figure"!

> **Suitcases**
>
> The five W's are also a great place for a comedy writer to start looking for jokes. One question comedy writers often use to get their creative juices flowing is one of the five W's: "What if?"

Remember, you'll be presenting your act as a comedy duo with your words, music, jokes, and behavior. You're going to determine behavior for yourself and for your figure by reacting to the spoken information, the jokes, and the sensory stimuli happening as you perform. There's always a lot of pretending going on: the figure, your relationship as a couple friends, the fact that you are onstage and telling jokes—it's all pretend. *Just don't let the audience know you know!*

Reactions That Get Laughs

It's been said that acting is reacting. That's especially true with ventriloquism; there's lots of reacting going on because there are so many jokes.

Before we get too far, let me say this: there's one type of reaction that can be a negative and take away from your set—overreacting. Many ventriloquists fall into the overreacting trap and make their figure's punch lines and punch words too far overblown. Let's see what we can do to help you avoid falling into this trap.

Act (and React) Naturally

When the figure delivers a punch line and the audience laughs, it's a natural (or nervous) reaction for you to say something like, "Will you stop?" or "Cut that out!" or "I can't believe you said that!" Fight that urge! For one thing, you're going to be stepping on your figure's line. You're also taking away from the joke by throwing something else into the mix for the audience to listen to.

The better choice is to sit back and either look at the figure or at the audience. Think about what you do when friends tell a joke when you're just hanging out at a restaurant. That's the better reaction; it's more natural and comfortable.

Practicing Some Moves

Studying the way people react is going to help you come up with some moves you can give your figure during your show. Rehearse these moves the way you rehearsed the lines you memorized for the first big show.

If you haven't done so already, put your figure on your hand and put your other hand underneath or behind the figure. Move your hands in opposite directions (this won't work for sock puppets). Essentially, if you're right-handed, and your right hand is in the figure's body or head, you'll move that hand to your left. Your left hand is underneath the figure or behind it, supporting it. Move it to the right. What you will get is an odd body movement—the top is moving one way and the bottom moves the other, almost against it—which is probably going to be funny.

Obviously, you want to give your figure lifelike motions and body movements, but it's always nice to get laughs at the same time without having to say a word. You're in

Pull Strings

Here's a funny reaction movement: pretend an army of roaches is climbing up your figure's leg! What does it do? What do you do? What if the roaches were climbing up your leg? What would the figure do? Practice those moves—the way you and your figure would act in that situation—and you'll probably come up with a move that will make people laugh.

luck, because the ventriloquist figure was made to do that! Here are some ways you're sure to get laughs with few, if any, words:

The slow-motion mouth: The ventriloquist says something and the figure slowly turns its head toward the vent and then slowly opens its mouth. The slower you do this, the more tension it creates and the bigger the laugh when the figure begins to open its mouth.

The mouth of surprise: Similar to the slow-motion mouth, this move can either feign surprise or be the real thing. The figure learns a new piece of information, does something wrong, or loses control of the situation. It stares straight ahead and opens its mouth, trying to imitate the Edvard Munch *Scream* painting without putting its hands over its ears.

The intense look: This is an important move many vents don't have! Get your hand inside your figure, and lean its head directly over its shoulder so its head is perpendicular to its body, looking at you over its shoulder. Cock the head down so it's looking at you through the tops of its eyes (the way some folks look over the top of their glasses when they are talking to you and want to make a point). You can use this with the figure looking the opposite way, too, giving your figure another move.

The rhythm: I spoke earlier about having your figure sing, even if you cannot. Well, your figure can also show it's got rhythm, even if you don't! There are a few ways to do this that can elicit laughter from your audience. One is to have it bob its head up and down. If music is playing, there's a definite opportunity for the figure to bop and roll as the music plays, keeping with the drumbeat. You can experiment with this in many ways. Move just the body as the head stays still, facing forward. Wiggle just the body, not the head. Experiment!

Overexaggerated head turns, rolls, and shakes: Especially when accompanied by any loud sound, these are usually good for a laugh, too. These can't be repeated because once they've been used the audience has seen the bit and you can't go back to that well for another laugh. Some vents will spin their figure's head all the way around, but that breaks much of the reality from the audience point of view, so you'll have to decide if that works or not.

Nose-to-nose: Bringing the figure nose-to-nose with yourself, so you're staring at each other the way boxers do at a prefight weigh-in, is a dramatic visual that might get a laugh if your personalities are defined for the audience.

figure with mouth open denotes surprise, shock, happiness, and with some head movement, laughter

The figure's basic head moves. Experiment with head movements, and get as many emotions out of the figure as you can.

figure with head cocked down, chin on shoulder, shows intensity, skepticism, or one-upmanship

figure with head cocked to one side could mean interest, confusion, or frustration

It's just as important that *you* react to what is going on, too. There will be times you'll want to roll your head, slowly turn and look at your figure, or let your mouth drop open in surprise. Give yourself an opportunity to play-act and get laughs without words the same way your figure is.

Pull Strings _____

Comedians refer to the laugh you get without having to say anything as "getting a laugh on character." I'm not talking about a guy bending over a water fountain and getting sprayed in the face. That's slapstick. Getting a laugh on character comes when the audience has learned the behavior and personality of the person or figure onstage and laughs at actions, reactions, or body language rather than the spoken word or punch words.

Acting is reacting. You call on the skills and techniques you have learned to acknowledge what is happening during a performance and behave accordingly.

In the same vein, you've put in the time and effort to become a good ventriloquist, and with the help of this book, you've got some tools and skills to realize that dream. Completing your ventriloquism course will come the day you start getting regular bookings and earning some money. And that's going to happen!

Everything Means Something

For the ventriloquist, everything that happens onstage is part of the show. The more you leave to chance and improvisation, the more you open yourself to making mistakes. The best way to improvise comedy is to have a set routine—a couple jokes or an entertaining song you can use just in case your "off the cuff" stuff isn't working. Otherwise, the audience is going to know you're not prepared. There's already a healthy amount of skepticism surrounding ventriloquists, who are often the butt of (sometimes very funny; sometimes just very mean) jokes. You won't want to leave anything to chance.

Successful ventriloquism starts with the relationship between you and your figure and the way you manipulate it or fail to manipulate it. Should the figure sit like a bump on a log (ooh, bad joke) and answer your setups with good punch lines, chances are audiences will laugh, but they won't laugh as hard because the figure doesn't seem alive or engaged. The same goes for you, the ventriloquist. You need to be "in the moment," performing to the best of your abilities until your set ends.

Another name for this section could be "Everything Is Connected to Everything." Start with the premise that we're going to turn your entire program inside out, concentrating on your technique (lip control, manipulation, and acting) and the material you're going to present.

A Tale of Two Gigs

Let's visualize for a moment. You booked a gig at a local establishment—say, a coffeehouse—that offers an *open-mic night* once a week. You went, you performed, you had a very good experience, and you even got some feelers for future bookings. Start here and work backward. You had worked on specific manipulations and movements for your figure. You took the time to memorize and edit your script, and your prep work paid off. You were confident in your abilities as a vent because you nailed the pronunciation of hard-to-do letters and those replacement sounds. You took the time in each of the chapters to become proficient, and you learned to *enjoy* the process. As a result, your jokes flowed perfectly in a seamless, airtight 7-minute set, during which you got laughter and applause and had great timing to go with the material and manipulations and body language.

def•i•ni•tion

> **Open-mic nights** are live performances in which audience members or performers who have signed up in advance get a chance to perform. Comedy clubs have these on occasion, as do other venues. These nights give inexperienced acts a chance to practice and improve. New acts are usually given 5 minutes of stage time, while more experienced performers are given longer sets.

Everything is connected to everything.

Now let's do it the other way, with the same setup. You went to the coffeehouse and had a bad experience, mostly because your figure and you did not appear to be much of a team. Your jokes were okay, but you sped through your set. The figure barely moved, even when it spoke. Your technique was good, but some of your words sounded slurred or unintelligible. You might have overcome those problems, but you hadn't put in the hours of rehearsal and preparation in front of the mirror, so you felt awkward and uncomfortable onstage.

See, everything is connected.

The best way to clean up your mistakes—and you *are* going to make some; it's very rare that even the most seasoned pro does the "perfect" set—is to record your performances. Audio recording is great, but video is a little better. The sooner you get into the habit of listening to or watching the playback after each of your shows, the stronger your act is going to become.

Dress the Part

What you wear and what your figure wears are important as well. If you get booked at a Rotary luncheon or a Kiwanis breakfast, it probably isn't going to help you to show up wearing cut-offs and sandals. "Dress for success" might sound a little bit conformist, and maybe it's not your style, but you're in show *business*.

If your act depends on you wearing cut-offs and sandals, you need to find work in venues where those kinds of clothes are appropriate. If you want to get paid big bucks to work for major corporations, you might as well get used to the idea that a shirt, sport coat, and slacks are *de rigueur* for the market. At the same time, a T-shirt and blue jeans are perfect for a college tour.

But dressing for your audience is the tip of the "everything is connected" iceberg. As you become more proficient onstage and find yourself getting phone calls requesting your vent services for various events, you will not only dress for your audience, but you will also write for that audience. "Know your audience" is an important part of your job from now on. You can do your jokes about going to college in front of the college crowd, but they'll fall on deaf ears at a kid's birthday party. A routine about selling insurance probably won't work with college kids because they don't have any interest.

You Are the Writer, Director, and Performer

Perhaps the biggest perk that comes with being a great ventriloquist is your workload, particularly the multitasking you get to do. This should not seem overwhelming; it should feel exhilarating and thrilling!

def•i•ni•tion

A **niche** is a specialized market. The comedy business has stratified and become a business of niches. You could position yourself in a variety of niches such as by location ("I'm only working within 3 hours of my house"), by style ("I'm the vulgar ventriloquist"), or by age group ("I only do shows for senior citizens").

You are directing your own show. You choose the material. You get to say what you want to say (albeit through your figure). You're in complete control from the start—what you wear, what kind of figure you work with, what material you do, what audience you want to *niche* yourself with, where you want to work, and everything else. As director, you have creative control, and everyone listens to you!

As director, you have a few things going for you that other kinds of acts don't. For one thing, your lead actor is yourself. Nice, right? What's more, the other "actors" are your ventriloquist figures. They'll show up when you want them to, they'll do exactly what you tell them to, and you can actually put words right in their mouth! What director wouldn't want to work under those conditions?

As the head writer, you are your own censor. You decide what topics you'll talk about, what you'll share with your audience, what words you'll use, and what the arc or story line of your performance will be.

Finally, as performer, you get to use all your skills as an entertainer, bringing life to the vision of your director and the words of your head writer—all three of which are you!

A ventriloquist is truly a one-man show (albeit with different figures) every time he or she takes the stage and performs. More professional ventriloquists are working today than ever before, and many of them share your love of the craft, the enjoyment of the entertainment value it has, and the autonomy a vent enjoys.

Director, writer, and performer—you could make a case that these are three dream jobs many people would do just about anything to have. You, as a ventriloquist, have the honor and responsibility of holding down three dream jobs. Don't waste the opportunity.

The Least You Need to Know

- ◆ Manipulating your figure is key, particularly if you want to become a good ventriloquist.

- ◆ When it comes to figure manipulation, practice makes perfect. There's no way around that.

- ◆ Everything that happens onstage has meaning, or is connected to everything. Your success depends on you perfecting as much as you can.

- ◆ As a ventriloquist, you hold down three jobs: director, writer, and performer. You call the shots.

Part 5

Ready for Prime Time

Are you ready? If not, you're awfully close. So now's the time to get a resumé, picture, and contacts list together. It's also time to meet a booker or an agent who can help you get onstage a couple times and get your feet wet. It's time to audition for work!

Money shouldn't be a factor at first because it takes time to develop an act that can command thousands of dollars or get fans to shell out $20 or $50 or $100 to see you perform. The key to success, eventually, is *stage time*. So you need to get onstage as much as possible.

There are lots of opportunities for ventriloquists today, including cruise ships; Las Vegas; TV; comedy clubs; the college circuit; churches, temples, and synagogues; and so on. Corporate shows, dinner theaters, and TV commercials use ventriloquists as well. And an underrated calling for the working ventriloquist are "kid shows," including libraries, schools, and birthday parties. This can be a lucrative market. With so many options available, you're sure to find your best fit.

Chapter 17

In Search of an Audience

In This Chapter

- ◆ Putting together your promotional package
- ◆ Advice for auditions
- ◆ Agents, bookers, and personal managers—what's the difference?
- ◆ It all comes down to who you know and networking

It's time for you to go out in search of an audience. As a ventriloquist, your job boils down to getting your next job. As a beginner in the world of paid professional entertainment, you're only as good as your last live performance, and you'll never be better than your upcoming gig. But that's not a negative! It just means you're working.

To book gigs, you'll be dealing with people whose job it is to put different entertainers and performers on stages. This chapter is going to arm you with vital information you need to deal with these folks on their terms.

Finally, you'll get some real data—some names and numbers of people who book acts. Be forewarned: this is one of the most competitive industries in the world. Your competition will be talented, aggressive, focused, and prepared. You need to be, too.

Must Haves: Photo, Bio, Resumé, and Video

There are a few essentials you'll be asked for when you get booked for personal appearances:

- 8×10 glossy photo

- One-page bio

- Resumé

- Short video with highlights from a live performance

The sooner you put these together, the better. There's no comeback to the line, "Uh, I don't have a photo," or "I don't really have a resumé yet." Don't get caught unprepared!

Say "Cheese"

Let's start with your 8×10 glossy photo. With modern-day technology, the affordable availability of home computers and printers, and cameras in cell phones that take very good photos, getting an 8×10 should not be a problem. A do-it-yourself photo and reproduction isn't a bad way to go, especially at the start of your career.

You need a couple shots that will appeal to the people who book acts and to the people who promote the shows you'll be doing. You should take this seriously. Dress as you would dress for a performance. Take at least 10 to 15 photographs of you with your figure. If you use more than one figure in your set, take pictures posing with all of them.

You also need a picture of yourself, called a "headshot." Even though you're a ventriloquist, it's a good idea to have one picture of you alone. You might change your act so the figures you're using onstage are not the same as the ones in the photos. Or the people you're working for may not want a picture that has any props in it. Maybe, if you're doing media and press coverage for your performance, the newspaper or publication might not want a pic with puppets, for whatever reason. Yours is not to question why; yours is to supply whoever wants it with the kind of promotional material they can use.

Obviously the best of all possible worlds is to go to a professional theatrical photographer (not a "family portrait" photographer) and do an honest-to-goodness photo shoot. A theatrical headshot photographer will take 50 to 100 shots of you and you with your figures for a fee, usually starting around $100 or more, and they will send all the shots to you. You can then choose the photos you like and have those made into 8×10s. It's much more expensive, but the payoff is that you will have very nice, professionally done photos that (hopefully) jump off the page and grab the viewer's attention.

A professional photographer will offer ideas, give suggestions, and have backdrops and lighting and all kinds of ways to make you and your figures look great. They've done this before (that's why they charge so much), so their skills match up perfectly with the ventriloquist, whose act is at least 50 percent visual. To work with a pro, instead of a friend or family member taking pictures, means that little things like bad lighting, a hair out of place, poor choices in clothing, or a backdrop are eradicated.

Pull Strings

After your shoot is over, look to the Internet to find some great deals on editing, copying, and re-touching photos. Most photographers will send you every one of the shots, which you can edit on a computer yourself if you want to!

It's your call, of course. Particularly in the very beginning, there's no need for you to spend lots of money on your pictures. You need something, but you don't need anything spectacular. As you pick up more and more jobs and your promotional needs (and the promotional needs of your clients!) become more acute, you'd be well served to get some professional pictures done.

All About You

Your biography, or bio, and resumé will start out a little short, but quickly grow as your career gains momentum and your workload increases. Continually update and revise both, particularly your resumé, as you pick up career-enhancing jobs and events. Your bio doesn't need to be updated but once a year or so. Your resumé will change more often.

Your bio should center on *just* your show business career. Keep it short (about 1 page) and to the point, expressing why you got started in ventriloquism, what you hope to do, and what your favorite experiences are (so far). It's always a good idea to put a joke or a funny line in your bio. After all, if you're in the business of making people laugh, why not put something funny in your bio? If you have a favorite line from your stage act, or a favorite line your figure says, put that in your bio, too. If you want to get creative, you can always write a bio for the figure or figures you work with!

The same goes for your resumé, which, like the bio, should be kept to 1 page. While your bio is written as a kind of short story of your career, your resumé lists your accomplishments and work experience in the various venues you've worked or shows you've done—again, only those related to your show business career. It has your contact information, your mailing address, and other vital information. Some acts include their height, weight, eye color, hair color, and so on. This is especially important if you're auditioning for film and TV commercial work.

> **Suitcases**
>
> Your entire promotional package—your bio, resumé, and video—is often called your "promo kit."

Your resumé lists the places you've worked, under titles like: "Theater," "Clubs," "Television," "Commercials," "Film," "Miscellaneous," "Corporate," "Colleges," "Cruise Lines," and "Casinos." You can add a category called "Other Skills" that would feature things you can do that might or might not be related to ventriloquism. "Handles farm equipment," for example, or "World-class swimmer."

You, on Film

The final must-have piece is a video. The video is the modern-day business card for a ventriloquist. It enables a booker to show clients exactly what you do, how you do it, and just how good you are at your craft. Not having a video is akin to saying, "I don't want to get any bookings."

As with photographs, you can film your first couple videos with your own small hand-held video recorder and edit it yourself. You need to be sure the lighting is very good, the audience can be heard laughing, and your audio is clear. It might take a couple videotaping sessions to perfect the technical aspects of recording yourself, but it will be worth it when you start getting bookings because people enjoy seeing your taped performance.

Needless to say, you don't want to make a video recording until you have a solid 15-minute set, well rehearsed and practiced in front of a couple live crowds. Giving the gatekeepers (agents and bookers) a poorly produced or badly performed comedy video will not only hurt you in the short term, but these people will remember you as the guy or girl who sent in the terrible video.

Obviously, having your video professionally filmed and edited will show you in the best possible light. It can be costly, but professional videographers set the lighting, mic the audience, stage your set, and make you look and sound great. The pros might use two or three cameras to give your set a slick, polished feel. When they edit, they'll add state-of-the-art graphics and text. And they'll package it in a way that makes yours the first video bookers might grab out of a stack. Again, this is expensive, but the payoff is worth it.

Suitcases
Many acts no longer send or give out bios, resumés, or even videotapes. Instead, many are opting for e-resumés. Thanks to the magic of websites, social network sites, and YouTube, you can put your resumé and bio online.

How to Get—and Ace—an Audition

Here it is. Before you become a headlining act or a mainstay in Vegas, you have to break in. That's where the time-honored tradition of auditioning comes in.

First things first: you have to get the audition. You need to get used to this because you're probably going to be auditioning for the rest of your vent career. Obviously, you'll be starting small, working your way up to auditioning for TV shows, Vegas production shows, etc.

Where to Start

The best place to start is … wherever you can start! Big-city comedy clubs offer open-mic nights during which you can get up and do 5 minutes in a cattle-call for comedy acts (of which there might be 20 on any given night). You can always ask to be the "opening act" for events at your local library, church, or school. Rotary Clubs, Kiwanis Clubs, and Jaycees allow acts to come perform at their luncheons and functions on occasion.

Your first few jobs will be the "I'll take anything I can get" variety, which is fine because you have to start somewhere. This kind of work isn't so much an audition as it is an opening into the world of show business.

Eventually you're going to take your act to the next level, and you'll have to audition for something meaningful. After you've done a number of "beginner" shows, you'll have met a few people, you'll have made some contacts, and your network will have started to grow. Chances are you'll be given more work in these small venues, where you can keep your ears open to what else is going on and where else you might work.

> **Suitcases**
>
> The more you work, the more opportunity you'll get to work. When you do get a break, you'll need to remember you're being given a chance to move to the next level.

It's not hard to find the people who have access to real paid work. If you're doing good shows, word will get out and other folks will recommend you or want to book you.

After you've done 5 to 10 shows, you should have a good idea of your best 5 to 7 minutes of material, and that will be your "audition set." If you're in a big city where there are comedy clubs, you might be asked to come in and do a spot on a regular comedy show on a Friday or Saturday night. That means the club is interested. Or you might get the opportunity to be the opening act at a fair or a festival in your town. You need to know when a big occasion has come up for you and be prepared to take advantage of that. Do the best show you can, wherever the audition.

Building Your Network

In the beginning, you're going to feel that every performance is an audition, and there's some truth to that. But you will also soon be doing more open mics and getting asked to perform at fund-raisers, parties, and other free events, where you'll hone your skills, edit your jokes, and end up with a solid set.

As you're doing this, you'll be networking with other acts and the people who regularly attend and watch these shows, and the names of bookers will come up again and again. That's true no matter where you are: city, suburb, country, or middle of nowhere. A man or woman exists who always puts shows together.

Getting Auditions

You're going to have to call the booker, agent, or comedy club. They'll want a bio, a resumé, and a video. Send them the best ones you have. One of three things will then happen:

- You won't hear anything for months and then you'll get a call out of the blue.
- You'll be rejected with a "we're not looking for your kind of act right now" line.
- You'll be granted a chance to go to the establishment and/or the person and perform.

I must warn you: the audition might be a bit awkward. After all, they don't know you, and you don't know them. It's a little intimidating, but so what? When you're introduced you'll go on and do the best you can. No matter what happens, you'll be back. You'll persevere.

Getting a call back is a good thing. It means you'll get another chance to impress the powers that be. And if that goes well, you'll get a job. That job will lead to more opportunities and more auditions. Those will lead to more auditions. In the comedy business, an "audition" might last for one set, two sets, or an entire week of sets, as a producer or agent watches you in front of different audiences.

There are other ways to secure auditions, of course. A quick look in the phonebook will reveal "party planners," "mobile deejays," and other entertainment-related businesses. You can always give them a call and direct them to your e-resumé or send them your promo kit. Some of the comedians, musicians, and other acts you work with will also book rooms and events that use entertainers. And there's always the most straightforward method of getting an audition: you find a venue where you want to work, you walk in and ask to see the manager, and you set up an audition for yourself.

Pull Strings

The Internet is an especially valuable tool for the working ventriloquist. With a simple website, you can create an "electronic resumé." On this site, booking agents can view and download your bio, pictures, video of your performance (i.e., an audition), and a schedule of your booked and open dates.

Venues: Your Workplace

This brings us to venues, the places where you're going to work. This is just a brief overview of 10 places and settings that might use someone with your abilities, just so you have an idea:

Casinos. This includes but is not restricted to Las Vegas. Casinos from Atlantic City to Reno use ventriloquists as lounge acts, club headliners, and featured performers in song-and-dance revues. It's a viable market for what you do, and it always has been.

Churches, synagogues, and temples. This market is very big and very broad, and it offers a real opportunity for a ventriloquist who can work without using profanity and/or controversial material. A working knowledge of the faith you're performing for is a plus.

Colleges. Colleges regularly book ventriloquists as part of their entertainment for students, but becoming a college act takes a particular skill set, and you'll need a college agent. You'll end up showcasing for college activities directors at a conference; from there, you will (hopefully) get lots of bookings.

Comedy clubs. The best-known and most viable way of breaking into the comedy business is a comedy club. There are four types of rooms:

- *Showcase clubs,* found in New York City and Los Angeles, where 5 to 10 acts perform on a show any given night, working on their sets and trying to attract attention from TV/movie/big-time showbiz types

- *A rooms,* which use big-name comedy talent as headliners and one or two opening acts

- *B rooms,* which use established-but-not-yet-household-name acts as headliners, with one or two opening acts

- *C rooms,* which are usually just bars or small establishments that offer a "comedy night" once or twice a week

In most comedy clubs, you don't have to have a clean act and can pretty much say or do what you want as long as it's funny. The clubs are competitive and vital for anyone in the comedy business.

Corporate events. This is a lucrative place to make a living, but it's also very competitive. The corporate world has a certain feel to it. Businesses might hire a ventriloquist for any one of a number of reasons. Perhaps a vent falls into the theme of their event, or maybe they want you to write a specialty show just for their people, featuring a figure as a competitor or a company rep or employee. Or maybe they just want an evening of laughter and entertainment. It's best to work clean for this group, and it would make sense to be politically correct. The ability to "read the audience" is key, as is an understanding of your client and what they want before you do your program.

Cruise ships. Ventriloquists and cruise ships go together like fish and water. Right now, somewhere in the world, a ventriloquist is onstage in the theater of a big ocean liner. Like other locales, breaking into the world of cruise ships is competitive and requires perseverance. Some agents handle nothing but booking acts for cruise lines. Once you're in the rotation, however, you'll have a full schedule and the basis for a long career.

Hiccups

Fairs and festivals are hard places to break into, and the setup and surroundings can make it hard to do a solid vent routine.

Fairs and festivals. From doing your act on a hay wagon at the state fair to opening for a big-name music group at an outdoor music festival, this is a market that has used vents over the years. Getting booked here is going to take some patience because most of the booking agents for these kinds of events already know who they want and who they're going to use, and it's often celebrity and/or name recognition acts.

Kids' shows, libraries, and schools. These are specialized shows in which your routine will usually have a story line ("Safety First!" or "Don't Use Drugs!") to go with your act. If you can combine a theme or message for young folks with your 40-minute set, you can fill your calendar with work! This is also the setting for a ventriloquist who wants to be home every night for dinner because you can book yourself within 75 miles of your house, work during the day, and be home for dinner. Sometimes, the producers of the show will give you the routine and you just memorize the script and go perform! This isn't as competitive as other markets (more on this in Chapter 21).

Theaters. Many small towns around the United States have theaters with subscription series where touring Broadway shows come. On occasion, these theaters will have a comedy night or a vaudeville night during which a ventriloquist might get a chance to be one of the main performers. These usually depend on a producer working with a number of acts and theaters, and getting to know exactly who these people are is a career in and of itself. Getting in with this group is tough, but it's a perfect setup for a ventriloquist!

Theme parks and zoos. Similar to cruise ships and kids' shows, getting in with a theme park means you'll have steady work and a regular audience. Some parks and zoos will want your act to revolve around animal figures or the mascot of the park, which means you'll either be given a script or you'll have to write a specialty act for them. Either way, it's steady work and decent pay.

There are 10 spots that use ventriloquists. This doesn't include TV, which uses vents as guests on variety shows, in commercials, and on sitcoms. Also missing from the list is the birthday party circuit, which does not offer great pay but does offer stage time to the beginning vent. Another way ventriloquism is used is in the walk around–type show, where a ventriloquist is asked to—you guessed it!—walk around and perform for people at outdoor fairs or street parties.

First and foremost, you need to get stage time, and all these markets offer you that. After you've established yourself and built a little resumé, you'll move on to the next step: getting paid. (More on that in Chapter 18.)

Necessary Evil: Agents and Bookers

Someone has to find talent, contract talent, and get talent to the venue for the show. That's where agents and bookers come in, accessing people who can do what you do and booking them. Okay, they're not really evil. They're just wicked! (Joking, joking ....)

You should stay away from being "exclusive" with any one agent for as long as possible. A booking agent is in the business to make money. You will be, too, eventually, but in the beginning you're just looking for stage time. Signing on with an agent early in your career changes the way you go about your business. Your agent is going to try and earn money for you, and in turn make money for himself.

Who's Who?

An *agent* is a representative, usually for a few acts, and he books them into venues, earning a percentage of the income for the performance. This can range from 5 to 30 percent for the agent, depending on the market and the amount of money being made. Most agents carry a number of acts, anywhere from 3 to 50.

The *booker* does just that, and only that. A booker usually doesn't so much represent people or acts but instead represents a market—say, a comedy club. The booker has a deal with the club, whereby he or she talks with agents and gets a price to bring a certain act into the club, theater, or casino. Bookers are paid by the venue.

The *personal manager* handles a couple entertainers, maybe as few as four or five, and makes a living by keeping his clients booked, busy, and happy. The personal manager is fundamentally dedicated and linked to the acts and everything they do. A good personal manager oversees everything in the act's career, from choosing dates, to helping with material and routines, to dealing with travel, to suggesting what to wear. An enthusiastic and completely committed personal manager alleviates many headaches that come with show business and provides a sounding board for ideas. Personal managers oversee the entire operation for his or her couple of acts. With such hands-on work, they're hard to get and hard to come by!

You're not alone if you're thinking these three different jobs seem awfully similar and are hard to delineate. Frankly, most agents and bookers have no idea what the differences between their jobs are because there's so much crossover. The one that stands apart is personal manager, who has a deeper, more vested interest in his or her clients and their well-being.

You could make the case that most bookers and agents want to be personal managers. Personal managers often become producers of the big shows or movies or whatever creative product their clients put out. Personal managers also often earn 20 percent of their client's income, which goes down as their main client makes more money. For example, when a client is earning $1,000 per week in a comedy club, the personal manager will take $150 to $200 of that. When the client is making $100,000 per show, the personal manager will cut back to 5 to 10 percent of that.

Dealing With Agents, Bookers, and Managers

The best way to deal with these three different types of showbiz people is to be honest and ask questions. Bookers usually contact agents, so you'll probably run into agents first.

An agent might have a roster with 20 or more acts, so when you meet him or her, first ask how many acts he or she handles. You won't get a straight answer, but if the agent says "I only book four or five people," you should look at that with some skepticism. It's a numbers game; if an agent is only booking four or five people, one of those acts must be a multimillion-dollar act because you can't live off 10 percent of what five small-time comedy entertainers make. If the agent is honest, they'll tell you "I book 20 or more acts right now ...." Good answer. Now you know at least this much: the agent is not trying to lie, show off, or worse—rip you off!

> **Suitcases**
>
> There are more agents in Hollywood, New York, and Nashville, Tennessee, than other places in the country, just because more people are involved with live appearances and show business in those places.

The agent needs acts to book, and therefore needs to book you because that's how he or she makes money. There's no way around it: a good agent definitely provides a service, makes clients (audiences) happy, and has good reason to charge 15 or 20 percent commission on the income the act earns.

The booker usually works for the venue. They'll tell you what they can afford to pay, and you'll agree or not agree. Because the venue pays the booker, you don't have to pay him or her a commission. There will be times when you'll pay a booker a commission, and there will be times that agents book you into a room and you won't have to pay them anything. And there are times when a booker will get you a job somewhere, get paid by the venue, and get a commission from you as well—it's called "double-dipping."

You will, of course, know what's going on from the outset. You will ask questions. You will learn who you can trust and who you can't trust, and you'll end up working with a certain number of people over the course of a couple years. (Everything is connected to everything, remember? In show business, everyone is connected to everyone. There are 6 degrees of separation for Kevin Bacon, but just 2 degrees between your agent and the head of the William Morris Agency.) You need to establish exactly what you'll be earning and what the agent or booker will be earning as a result of your paycheck. Don't be afraid to ask questions!

Hiccups

Before you start thinking *This sure is a sleazy business,* be assured: you're exactly correct. This is no more evident than in the corporate world, where a party planner will put on a gala event for a huge conglomerate, charging an incredible amount of money for what they're going to be doing. The planner gets an act, pays them a pittance, and pockets a couple grand after telling the client that the ventriloquist was very expensive! Yes, you can fight this. Yes, it is not fair. No, it's not worth your time to investigate.

There are only a couple ways to make money in show business. You find an audience that likes what you do, you go to the venue and/or the place where that audience is, and you work for them. If you're working regularly at a theme park or with the corporate market, you can always take a survey at the end of your program by asking people simple questions as they walk out: "Did you have fun? What was your favorite part of the show? What didn't you like about the show?" You will soon start getting booked into one of the 10 markets previously mentioned. Then you can dedicate yourself to making that core group of people laugh and enjoy your show.

There's one more way to make money as a ventriloquist in the world as we know it: work closely with a personal manager, who gets you booked at venues where the people who want to see you and your act are. You build an audience who buys your DVDs and your online products, not to mention tickets to your live shows, and you sell out every seat in big theaters across the country. That comes with lots of shows and lots of travel to lots of different places and lots of work in different markets.

It's always a good idea to get feedback from the men and women who book you into the rooms you get to work, but it's also important to talk to the venue employees, including the bartenders, ticket takers, and bands who play as you walk on. These people see lots of entertainment going in and out of that venue every week. They know what works and what audiences like. Ask them!

Clubs and Organizations

There's never been a better time to be a ventriloquist. The art is steadily gaining popularity, more people are doing it well, and the number of places for you to work are nearly endless. And there's no doubt about it: if you become a professional working vent, it's partially because there's a strong network of people who can and will help you.

Here are some clubs and organizations that have information on all things vent related:

Cyber Vent

www.ventriloquist.org

This site is dedicated to ventriloquism. Log on for message boards, blogs, current updates on ventriloquist happenings, and more.

Maher Ventriloquist Studios

www.maherstudios.blogspot.com

This is the number-one site for ventriloquist supplies, figures, puppets, information, and everything else ventriloquist related.

One Way Street

119999 East Caley Avenue

Centennial, CO 80111-6835

1-800-569-4537

www.onewaystreet.com

This company offers resources for puppetry and ventriloquism with a focus on materials for the Christian church.

Vent Haven Museum

33 West Maple Avenue

Fort Mitchell, KY 41011

859-341-0461

venthaven@insightbb.com

Home of the Vent Haven ConVENTion, a yearly get-together of the best and brightest ventriloquists from around the world, this is the Super Bowl of ventriloquism! This convention takes place every July in Fort Mitchell, Kentucky. No other event in the United States focuses on ventriloquists and ventriloquism the way this one does. Not only do the most famous and most popular ventriloquists of the day perform, but there are also workshops and sessions taught by the best ventriloquists from around the globe. The "Dealers Room" features figure-makers who have examples of their work for you to test. The vent community is fairly small, and this celebration allows beginners and newbies to rub elbows with established greats and those few who have attained some notoriety. If you are a vent, want to be a vent, or like ventriloquism, you need to get to Fort Mitchell this year!

Some Contacts to Get You Started

There are a few other organizations that feature or relate to ventriloquists, and some are probably in your neighborhood. Magicians and magic clubs are often open to vents being part of their group because the art is so much like magic (it depends on diversion and illusion). You can find online blogs and chat rooms for ventriloquists as well, among them:

Puppeteers of America
www.puppeteers.org
This organization is dedicated to providing information to the community of people who work with puppets. Ventriloquism is part of their program.

VentMail
groups.yahoo.com/group/VENTmail
This is another online forum for ventriloquists.

WorldVents
groups.yahoo.com/group/WORLDVENTS
This online forum and message board welcomes professional and amateur ventriloquists from all over the planet.

The Least You Need to Know

- To get gigs, you need to promote yourself. An 8×10 photo, bio, resumé, and video are your ventriloquist calling cards!

- You have to audition. There's no way around it. But with some hints and guidance on how to approach auditions, you're sure to succeed.

- You need contacts, and you need to network. Finding the right people and places helps you get on the road to becoming a professional ventriloquist.

Chapter 18

Getting Paid!

In This Chapter

- How much can you expect to get paid?
- Discussing money with bookers, agents, and clients
- Tips for moving up in the "biz"
- Becoming the best ventriloquist you can be

Two words you'll be reading more of in the rest of this book are *stage time*. The beginning of your career as a ventriloquist has nothing to do with income. Your success or lack of success depend on how often you can get onstage and gain invaluable experience as you refine your material.

Show business is similar to every other business in many ways, especially when it comes to money. Everybody wants something for nothing. And, in the beginning, you should be very happy to give exactly that—your best something—to the folks who give you nothing but stage time.

The Pay Scale (Who Can Live on *This?*)

You will start by working for nothing. And you will like it! There is some significant and positive fallout that comes with working for free.

First of all, there's no pressure. You're not getting paid, so there's an unspoken understanding with everyone involved—the person who booked you, the other performers who might be on the same show with you, and maybe even the audience—that it's not a "professional" job. Frankly, you can't lose in these situations!

Second, because you're not getting paid, everything you do is exceeding expectations. If your performance doesn't go well, there's no worry: no money was involved, so nobody lost anything. As a matter of fact, if things didn't go well, that's good for you: you learned what *not* to do! If things go really well, it's good for everyone: the booker/client is happy because they got a great show without spending any money. You're happy because you're doing good work, building your act, and now you have a positive experience to put in your pocket as you go on.

Third, and perhaps most important, every free performance is a chance for you to network. You'll give out your e-mail address, phone number, and all your contact information. You'll have a taped performance to study later. You'll probably be asked to do another show for another client or two (and no doubt you'll be asked to do them for free). You can get recommendations from the people who booked you, and you'll have started the process every ventriloquist goes through: using each job to get the next job.

From the start, you'll be asked to work for *benefit* shows. This is a show in which an organization, business, or group is trying to raise money. It's an apt word, *benefit*, because you stand to gain as much as anyone: stage time, meetings with new bookers and clients, not to mention the chance to work in front of a positive audience. That doesn't even include the fulfillment you get from breaking away from the norm and working for some project or cause that needs your help.

def•i•ni•tion

In showbiz terms, a **benefit** is the common name for a fundraiser, a charity program, or an outreach. Sometimes these are paid performances, but usually you'll work for next to nothing. These are usually lots of fun, though, and the opportunity to network is second to none. You often work with and meet folks you otherwise never would have come across.

So your first few performances will be freebies. You'll work wherever, whenever, and for whomever, just to get onstage and work your routine. Remember, you're building an act. Yes, a fortunate few go onstage and within a week or two are on TV, getting cast in commercials, and progressing on their way to a career. That's very rare, but it could happen!

If you're like most, you'll have to concentrate on getting your next gig, pleasing the audience, editing your act, and improving overall. There's a reason for the cliché "Pay your dues." Specifically, the dues you'll be paying are the many, many shows you'll do without getting paid.

When you do start getting some kind of payment, that first compensation might not even be real money. You'll sometimes work for a meal—probably dinner—when you perform for festivals, organizations, or charity events. Don't take this for granted. If nothing else, sharing a meal with a client or booker might give you a chance to introduce yourself to movers and shakers in local show business.

You'll eventually work into paid performances, but remain in the "don't quit your day job" category. Let's start our look at paid performances in the most obvious of show business outlets: comedy clubs. As mentioned in Chapter 17, comedy clubs break down into three categories: A rooms, B rooms, and C rooms, the C room being the lowest rung on the ladder of stature and cachet.

> **Pull Strings**
>
> You should have a business card with basic contact information on it, such as your phone number and e-mail address. As your act gets better and you gain experience, people will ask you for your info. Be ready to hand it over!

The C Room

C rooms are usually open for comedy one or two nights a week. These establishments offer other services to their clientele during the week; it might be a bar that has "comedy night" every Wednesday, or a hotel that has a couple comedians work an otherwise-empty conference room on the weekend. Comedy is not the focus of the C room; it's just a way to get people to come in and spend money at the bar, restaurant, or hotel. Nobody gets rich doing comedy in a C room. The pay ranges from $50 (or less) for the *emcee* and/or middle act, up to $200 to $350 per show for the headliner.

> **Suitcases**
>
> Comedy clubs follow a rigid protocol for shows. Usually an emcee goes on, welcomes the audience, does a few minutes of warm-up, and then introduces a middle act. The middle act does a 15- to 25-minute set, before the emcee comes back and introduces the headliner, who closes the show with a 45- to 60-minute performance. Sometimes there's no middle act, and sometimes there's an added act or two. But the emcee-middle-headliner setup is pretty standard these days.

C rooms can be tough. The audience is usually very young, a little rowdy, and very demanding. They might heckle. Often there's no cover charge, meaning anyone can go to the show, and there's usually no vested interest in whether the performers are any good because the show didn't cost anything.

def•i•ni•tion

An **emcee,** short for "master of ceremonies," is the host of a show or presentation who introduces other speakers, presenters, or performers, and acts as a kind of thread from the beginning to the end of the show.

So why play a C room? Simple: if you can do solid, funny, entertaining shows in a C room, you're going to be very successful in the B and A rooms. Because the C room is at the bottom of the comedy club ladder, it's a good place for a ventriloquist to start. Similar to the "free" shows you start your career with, there's very little pressure in the C room. Most of the acts work very blue (that is, with profanity), trying to appeal to the lowest common denominator and just getting through their time onstage.

Your job is to continue what you've started by editing, rewriting, and re-editing your show. Focus on your technique. Prepare your presentation, execute it, and then network and share notes with other entertainers and bookers involved with the shows. Make no mistake: if you do solid shows and work hard, you will get more bookings!

The B Room

B rooms are a step up from C rooms, but they are still a step below A rooms. Some B rooms are C rooms made good, and are located in bars and restaurants or other establishments. These are sometimes full-time comedy clubs open three to five nights a week, similar to A rooms, and they follow the same emcee-middle-headliner format for shows. While the C rooms are using comedians and entertainers who haven't yet hit the "big time," B rooms offer audiences a solid show with good performers, even if they're not celebrities or household names.

Pull Strings

Emcees and openers get short shrift in the comedy world, but these are important spots, not to mention great opportunities for a ventriloquist. The headliner often performs for 45 minutes. That leaves another 45 minutes for two or three other acts to perform; this is where the emcee and opener fill in. For you, emceeing and opening mean one thing: stage time!

You can make a little more money in B's because the clubs charge a cover (especially for the weekend shows), and audiences come for the comedy (as opposed to C rooms, where the audiences come for anything but comedy). Because comedy is the product, the acts are paid a little more. Emcees and openers can earn $200 for the week; middle acts can make up to $500; and headliners get $800 to $1,500. Payment depends on how many nights the room is open and how many shows are offered. It's not unusual for a comedy club to have one show on Wednesday, one on Thursday, two on Friday, and two or three on Saturday! For a beginner ventriloquist, the chance to work five to eight times a week is incredible. To be paid for "practicing" is even better!

The A Rooms

The A rooms are the premier comedy clubs in the country, featuring big-name acts and celebrities on a regular basis and filling out their schedules with established touring comedians. These are bars and/or restaurants with a high-quality sound system in the show room, TV-ready lighting, and great sight lines for the audience to see you onstage. A rooms make their money on who is playing the club that night, and they sell particular comics, entertainers, and celebrities.

A rooms are the top of the comedy club food chain. Many are franchises, and can be found in many cities around the United States—The Improv clubs, for example. These full-time comedy clubs, open six or seven nights a week, have at least one show and often two, three, or four shows, depending on the night. The pay is a little better here than in the B room: $300 for the emcee and/or opening act; $500 to $700 for the middle act; and the headliner usually works out a deal with the club booker/manager in which he or she gets a percentage (or even 100 percent!) of the door (all the money taken in cover charges from the paying audience). It's not unusual for a well-known comedian to play a comedy club and earn $20,000 in a 3-day run. Of course, he or she does anywhere from three to six shows for that money and draws his or her own crowd due to name recognition.

Showcase Rooms

Showcase clubs are found predominantly in New York City and Los Angeles, and the setup here is very different from the A, B, and C rooms. Showcase rooms have their own agenda, which is to find comedy stars of tomorrow. Competition is fierce, and stage time is precious. It's very hard to break in.

The setup goes something like this: there is an emcee—just like the A, B, and C rooms—but he or she handles the job much differently. For one thing, there's much more banter between the emcee and the audience. Often the emcee is a seasoned, touring, headlining comic who spends his or her "off" days in a showcase room, refining new material, networking with the powers that be, and keeping up their chops in front of discerning audiences. Instead of opening, middle, or even headlining acts, a number of comedians perform—at times, there are as many as 10 to 15 acts! Beginners, established pros, and comedy stars alike go on every night, playing to audiences that resemble a TV crowd because they're usually from all over the country.

> **Suitcases**
>
> Why would anyone work in New York for $20? Because there's always the chance you might be discovered by a TV scout or motion picture producer. You sacrifice income for the opportunity to be seen. This is showbiz, and it is very competitive!

Showcase clubs are where new talent is often discovered. Agents and bookers for mass media and personal managers often hang out and shake hands with the acts before and after. The pay scale on both coasts might surprise you: everyone gets paid the same, and it's usually in the $20-per-set range and maybe as much as $50 on the weekends.

For you, the beginning ventriloquist, I have a few suggestions. First, don't be afraid to be an emcee. Many people overlook the advantages to emceeing, but this is a skill that will make you valuable to a booker in many ways, not just as a ventriloquist.

Being an emcee forces you to write material because you're always trying to balance things onstage. If the crowd is quiet, you need to get them rolling. If they're particularly loud and appreciative of the middle act, you need to calm them down, change the mood a bit, and prepare them for the headliner. Emceeing forces you to work as a stand-up comic, without your figure, which helps make your ventriloquist act stronger because you become a better performer.

It's also true that the emcee earns the least amount of money. But don't let that dissuade you. You can't make much money at first anyway, so you might as well emcee and learn the trade while stretching yourself.

Finally, comedy clubs are kind of like comedy college, where you can immerse yourself in Comedy 101. Your tuition is not so much the money you pay out (and you're certainly not making much), but rather it's your time spent in and around the clubs that represent your investment. The only way to make that pay off is to use your stage time as best you can! You could even compare the clubs to professional baseball. If you think of comedy clubs as minor league baseball, C rooms are single-A ball, B rooms are AA, and A rooms are AAA! The major leagues are Vegas, big theaters, TV, and motion pictures—the places where you make the big bucks.

There are major financial drawbacks to comedy clubs, of course. If you're not near a big city, you probably don't have a club in your area. It's a major commitment to drive 1 to 3 hours (or more) into a city to work a club a couple nights a week. And you have to consider the pay because working for free or for $20 a night—when you spend that in gas to get to and from the venue—doesn't make sense.

Kid Shows

The children's market isn't talked about much, and as a career it flies under the radar, but there's no doubt about it: you can make money as a children's entertainer. Birthday parties, schools, religious organizations, theme parks, and fairs book children's entertainment.

Doing birthday parties is the best way to get started with kids' shows. You only need 15 to 20 minutes of material, and you don't have to be the greatest entertainer in the world. Audience participation works with these parties, so if you can get the kids singing along with you and your figure, you're halfway home.

Children's shows can bring pretty decent money, but you'll want to start small: $25 or $50 for a show. You'll eventually raise your fees, of course, but start small until you get more established. The same thing is true of bar and bat mitzvahs: start small, with $50 as your high point, and use your shows to grow your act and get better jokes.

Schools are always looking for quality programming to come and perform for the students. These shows are sometimes booked at big school showcases, where different acts (musicians, jugglers, magicians, ventriloquists, etc.) get up and do a short set of what schools might expect to see if they book a particular act. These entertainers make $300 to $500 per show, sometimes doing two in a day and as many as five or six in a week!

There are also organizations that will hire a ventriloquist to perform a prewritten, school-accredited script dealing with bullying, drugs or alcohol prevention, or making friends. The same applies here: you can earn around $350 per show and work 12 to 20 shows a month.

Expenses can be pretty steep for this market (you'll be driving *a lot*), but kids' shows fill your calendar and allow you to put together your act, and you'll certainly have opportunities for more work as your reputation gets around and clients begin to ask for you by name!

> **Suitcases**
>
> Many kids' show entertainers will tell you they didn't plan on getting into this particular market, but once they did and really put their minds to work, they can't see leaving for any reason. There's something very fresh and vital about working for kids!

Churches and Religious Organizations

If you are called to a particular faith, there's a good chance you can turn your ventriloquism skills into a way to earn money within your religion. Religious groups are always looking for entertainers who can talk to their followers. There are great opportunities for working with children here as well.

The religious market doesn't pay well at first (recognize a theme here?), but it can be lucrative as you become more well known and accepted into the community. It's not unusual for faith-based entertainers to earn $500 per show, and that might be a little low. There are, within each religion, particular singers and performers who command very large sums for live appearances. To start, most religious acts do what everyone does to start: they work for nothing or for food and maybe a recommendation. As their reputation spreads, job offers come in, and eventually the money gets to be something respectable.

One advantage to the religious market is that you can move up the ladder quickly—from beginner to major headliner—in a couple years. But you'll also niche yourself within your religious group, and it's hard to break out of that.

At the same time, everybody wants programming for the young people within their faith, something representative of doctrine or religious views. A solid kids' program in this market can earn a vent something close to $3,000 and more per show, if he or she gives the church, synagogue, or temple exactly what it's looking for.

Theme Parks, Festivals, and Fairs

Breaking into this market depends on who you're dealing with, how much name recognition you have, and the event itself. For example, working with one of the major theme parks in North America—Universal Studios, Disney, Six Flags, and Sea World—earns you a little bit more money (and viability) than a county fair. Theme parks often have a stage with state-of-the-art lighting and sound, and you can do three or four shows every day for 5 or 6 days of the week.

The money can be pretty good—as much as $1,500 to $2,000 per week, and sometimes more than that with certain parks. The keys to making money in theme parks are pretty simple: have some audience participation, have great energy, and offer child-friendly material.

Fairs and festivals are a different story. The setup usually isn't as nice as you might find at a theme park. You're often working in the dead of summer, which is hot and uncomfortable. The booking might ask that you do a walk-around performance, where you're walking around talking to people with your figure, and that can be awkward. The pay is something in the $100 to $300 range for a day or two.

Naturally, if you're a headlining act with a big name, you're going to play a theater or a soundstage at a festival or fair, and the stakes—and the money—are higher. For the beginner, it's a tough call. You want to work, but the conditions aren't going to be the best in this market.

Colleges

Successful college acts do very well financially. This is another very competitive market, where lots of entertainers are vying for the student dollars that come with college shows.

There are big events in the fall and spring of the school year during which acts showcase for the kids involved with student activities at their particular school. Naturally, the students want to bring in the biggest stars and most popular icons of the day, but the students find those artists want too much money. So acts like yours get an opportunity to show what they can do in a showcase, usually in about 20 minutes of stage time.

Colleges typically pay $700 to $1,500 per performance. But those numbers are misleading. What happens is something like this: You go to a showcase. You do your set. The students love you. Thirty-five colleges request that you come to their school. They have a meeting and try to route you so you can play all the colleges in western Ohio in a 1-week run. So in 6 days, you do seven shows: six performances at colleges from Dayton to Toledo in six straight nights, with a junior college in Columbus thrown in for good measure. Your price per show is $1,500, but because the kids got together and "block booked" you, you go for a reduced rate: $900 per show. You do seven shows, $900 each, and go home after the last performance with checks totaling $6,300. Not bad!

The problem with college shows is that you're often responsible for your own airfare, hotel, and rental car. The college circuit is all about driving from gig to gig, eating at the hotel, and catching crack-of-dawn flights to get to another show or back home. It's not unusual to earn $6,300 in 6 days … but lose $3,000 of that to airfare, hotels, rental cars, and agent commissions!

College shows can be lots of fun because you sometimes play beautiful theaters and venues that have every kind of modern light and sound technology available. You also get to play in school cafeterias and lunchrooms at noon, when kids have weapons, i.e. food, to throw at you. This is a hard market to breach, but once you're in, you'll be booked solidly into the next few months. Nice work if you can get it!

Cruises

There may be no other venue more closely associated with ventriloquists than the cruise line industry. Maybe it's because the vent figure is often made of wood and serves as a back-up flotation device? Whatever the reason, the cruise market has always been good to ventriloquists, and vents have been the highlight of many people's cruises for the past 30 years.

Like the college market, you will be hard-pressed to break into the cruise line industry without an agent. These people have worked with all the big lines, and they know what material does and doesn't work on cruise ships. Obviously, ventriloquism works because they keep getting booked!

The cruise industry is very close-knit, and they work together. You might switch cruise lines in the middle of a week, going from the Mediterranean to the Caribbean and performing the same night you flew in. On the other hand, you might sign a contract that has you performing on a ship for 6 straight weeks. A typical week might be as follows: a 10- to 12-minute welcome-aboard show the first night, a 45-minute main show one night in the ship's theater, and a hope-to-see-you-again part in the grand finale.

What can a cruise act earn? The really good ones with the top lines can earn more than $5,000 a week because they've been on the ship so often and draw a following! To start, and depending on the line you work for, you can earn up to $1,500 to $3,500 as a "specialty act." Some cruises require that you work as an aide with the ship's passengers, chaperoning them on short trips or walks to the local town when the ship docks. Other cruise lines pay you $2,000 for the week, and you work all of two nights.

Corporate

Getting into the corporate market takes patience and fortitude, a lot of talent, and the ability to work in various situations, not all of which are conducive to great ventriloquism. The keys to working for big companies and industry conventions, conferences, and meetings come down to two things: how flexible you can be and how you can tailor your set to their office or their people.

Your writing skills will come in handy here. You probably know the rumors: businesses and mega-companies are happy to pay top dollar for an entertainer who is funny, clean, and honest, and has broad appeal. You've done your homework in the comedy-writing chapters of this book, so now it's time to put those skills to the test and go get yourself a corporate booking.

The entertainer's fees for these shows range from $1,500 to $25,000 for either one or a couple shows.

Casinos

Casinos are kind of a cross between comedy clubs and cruise ships. Casinos usually have showrooms where something different goes on every night. Las Vegas has always been a home to ventriloquism, and now that casinos dot the entire country, you have another opportunity for work.

There are different kinds of shows for a ventriloquist to fit into at a casino. There are music revues and floorshows featuring dancers and singers. Some casinos hire a ventriloquist as comic relief during a particular program. Your set will probably last in the 15- to 20-minute range, and you'll do some eight shows a week. The pay is $500 to $1,200, depending on the

> **Suitcases**
>
> There are comedy clubs in many casinos, especially in Vegas and Atlantic City, and they follow the same rules as the B rooms covered earlier in this chapter.

casino, the length of your show, and the size of the showroom (that is, how much money they can charge and how many seats they have to fill).

There is also the opportunity to be the opening act for headliners in the big showrooms. Those pay $350 to $500 for your set, plus you get a nice credit for your resumé!

What to Ask For, What to Expect

There's no right answer here. Every situation, every venue, every booker, and every agent differs. The best rule of thumb is to work for as little as possible in the beginning. You want to get to a point where your act is so good that you *force* a club, church, or cruise line to pay you more because you're doing such good work.

Of course, if you're doing great work, you'll begin to draw an audience—people who will be happy to pay to see your ability and your talent. At that point, you'll be haggling over how much tickets are. But that's a different book! At some point, you'll be forced to discuss money with the person who requested your services. It might be good to know some ways to get as much money as you can from each performance, right? I have it covered.

Negotiating Your Pay

Use the price-point examples I gave earlier in this chapter when you're haggling with bookers or agents about what you should be paid. If the audience pays a cover charge at the door when you're playing, you should make at least a little bit of that cover.

Many comedy clubs don't haggle over price; rather, it's a set fee: "We pay our middle acts $50 per show. We're doing eight shows this week, so he or she will get $400." Much of what you'll be doing at the start is all about the set price clients such as comedy clubs have determined is the going rate. The only way to beat that is to become a draw by getting your act seen on TV, video, or YouTube.

In the beginning of your career, don't expect very much haggling over price. The club offers a set amount, and that's what everyone makes. Period.

When dealing with churches, synagogues, and schools, you have to stay strong with what you believe is fair and equitable. If you're doing a 30-minute show for a bar mitzvah and the person booking you says, "There will be 300 people there," your comeback should be, "I'd like to make $1 per person." Who can argue with that? You're a fledgling act, and you're not asking for much—just a couple hundred bucks based on what the person who booked you knows.

Comedy clubs operate similarly, and you'll have to stick up for yourself and say, "I'm happy to book the third weekend next month. I need $400 for the four shows." The club owner might go nuts. He might give you the $400 for the middle spot in four shows. He also might fire the emcee and just have a two-person set, making you the emcee. Or maybe he won't book you just because you asked for too much money!

Send In Your Agent

You're going to need an agent sooner or later. The agent can argue about money on your behalf. Agents are already aware of what clients earn at all these various venues because they talk to club owners and important event coordinators about pay all the time—it's their job!

Pull Strings

Yes, sooner or later you will need an agent to work with bookers in the various arenas: college, club, church, casino, corporate, etc. What you really want is a personal manager (see Chapter 17).

When you begin to work with one or more agents, they'll explain to you what the going rate is for each individual job. You have every right to ask for more, or ask for a *lot* more, and ask why the fees are set the way they are. Always ask, "How much does this club/casino/college usually pay per audience member?"

Experience Pays

One of the reasons you want to network and hang out in various venues with other entertainers is to get an idea what people are being paid. You will have some idea after working a few paying gigs because everybody usually knows what everyone is making in show business.

As your act improves and you become more comfortable and successful onstage, you will begin to ask for more money in return for your services. Frankly, that will happen whether you ask or not. Every venue wants to host great shows, and people are willing to pay a fair price to get the best. The truth is, you will earn more money and become more profitable the more you work and edit and focus on your act.

Working Your Way Up

The comedy club model is the easiest to use as an example to illustrate how you might work your way up the pay scale. Let's take a look.

You put together your 5-minute audition set. You rehearse it and get a spot at open-mic night at a comedy club. You go on and get some laughs, and the club manager asks you to come back next week. So you do.

Things go a little better this time, and the manager asks if you'd mind coming in and performing a set on the weekend. You agree, and instead of waiting until the weekend to perform, you go to a coffeehouse and perform as part of a poetry reading (you get onstage by telling the poetry coordinator you do poetry reading with your figure—which you do by writing a short comedy poem, performing it, and then running your regular 5-minute set). When you get to the club on the weekend, you're totally prepared and you have a really great show.

The manager asks if you would do a week in the club. You agree. How much?

"First-timers always make $250 for the week—eight shows," says the club manager. You agree. You come in, do the week of shows, and then emcee the last show on Friday and both shows on Saturday when the original emcee gets called out of town. The club manager is impressed with your work, and a local agent hangs out to talk to you after one of the shows. The agent has a room 30 minutes away, which you play the following weekend. It's a $300 payday on a Thursday, and an easy show for some senior citizens in a home. After that show, a woman asks if you'll come do her senior center. "How much is your show?" she asks. You ask her how many people will be attending the performance. "About 200," she says, "maybe more." You reply, "I like to get $1 per person." Your new client is ecstatic: "*Done!*" she shouts.

Your phone rings. One of the comics you've done open mic with is calling with news that a club 3 hours away has an opening for a middle act. "How much?" you ask. "$500 for Thursday through Saturday," says the comic. You take the gig, and you're on your way!

After the weekend, you get a call from someone who visited your website. She wants you to perform at their homecoming concert in the campus sports arena. "How many people?" you ask. "3,500!" she says. "I'd like $1 per person," you say, swallowing your words. "I think I can do that," says the voice.

No, it is not a common occurrence to have all that stuff come together just that way. But it *could* happen!

It's Not About the Money (at First)

It really isn't about the money. It's about stage time. It's about making mistakes, correcting those mistakes, getting your set down tight so you can audition, and coming off looking professional. The money will come as you improve, stay focused, and become a top-notch ventriloquist.

You've heard the stereotype: "5 percent of the people make 95 percent of the money in showbiz." That's the cynic's way of looking at the world. For you, it's not about being one of the 5 percent—it's about being the best ventriloquist you can be and taking that as far as you can take it. The money will follow!

The Least You Need to Know

- You won't make much money at first, but you need to do free jobs to get stage time.

- As you start taking on paid jobs, you will find that there is already an unwritten pay scale. You'll fit into the format at the start.

- You can work your way up the pay scale, or you can force the issue by asking to make "$1 per person," or even "$5 per person." All the client can say is "Yes" or "No."

- It's not about the money at first. It's about—let's say it together—*stage time!*

Chapter 19

Putting Your Act Together

In This Chapter

- ◆ Staging your act
- ◆ Advice on maximizing microphones and lighting
- ◆ Putting your off arm to use (or not)
- ◆ Setting some performance goals
- ◆ Tips for working with the audience and having fun

This chapter could be retitled "Tech Rehearsal." In the following pages, you'll learn about basic stage direction (downstage, upstage, stage left, stage right, and so on). Staging your act might sound simple, but the successful ventriloquist leaves nothing to chance, so he or she runs through the set with the tech crew, starting with how the show will be set up so the audience can best enjoy it.

Just as important is the sound and light that will be used (or not used) during your performance. Ventriloquism is based on seeing and hearing the performer, and because part of your success depends on subterfuge and deception, it makes sense that every time you walk onstage, you have the optimal system in place to execute your presentation.

There's also the little matter of your "off hand"—the one not manipulating your figure. I deal with that here, too, and give you some suggestions for how to best use that hand to support and augment your program.

This chapter ends with a discussion of the concept of your show. How much, if any, does the audience participate? Are specific light cues and sound cues necessary for the show? How can staging best strengthen the program you've put together?

Staging 101

You'll encounter a variety of stages and performance spaces during your career, and there are some basic rules you'll want to follow no matter where you go. First, the audience should be seated in front or to the sides, but not *behind* you, so they have the best view of your and your figures, without seeing your hand going into the back of your figure. (Keeping the illusion!)

Second, some staging depends on *you*, the entertainer. You'll want to include everyone during your set. Make eye contact with someone (or something) in every part of the audience. A good rule of thumb is to pick someone to your left, someone directly in front, and someone to your right as you work. You can look at them without really looking at them. Pick a spot just above your mark's head, and look to that spot as you talk or have your figure talk.

Pull Strings

A good way to "pick a mark" (someone to look at during your show) is to watch the audience before you go on. If there's an opening or another act before you go on, watch the audience. Try to find one person to your right, one in the center, and one to your left who appear to be enjoying themselves, and play to them when you're on.

Remember *you* are the director. Don't be afraid to ask for the minimum requirements you need in staging, lighting, and sound. These are essential to giving your act the best chance to succeed!

Depending on the venue, you'll work with a stage manager, a lighting director, and a sound engineer. Sometimes this is one person doing all three jobs. Sometimes you'll be responsible for everything on your own. No matter what the situation, you are responsible for setting the stage for success—literally. Often you can ask the professionals for their opinions about how to best prepare the stage. They know their theater, club, or performance space better than you do. Listen to what they suggest, ask questions, and do what you think best represents your act.

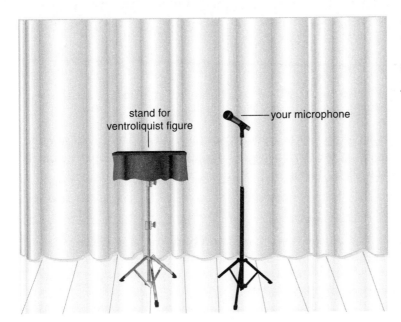

stand for ventroliquist figure

your microphone

Stage setup is the first order of business in creating the best environment for your act. In most cases, you're responsible for setting the stage.

You'll likely work a variety of stages throughout your career, including these:

- ◆ Floor
- ◆ Risers
- ◆ Stage
- ◆ Soundstage

Let's look at the setup for each.

Down on the Floor

In this situation, you're playing to an audience that's seated on the same floor you're standing on. The best way to set up is to seat the crowd in front and at a 45-degree angle to the sides from where you stand. This means that, if the audience numbers more than 100 people, you might lose the attention span of those folks seated in the back. They're far from the action, and they can't see you well because people are seated directly in front of them and you're not elevated.

The sound system is usually on the floor with you, which means you need to be sure it works, it doesn't produce feedback, and it's not too loud or too soft. Feedback can be a problem in this situation. The same goes for lighting—the lights have to be set so everyone can see you.

A Little Higher: Risers

Risers are used in hotel ballrooms, at school assemblies, and in places unaccustomed to having performances. Always be sure the riser legs are stable!

There are usually stairs set to the left or right so you can get onstage. If you're using audience participation, having the stairs *downstage* makes sense, so audience members can get right up and on without having to walk around to the back of the set.

def•i•ni•tion

Downstage refers to the front of the stage, closest to the audience. *Upstage,* then, is the back of the stage, farthest from the audience and/or closest to the back wall. *Stage right* is to *your* right as you face the audience. *Stage left* is to *your* left as you face the audience. *Center stage* is, you guessed it, the center of the stage.

As with the floor, be sure sound and lights are set so the audience can see and hear you with no problem.

All the World's a Stage

The best of all worlds is a professional stage, with lighting and sound that's already part of the physical structure of the venue. A professional stage can handle all your needs and often has the added benefit of professional staff who have experience and expertise.

The Soundstage

This is a soundproof structure with high ceilings and plenty of space (think airplane hanger) used predominantly for TV and film recording. You'll find yourself on soundstages when you perform for TV, and there's no better situation for a ventriloquist because you're the focus of everything.

Follow the simple rules you've already learned for setting up a soundstage: tell the stage manager, sound director, and lighting director what you want and then follow their suggestions. They've seen what does and doesn't work in this space.

A Few More Thoughts on Stages

It's always a good idea to get to the venue where you'll be performing at least 1 hour (if not 2) before show time. Some of the venues you'll play will have a "call time" 4 to 6 hours before you actually go on. This is the chance for you to go over your set with the tech staff and run through your needs for a successful performance.

By definition, a ventriloquist is a prop act, which means you'll require some planning before you go on:

- Where do you set your case with the figure(s) when you walk on?

- Where's the microphone onstage?

- Is your figure going to sit on a stool or a stand?

- Do these props need to be pre-set by someone (like a stage manager or assistant), or will you carry them on yourself?

- How will you close your set? Will you take your props off stage on your own, or will you need help?

These questions are going to become routine for you, but in the beginning, write them down as a checklist and go over them one by one with the stage manager you're working with. This isn't something you can leave to figure out as you're performing. This checklist needs to be part of your pre-show routine, the way a pilot goes through a pre-flight protocol before taking off.

Depending on the amount of time you're performing and the number of figures and cases you'll be using, each performance varies according to the stage and the material.

Check One, Two, Three ...: The Microphone

The microphone is more than the amplification system. It's similar to an instrument for a musician, and as a ventriloquist, you have to use and adjust it to your needs because sound is so important to your act.

As a vent, you'll likely work with a few different styles of microphones.

Wired Microphones

A wired microphone is the classic microphone you've seen used by everyone from recording artists to stand-up comics in your local comedy club. The microphone sits in a clip on top of a mic stand. A wire runs from the microphone to an amplifier, which is connected to a sound system, which sends a signal to speakers, which fill the room with your voice(s).

Wired microphones are analog rather than digital, but the wire makes it a safe bet that there will be sound—one way or the other—coming out of the speakers.

Wireless Microphones

A wireless microphone is the same as a wired microphone; a wireless mic sits in a clip on a mic stand, and you can take it out or leave it in the clip to perform. One advantage of the wireless is the ability to move around without an annoying wire getting tangled in your feet. Another advantage is that you can go just about anywhere and you don't have to worry that the cord will pop out or get pulled too tightly and break.

The disadvantages stem from the battery and the wiring in the wireless microphone: you have to be sure the battery is fresh and won't die as you perform and there's no "interference" if you walk around on the stage as you work. These days, wireless mics pick up phone conversations, Internet correspondence, wireless information networks, and even car radios! Be sure you sound check and ask questions before you go on!

Sometimes a wireless microphone requires that you wear an amplifier or battery pack as you work. This usually fits in your hip pocket or on your belt. You can also ask to have an earphone or earbud that allows you to listen to yourself when using a wireless mic. (Think of it as a personal in-ear monitor.)

Headset Microphones

For this type of microphone, a headset attaches to your head with a stabilizing headband, and the microphone is on the end of a small rod, often picking up your voice from the side of your mouth. The headset is ideal for a vent who wants to show off his lip control and technique. It alleviates the problem of the microphone stand and having to pick up and replace the microphone, and it's a popular choice for many venues.

The biggest drawbacks to the headset mic are similar to the wireless mic (picking up interference and battery life), with the added problem that the location of the microphone (near the side of your mouth) can cause volume and enunciation problems.

Also, be aware that the headband is not always secure and immovable. Headset microphones are notorious for falling off, moving slightly so you become unintelligible, and losing volume during performances. As always, do a thorough sound check and ask questions!

Lapel and Clip-On Microphones

Lapel and clip-on mics attach to your collar or necktie, and a wire runs underneath your shirt, connecting to a battery pack or amplifier.

These microphones are not made for people who use dynamic voices, music, or any kind of polyphony in their production. If you use any of these elements, I highly suggest you use another microphone system.

Pull Strings

Some ventriloquists use two microphones: one for themselves and one for their figure. This is a good illusion that helps bring character and life to the act. Of course, using one microphone on a stand can also make your figure more lifelike as it leans in to the mic and talks—louder as it gets closer to the microphone, softer as it moves away. The microphone can be used as a prop (it's an instrument, remember?) and help create character!

Make Friends with the Sound Tech

Without question, the sound technician is going to be your best friend, regardless of the venue. Having clear, distortion-free, and perfectly mixed sound is essential to an act such as yours, which requires the audience to listen and hear everything.

You'll want to go over your act with the sound tech in some detail, maybe even running through some of it so he or she can better understand your needs and what your act is like. If no sound tech is available, ask someone to stand onstage, using the same microphone you'll use, and let them talk and sing into it. You can then walk around the room and get a feel for the acoustics, what sounds good and/or bad, and how you want to set your levels.

If you're doing lots of music in your act, a sound tech is even more valuable to you. The tech can set levels and equalizer positions so everything sounds good in the audience. If you're using music, chances are you'll have some sort of accompaniment; perhaps there is a band you work with as you and the figure sing. It's imperative that the sound technicians mix things so your vocals are easy to hear and understand. It's hard to do a comedy show and tell jokes if the punch lines are drowned out by a bass guitar or awkward moments of feedback.

You might be using cuts from a CD or digital download music player. Of course, it is possible to access this onstage during your performance (it's one use for your off hand), but having a short rehearsal with the audio people so they hit the play button when you need them to is just as good if not better.

This rehearsal, going over cues and prompts for the sound people, should be very methodical and detail-oriented so there are no questions as you're performing. Nothing is worse than getting ready to sing a song but having no accompaniment because the tech went to get a beer.

See and Be Seen: Lighting

No matter where you're working, you want the audience to be able to see you. Period. Lighting isn't as important as sound, but it's a close second. Ventriloquism is creating diversions, and it's hard to create those when you're in the dark.

Most of the venues where you'll work will have some kind of lighting. The best lighting is a spotlight or theatrical lighting focused directly on you. Working with the lighting director at a theater helps you find the best spot onstage for your act, and this will vary from place to place.

On occasion, you'll have to "find the light." For example, you might walk into a theater or a venue where the stage is perfect, but as you stand downstage center, you realize the spotlight is focused to your left and a little behind you. There's no lighting director, and nobody knows how to change or move the lighting. In other words, the best place for an audience to see you is going to be where the light is pre-set—in the center of the stage, a little to the left. Although that's not the best place for your act (you'd much rather be downstage center), you have to work with the situation. Do your act where the light is best, and figure out how to make all your bits and routines look good from there.

If you're using lots of audience participation in your act, go over those cues with the lighting director. You don't want your victims … er … helpers to trip or stumble as they're getting up onstage or going back to their seats. Good lighting is essential for all interaction between yourself and the people in the crowd.

Most lighting is self-explanatory and easy to figure out: can the audience see you? If not, get some light. If they can, you're set.

> **Suitcases**
>
> A *spotlight* is usually very bright, pinpointed on a single spot, position, or performer. *Wash* lighting covers all or part of a stage. The wash can be "hot" (very bright), "warm" (this is the norm—not as hot but still bright enough for everyone to see), or "cool" and "soft" (popular as backlighting for performers who are out front in a spotlight or hotter wash). *Blackout* lighting refers to when all the stage lights go out, leaving you and the audience in total darkness for a few seconds. Only use this in specialized situations.

A couple notes on lighting: spotlights can be very hot, so be prepared to sweat. And it's never a bad idea to have the audience at least somewhat lit. Some acts like to have all the focus on themselves, but it's never a bad idea to see the people in the crowd, especially if your act includes audience participation.

What to Do with Your "Off" Arm

You've got everything set. Your technique is faultless. Your material is hilariously funny. You're prepared for the big audition set. You get onstage, the first joke is a hit, and you're basking in the laughter and applause when you realize the hand not working your figure is twitching. It's kind of flapping nervously against your leg, drawing attention to itself and away from your act.

There are no fine points to ventriloquism. Your off arm—the arm not manipulating the figure—has to be part of the performance, rehearsed and prepped the same way the rest of your show was built. Fortunately, this is not an overwhelming task. With a couple suggestions and directions, you'll be good to go.

Get It Involved in the Act

You could use your left hand as a pointer. When you ask your figure a question with the word *you* in it, point! For example, you might ask, "How are you?" and point right at your figure. To make the illusion even more realistic, have the figure look at the finger that is pointing.

You can always use your off hand as a cheerleader. For example, if you introduce your figure to the crowd, you can use your hand to coerce audience applause. "I want to introduce you to my figure," you say, "Won't you help me welcome my figure!" Then motion to the audience, using your off hand as if you're asking someone to come toward you. You're waving and encouraging applause. Easy, right?

Hand motions with your off hand can only enhance your set. You can throw your hand up in the air in disgust or hit your forehead as if to say, "I can't believe it!" Make a fist and threaten your figure, rub your head or your figure's head, or pull your figure's arm as if to say, "Come back here!" Naturally, you can always put your hand in your pocket, behind your back, or at your side.

The biggest thing you'll want to do with your off hand is to make it look unaffected and spontaneous. Don't overanalyze what to do with your off hand. Do what feels right.

Working With a Rod Arm

Many ventriloquists use rod-arm figures, where one or both of the figure's arms are attached to a long, thin metal rod. The ventriloquist holds this rod (or, on occasion, two rods) in his or her off hand and manipulates the figure's arm(s).

Rod-arm figures add an extra dimension to the illusion that they're alive because they can move one or both arms, making gestures and arm movements. When you use rod arms perfectly, your act seems that much more realistic and is more enjoyable for the audience. Done well, it's fun to watch. Done poorly, it's frustrating for the audience because it's almost impossible to not pay attention to the ventriloquist manipulating the figure. (There's an old showbiz rule: "Don't let the audience see you working." If people are paying more attention to your work with the rod arms than to your routine, you're doing something wrong!)

Rod arms are usually used with soft, Muppet-like figures, and the rods are often attached at the figure's elbow or wrist. The best way to work with rod arms is to practice in front of a mirror. Your inclination will be to look at your hand as you push and pull and turn the rod, but don't. You're directing the audience to watch your off hand as you move the rod, and that's not what you want.

As with most figure manipulation practice, you need to practice and become comfortable with the rods, the way your figure's arms move, and integrating this into your performance. I can't teach you how to learn rod-arm manipulation. You just have to practice in front of a mirror, with your script, and make hand-and-arm movements in coordination with what's going on in the script. Do what feels and looks natural to you, and chances are it'll look good to your audience as well.

You can use two rods in your off hand and control both of the figure's arms—think of it as using giant chopsticks that bring the figure to life! Again, this requires practice in front of a mirror as you try to coordinate movements.

Hiccups

Because the audience will see you using the rod arms, it might add to the illusion you're trying to create, or it might hurt it. Think long and hard before introducing rod arms into your act. Remember, it's just you and your figure and the mic up there on the stage, and the audience can see everything, including you working the rod arms. Rod arms can be a very big accessory, but they're not a necessity.

As with all your ventriloquism tips and directives, doing what comes naturally and what is within your abilities will be the best action you can take.

What Are Your Performance Goals?

Each performance, each booking, and each opportunity you get to perform is precious. Stage time doesn't come easy, particularly when you're starting out. You need to identify and focus on specific ideas and concepts every time you get up in front of an audience.

Yes, you always want to give a great performance. As with everything else you've learned about ventriloquism, you need to break that down. What gets you to a great ventriloquist performance? It's a combination of your lip-control and figure-manipulation skills, joke-writing, script-writing, script-editing, stage and show preparation, and concentration. Specifically, concentrate on one particular facet of your work with every show.

This doesn't mean that you're forgetting about lip control when your goal for the set is using your off hand better. You want everything to work in synch. You're just picking one of the areas of ventriloquism to work on with each live presentation.

Start with this: your first-ever live show takes place at a business luncheon. You are given 15 minutes. It's your first time in front of people with your figure, your jokes, and your act, so you're nervous. Your goal? You want to give the audience a chance to laugh, so you're not going to speed through your material. You're going to try to get through the performance at a nice, even pace, maybe speeding up at the end to close big.

This is hypothetical, but let's just say you have a decent set for the lunch crowd. In fact, the highlight comes in the first 5 minutes, when the audience is receptive and attentive, laughing at your first few jokes and enjoying your talent. The set lags, however, and you feel as if it dragged for the last 5 or 6 minutes.

You recorded it, of course, and the playback reveals that you started strong, the audience loved your first 5 minutes of stuff, and then came a steady decline in laughter and attention span. So you have some work to do.

Go over the last few minutes of the set. You might have to edit or change material, or write all new jokes. Maybe you slowed down too much. Maybe you lost energy after the initial rush of excitement when you went onstage. So your next job will be all about starting off the same way, really well, and maintaining that energy and focus for the entire time you're onstage.

As you become more comfortable with your work and as you gain confidence, you'll have different goals with each show: maybe you'll want to nail down your TV audition set. Perhaps you think you're losing laughs because the figure isn't animated and moving enough, so you'll have to spend a couple shows getting into figure manipulation. Whatever it is—jokes, script, figure manipulation, your off arm, lip control, or other techniques—you always want to have a specific goal and area to work on. When you get something down pat, where you think it's as good as it can be, pick something else and work on it.

Every time you get to go on stage and do your new job, you are facing an obstacle course: the audience, the stage, the lighting, the microphone, the other acts, and the anxiety and nervousness you feel. Forget all that! Just pick one area to work on and make it happen. And remember to love the process!

Making the Audience Feel Comfortable

Some performers are not all that talented or skilled at what they do, but their ability to make an audience feel comfortable is second to none. This is one of those traits that come naturally to some and is harder for others. Here are some easy ways to make an audience feel comfortable as soon as you walk onstage.

First, smile! It seems like such an easy thing, something so obvious you don't have to think about it. But beginners often forget to do this, sometimes for their entire first few performances! Smiling for the audience after being introduced is a great way to put people at ease.

It helps to pretend it's a party. Your approach to a performance should be similar to the way you'd act and do things if you'd just been introduced to some strangers at a party. You want to make a good impression. You want people to like you. You want them to get to know you as quickly as possible, and you have a surprise to share with them.

Most of all, enjoy yourself. Perhaps the best way to make people feel comfortable with what you're doing is to enjoy yourself as you're doing it. Yes, there will probably be some tough shows. You might face technical problems or a rowdy audience, or you might have to follow someone getting a standing ovation. Great! All these are good experiences and the kinds of things that will make you a better ventriloquist and performer.

Stage Presence and Having Fun

Stage presence is all about audience perception. Rock stars have it. TV talk show hosts have it. Some comedians and politicians have it. You can have it, too. It's a skill that comes with stage time and practice, one that can't be taught.

It's really kind of a catch-22: you can't learn stage presence unless you're onstage performing, discovering what works and what doesn't. But you won't become a solid ventriloquist until you have great stage presence during your performance.

Don't let this deter you. Everyone goes through the process of developing a strong stage presence. Confidence will come with getting onstage and performing, having success, and seeing real results from the work you've put in. In the meantime, as you're putting together your shows, jokes, and sets; performing; and getting more acclimated to the stage, you might as well enjoy yourself! Have fun!

def•i•ni•tion

Stage presence is a quality a performer exudes, allowing him or her to command respect and attention from an audience through focus, expression, and confidence in his or her talent.

You need to know that, going into this career, there will be road bumps and dead ends. So what? Might as well enjoy yourself and everything you've accomplished. Don't forget to look forward to what you're still going to accomplish!

The Least You Need to Know

- Your preshow setup includes three basic must-haves for each performance: staging, microphone, and lighting. It's critical for you to be seen and heard.

- What you do with your off hand can enhance and intensify your act. It can also bring down your set a notch, so think carefully about what you want to do with it.

- Every time you take the stage, work on improving one area, be it lip control, figure manipulation, jokes, script, stage presence, or whatever. Don't waste stage time!

- You have to earn stage presence by performing, gaining confidence, and improving. It can be done.

- To make audiences feel comfortable, and to overcome any obstacles you might face, remember to have fun! Enjoy the process!

Chapter **20**

First Gigs

In This Chapter

- You picked up a booking! Now what?
- It cannot be stressed enough: stage time is everything
- On the lookout for places to work
- Travel tips

You've secured a booking and you're going to do the open-mic night to show the world your newfound skill. You're excited but also a little nervous. Don't worry, you'll be fine! In this chapter, I give you the ins and outs of what your first gig will likely be like so you know what to expect.

After that first spot is over, regardless of how it went, you now have the job of getting the next job. Here are those two words again: *stage time*. Stage time is everything! To help you to get out there and work, locally and farther from home, agents and bookers can assist you.

Your First Show

Here it is. You went to the local comedy club and signed up for open-mic night. Maybe you went to the coffeehouse and asked if you could open for the band on a weekend night. Or you've been asked to perform at the local grade school. You've taken the first step, and you're getting a chance to present your craft. Congratulations!

Regardless of where you're doing your first performance, you're going to be nervous. A little bit of anxiety is all right! You're only human, and everyone has to start someplace. Show business is not an easy profession, but the rewards can be big. At the same time, the competition and the fight for stage time can be fierce. Your goals have to be clearly defined for this first appearance.

What Do You Want to Do?

First, because this is your own personal opening night, pick something simple to concentrate on. You've memorized your script until you're sick of the words and you don't know why you ever thought those jokes were funny in the first place. You've rehearsed and rehearsed, and your technique is perfect. You love the way the figure looks, you're going to wear something you like, and you're beyond prepared. So why not concentrate on having fun? You deserve this night. Your work and patience and concentration have led to a chance to perform, so enjoy it!

Second, it's very, very, very rare that anyone goes onstage for the first time, blows away the room, and some Hollywood agent from the back comes up after the show and offers a billion-dollar contract. It's also rare that a first-timer goes on, does an amazing show, and is booked for another show—although that does happen on occasion. More realistically, you will go on, you'll have some good stuff happen, and you'll see where you made mistakes and have things to work on. If you're lucky, you'll be able to go back and do another spot soon.

Third—and this is vital—you will have (hopefully) recorded your set. You need to be brutally honest with yourself, even if the audience is giving you a wonderful response! What things jump out at you when you listen or watch that first set? What could you have done better? You will see and/or hear what the best parts of your set were. But where do you need work? Make a short list and decide what needs the most work. Pick one area of expertise—technique, jokes, manipulation, lip control, your reactions to the figure, or whatever you deem the most important. Then work on that as you get ready for your second set.

Don't expect too much from yourself with this first appearance. Remember why you got into ventriloquism in the first place: you wanted to share the fun and enjoyment with people. So that's your goal.

The Venue

Where you do your first performance will dictate what happens next. The comedy club is the toughest spot. This is a professional room, where people earn the money they use to pay the rent, and you'll be judged much tougher here. You are going to be compared to other full-time acts who make their living in show business. And there are going to be lots of other acts on the same bill with you, all at different stages of their careers in the biz.

You need to block out all that and concentrate on what you do and how you present your work. With any luck, you'll get to do more open mics for this club and build up a little resumé with the booker there. That might lead to some more work.

Most of the other places you might do your first set will be a little more supportive and conducive to a good show. There won't be as much competition, and therefore you won't have the same kind of anxiety. When you do shows for a Kiwanis luncheon, a meeting at a church or synagogue, or even a coffeehouse show, you'll get a nicer crowd that isn't so demanding. That's fine. But you will eventually want to go onstage in front of that tough crowd and see where you stand. The sooner the better.

One last piece of advice regarding the first show: remember the ventriloquist's basic job. (No, it has nothing to do with lip control or jokes or the song you sing with the figure!) The job is: *getting the next job!* Do some networking and meet people when your set is done. You're always looking for that next gig. Start right now!

Stage Time Is the Key

I can't stress it enough. The only way to become a great ventriloquist is to get onstage and do your job. Stage time = improvement. Stage time = networking. Stage time = confidence.

There's no way to quantify how much stage time you need to become proficient and excellent in the art of ventriloquism. It takes a stand-up comic 5 to 7 years to become a bona fide headlining act. Musicians work for 5 to 10 years with a band or different groups before they turn into "overnight sensations." Screenwriters and directors take years to finally get their first film produced. Your road is probably going to follow those professions.

At the beginning of your career, you can't make mistakes. There should be no question as to whether or not to take a job. Money doesn't mean anything at the start—you're trying to get to the point where you can demand money for your service. So you need to take every job you're offered (within reason, of course). If you can perform at a grade school one day, a senior citizen home the next, followed by a comedy club and a coffeehouse the next, that's a good schedule. You're getting valuable experience in front of audiences, learning how to deal with different situations and refining your act.

Obviously, if you live in or near a big city and have access to transportation, you'll have more opportunities to get on a stage. If you're not in a big city, you'll have to make your own stage time somehow. Either way, the more you do your job, the more you'll see your mistakes, the better you'll get at correcting them, and the faster you'll move up the show business ladder.

Getting Stage Time

Stage time goes to the performers who do the best job, show up on time, do the time they're allotted, and act professionally when they're off stage. Clearly, the entertainers who get the best audience response are going to be asked to perform again, and talent always rises to the top. You're going to break into that niche—getting the best responses and showing off your talent—by working on your craft and improving with each show you do.

Particularly when you're just starting out, you'll want to be early for any one of a number of reasons:

- ◆ You want to prepare.

- ◆ You don't want to be late.

- ◆ Sometimes other acts are late and you'll go on earlier than expected, which is always a bonus.

If you have the reputation of someone who's available and always ready to get onstage, you'll earn more stage time!

Acting as if you belong is half the battle. So you might as well start your career acting as professionally as you can. Most professional and experienced acts of all kinds—music, magic, comedy, and acting—are complimentary and supportive. Watch any awards show, and you'll see the stars and celebrities back-slapping and enjoying each other. Even if it's just for show, that kind of positivity wears off. The idea that you're supportive of someone else is not a weakness. It means you're confident and secure in what you do. So treat everyone you work with—the other acts, the wait staff, the audience, whomever—with dignity and respect. This only serves to put you in a better light, and gives you a certain air of professionalism.

Most new acts and entertainers who have been in show business for less than a year have a lot in common. They're all trying to find their persona onstage, they're not being paid much to do their act, and they're still in the practice part of their careers. It's hard to be supportive and complimentary, so that will be part of your job: looking for the best things in other people's performances and giving them some encouragement.

Be an Emcee, Get Onstage

The fastest way to get stage time in any venue where there are more than a couple acts going on is to offer to emcee. The emcee job in a comedy club is by far the fastest and best way to get stage time. It's simple: if eight acts are going up during a show, the emcee will go onstage at least eight or nine times during the evening. Yes, sometimes he or she will only be onstage for a couple minutes. But there are also times that he or she will have to kill time and perform. That's stage time!

Emceeing is probably the quickest way to build an act. It's the fastest way to learn how to read audiences, work with difficult situations, and become a better performer. It's almost like a steroid for a performer: you're constantly going onstage, you're constantly in need of a new joke or new material because you're on so much, and you're always discovering something new in your performance. If you can get yourself an emcee job in any environment, it will make you a better ventriloquist and a better act!

The benefits of emceeing don't just apply to comedy clubs, although that's the best place to hone your emcee skills. You can emcee just about anything: local talent shows, church fund-raisers, battles of the bands, charity auctions, or wherever events require a host to introduce people and keep an evening of presentations or entertainment moving.

If emceeing isn't your cup of tea, that's fine. You can get stage time by making yourself accessible to a club or theater or performance space. Tell the venue you're willing to come in on a moment's notice to perform. This means you might be getting called to fill in for a cancelled act, and that call might come at any time of day. It means you might have to go onstage in tough situations, like at the end of a night of comedy, when the room is close to empty and has only a few people left.

Stage time is similar to a job interview. You're putting your best foot forward in the beginning, trying to make a good impression, while showing why you're more qualified for the job than the next act. You'll be tested and challenged. Many people are vying for the same thing you want, so all the little things will help make you attractive to the bookers: being on time, being flexible, doing the prearranged time and not going 20 minutes over, working well with others, etc.

Of course, the fastest way to get stage time is also the most difficult way. If you have an act that's so entertaining, so hilariously funny, so unforgettably well executed that audiences are shouting your name as they leave the show room, you won't have any trouble getting stage time.

Your goal is to have an act that is entertaining, funny, and unforgettable. You're at the starting line, and remember: this isn't a sprint, it's a marathon.

Finding Places to Work

Everything is connected to everything in show business. Once you've been bitten by the showbiz bug, once you've performed and earned some laughter and enjoyed some success, you're going to be desperate to repeat your experience. You're going to have to find more places to work.

And if you didn't have a good experience that first time onstage? Don't let that stop you from trying to find another place to perform, another chance to get onstage, another opportunity to ply your craft. It's almost as if you'll want to get back up there and prove to yourself that the first performance was a fluke. You're better than that, and you *will* do better next time!

Here's another way to look at it: you're going to work in every possible venue that uses acts like yours. Saying "no" to any possible job in the first few months or even couple years of your career is a step backward. Frankly, as a beginner, you don't have the right to say "no" to a decent venue and a request for your talents.

There are exceptions, of course. If you have no interest in performing for children, don't! If you don't want to be a raunchy comedy act, don't agree to do a show at a bachelor's party. This is common sense. But if you're offered a 15-minute set at a country club before a dance band goes on, you're foolish to reject that, especially if you don't have any other plans for that night!

Without question, you'll have more opportunities for stage time in big cities than anywhere else. You won't have a lot of places to work if you live in a rural area. It's up to you to do some research and find places that might hire a brand-new, just-starting-out ventriloquist.

City clubs and coffeehouses will have open-mic nights during which you'll have the chance to get onstage and begin working on your act. This is the accepted and traditional way to start a showbiz career, and it's worked for many decades as a way for people to break into a career.

> **Suitcases**
>
> It's true that booking agents are the best at what they do, but in the beginning, you don't need an agent to help you find stage time. In fact, it's better that you don't use an agent to start. You'll get an education in show *business* going it on your own, and you'll see how everything operates. Negotiating contracts and movie deals won't be part of your career in the beginning. Besides, you're not just building your ventriloquist act, you're building your livelihood. The more you know about it, the better equipped you'll be to make decisions in the future.

Theater groups and arts communities in metropolitan areas have performance spaces for solo performances known as *one-man/woman shows*. This theatrical performance is much more involved than the short 5- to 10-minute set you've worked on for your act. This unaccompanied program is much more ambitious, especially to start out, but you can apply the same techniques you've learned, while adding a story line or narrative to your performance (say, "The Life and Times of a Modern-Day Ventriloquist"). Performing a one-man/woman show requires building a relationship with the creative director at the theater and coming up with a script for a 70- to 90-minute performance.

def•i•ni•tion

A **one-man/woman show** is a theatrical form started as a performance piece for stand-up comics who deliver a monologue in front of an audience, usually centered around a theme so the jokes and stories accommodate a wider scope than just giving the audience some laughs.

These same kinds of places—clubs, coffeehouses, theaters—might exist in suburban or rural areas, but there definitely won't be as many. In that case, you will have to find your own audiences and venues. You'll have to be creative.

One place to start is your chamber of commerce. You can get information on local clubs and organizations that have meetings in various places close to where you live, and you can provide your services as a ventriloquist at their next engagement. Try the public library and the school system, offering to perform for free. Sometimes you can tie in your act with programs and themes they're running (which is a great exercise in writing comedy for a particular audience!). If there are local hotels and banquet halls, you can drop off your contact information and ask that if clients ask for entertainment, your name be thrown into the mix.

Although living in a major city makes it a little easier to find ways to get stage time, don't let where you live deter you from doing the act you've prepared. Don't be discouraged if it takes you a while to find that first performance, and if you can't find steady weekly work, don't despair! Do the best you can!

Finding Regular Work

Roughly, most novelty acts and/or comedy acts (including music) have careers that might work something like this: Pat, a ventriloquist act, begins working at an open mic in a restaurant/bar where locals can get up and perform once a week. Pat goes up three weeks in a row, improving a little bit each time, getting to know the folks who work the club. One of the reasons Pat has improved so quickly? Pat has also gone onstage in four other rooms around town during the past couple weeks. She has eight 10-minute performances under her belt, and she's getting used to being in front of audiences.

The club manager also handles all the bookings and has had a fallout—one of the comedians for next week's show has cancelled. So the manager asks Pat if she could come in and do two shows next Friday and Saturday nights. Pat asks if these are paid spots on the show. The manager says, "Not for your first time. I want to see how things go. If things go well, you'll get the going rate the next time you're booked." Pat agrees. She has to cancel a couple open-mic nights to do the weekend at the club, but that's part of the game.

Pat works as an emcee and opening act for all four shows that weekend. The sets go well, and Pat has fun talking with the audience and making the crowd feel comfortable, as she brings up the professional touring acts—a guitarist and a comic—during the show. The club manager offers Pat four weekends over the next 2 months, $50 per show, $200 for the two nights. Pat says "Yes!"

Two weeks later, Pat plays the same club but doesn't have the same success with all four shows as the first week. No matter. This is showbiz, and nothing ever goes perfectly. The first show Friday is okay, but the second show doesn't have the audience response she likes. Same with the first show Saturday, but the second show goes very well, so Pat is encouraged. She's more encouraged when one of the acts on the show, the "headliner," gives Pat the name and number of a booker. Pat calls the booker, who has a weekend gig in 1 month about 45 minutes away. The pay is similar: $50/show for three shows in two nights. Pat says "Yes!"

Six months later Pat takes stock. She's got eight two-night paid bookings over the next 6 months, mostly in the $50- to $75-per-show range. She's still doing three or four open-mic nights every month, not for the money (obviously) but for the stage time. With some 40 performances over the past 6 months, Pat has dropped most of her original material from that first set and now has a solid 15 minutes that get good laughs throughout, plus another 5 minutes she's working on.

The problem isn't money (Pat hasn't quit the ol' day job); the problem is the same one she started out with: stage time. The open-mic nights and paid weekend performances aren't giving Pat enough. So Pat contacts the guitarist from that first weekend gig at the club and a comic she's become friendly with, and the three of them pitch a show idea to a coffeehouse for a Sunday night performance, "Music, Ventriloquism, and Comedy: Three People Who Can't Grow Up." The coffeehouse agrees to the concept, paying the entertainers $50 each. They take eight straight Sunday nights to build an audience.

After the sixth Sunday night at the coffeehouse, Pat gets a call from a booker for a legitimate comedy club about an hour away. The run is Wednesday thru Sunday, eight shows, $300 for the week. Pat jumps at it. The week goes well, and the comedy club rebooks her for another engagement 6 months down the road. The booker calls the following Monday with another offer: 2 straight weeks of comedy club runs, $400 per week, in 4 months.

Pat has found a way to get regular work.

This is just an example, and it's not typical, because nothing is typical in show business. But the keys to finding regular work are very clear here. First, Pat found as much work as possible, not putting all her eggs in one basket at the beginning, working a couple different open-mic nights. When an offer came in—working an entire weekend for free—Pat didn't balk. Instead of saying, "I'm getting ripped off!" Pat went in, did a great job, won the manager's trust, and got another booking.

The weekend job led to a paid weekend job, which led to another paid weekend job. Pat had to do some thinking when it appeared she hit the wall, but by coming up with a show idea and a way to make it profitable for the coffeehouse, she was able to get offers to go on the road. All the while, Pat kept writing comedy and performance material (she had dropped all the original lines from the open-mic night by the second or third weekend job), and handled every situation professionally.

Pull Strings

In addition to stage time, here's another phrase you need to learn: *bookings lead to bookings.* Every time you get onstage, you're auditioning—even if you're trying some new material, you never know who might be in the audience! You never know what might happen. One of the allures of being in the business is that you could wake up tomorrow and everything has changed.

Pat's going to come to a crossroads soon: quit the day job and go on the road? Or stay close to home and keep working on material in the local joints where she can easily get work?

Hopefully Pat has some kind of web presence by now, a website or social networking page like Facebook where fans and people who enjoy her act can go, check her schedule, and maybe download some videos to show their friends and family. Because that's the next thing Pat will have to do: make a video. This video will help sell her act to future buyers and clients. Today, there's no more important tool for a ventriloquist—or any live performer—than a video. This can be a DVD Pat can send to prospective bookers or a digital download on a social networking site or webpage. Video is the modern-day business card.

There are a variety of ways to make video. The best of all possible worlds for Pat is to contact a videographer or professional video company to come and set up three cameras one weekend in the original club where Pat worked. The shoot would be advertised on Pat's website, and the evening would be promoted as a "live DVD taping!" To cut costs, Pat has asked two other acts to be taped and each pay for a third of the cost for the shoot.

The other choice is to do a one-camera shoot with a pro videographer or even have a friend do the videotaping. Pat doesn't have to stop there, though. With cheap and available digital video recorders, there's no reason Pat can't do some special recordings—just Pat and her figures, no audience, doing some short, 3-minute or less video blogs (or *vlogs*)—for the website. These comedy shorts work on a couple levels. They help prospective clients and fans see Pat at work, and this kind of stuff shows people in the TV and film industry that Pat can work with the camera.

Finding regular work is just as much a part of the ventriloquist's repertoire as lip control, figure manipulation, and script-writing. Combining professionalism, creativity, and a calendar of events means the working ventriloquist will always have a place to use his or her abilities.

From our little scenario with Pat, it would appear she is on the way to a career as a ventriloquist. There will be plenty of choices as her act grows and becomes more polished. Pat might reach the point where she either can't or doesn't want to do her day job anymore. Comedy clubs are an obvious choice for many ventriloquists, but Pat is probably going to be contacted by a variety of booking agents in the near future.

Cruise lines, for example, are always looking for quality ventriloquists. Some agents handle nothing but the cruise line entertainment industry. Once an act like Pat is in the cruise system, there's untold work available and it's easy to schedule an entire year (or more!) in advance. If that's the case, Pat has to decide if she wants to travel the world, leave the country for weeks on end, and commit to a certain lifestyle.

Theme parks, zoos, and other family-style entertainment venues are also great places for ventriloquists, offering the security of long-term contracts in lieu of advancing one's career on other fronts.

The working ventriloquist is in a unique position. His or her act can appeal to a broad part of society, or it can be a comedy club–style act that appeals to the shot-and-a-beer crowd. Ventriloquists are being featured on TV shows, and they're headlining Las Vegas. Cruise lines use ventriloquists in their advertisements. There's clearly demand for good ventriloquism, so it's up to you to follow the plan and find regular work!

Have Ventriloquist Figure, Will Travel

Travel—it's a nuisance for anyone who depends on personal appearances to earn their keep. To get a full understanding of what travel encompasses for the working ventriloquist, I've broken it down into four basic groups:

- Packing
- Flying
- Driving
- Hotel/rental car

Packing is the place to start, because it will take a lot of time and consideration.

Smart Packing

The discussion of cases in Chapter 2 gave you an idea of what your choices in cases are—custom, hard, or soft. Each has a purpose and a different role. The custom case is the ideal for the expensive fiberglass or wood-headed figures, made to order and perfectly fit. With a hard or soft case, you're going to have to pack these carefully with an eye on a couple things.

First, you want to "pack small and play big." That is, try to get as much into your cases or bags as possible: your figures, any props you need with the figures, your clothes and travel essentials, and anything else important. It's almost as if, with every trip you take to perform your job, you're taking a family with you. You'll definitely need to make a checklist and double-check that you've got everything. If your figure wears shoes, a hard hat, or something that can cause damage if it shifts in the case or bag, you'll have to secure it somehow.

Always pack your bag with the understanding that travel is subject to delay. Even with all conditions being perfect (weather, traffic, mechanical issues), there's still a chance you'll either be right on time for your performance or have just a minute or two before you go on. In those circumstances, you'll be well served to have prepared before you left. If you have packed so you can grab your figure and props and get them onstage in a matter of seconds without much set-up, your audience, your client, and you will all be happy. You arrived on time, or close to it, and instead of taking 20 minutes to set up, you were ready to go on right away.

When it comes to packing your figures, take nothing for granted and take every precaution you can. If you're using an expensive, custom-built fiberglass figure, there's no reason to pack the most delicate part of it in a case, custom-made or otherwise. A better choice is to invest in another bag, custom-built or not, that can carry the delicate piece of the figure—the head, with all its controls and machinery—independent of the case. This is particularly crucial if and when you're traveling by airline because so many bad things can happen to checked luggage. Even if you're driving from gig to gig, pack your figure's head (or whatever the most delicate part of the body is) separately. A lined bag or soft pillowcase that fits over the head inside this additional head bag (maybe we should call it a "head case"?) further protects bumps and nicks that might occur in transit.

It just isn't a good idea to check a soft case with a hard figure, especially the head. It's going to get jostled and pushed and dropped. If you're using soft figures, you still might want to invest in hard cases. The soft case can work with the soft figures, of course—especially if your packing is well thought out and planned. If you're packing clothing and essentials with your figures, remember to have everything in a place that can easily be unpacked if you need to get on stage in a matter of seconds and start your set! It's best to have your figure dressed and stage-ready right out of the case, but this isn't always possible. However you pack, planning ahead is essential!

These packing rules apply to both flying and driving. In the end, you need to do what is right for you and your figure(s). Common sense should prevail above all! Prepare!

Flying the Friendly Skies

Packing is the perfect lead-in to flying because you'll no doubt be checking luggage if you fly. The first red flag for the ventriloquist is the Transportation Security Association (TSA), whose job it is to protect us all and ensure we're safe when we fly.

The TSA baggage handlers will, no doubt, be opening your cases and looking through everything you've packed. You can leave them notes ("Please don't move this!" or "Please be careful if you pick this up!"), and they sincerely try to make as little change in the packing of every case they see, but there are always exceptions. It's very important you pack things in a simple, easy-to-get-to way. Not just so you can get onstage quickly in case you're late for a show, but to make things easy for the TSA handlers.

You'll also incur luggage and checked-bags fees with almost all the airlines now (unless you've flown so many miles with one particular airline and have joined its "elite flyer" program, whereby the luggage handling fees are waived). Be prepared to pay extra for every bag you check.

Suitcases

Each airline has its own rules about size and weight. For the ventriloquist, particularly the one using hard and custom cases, the baggage charges can be prohibitive. Check with the airline you are flying for any specific charges you might have to pay. Sometimes explaining the contents of your luggage will get you some points, and a reduction or erasure of the fee, but don't count on it!

Another choice for travel with your bags and cases is to use a delivery company like UPS or FedEx to deliver your bags to the venue for you. The charges for such services can be very expensive, but check into it. You might save some heartache and hassle by sending your figures—or at least the bodies—ahead of you.

If you have a booking well ahead of time, it makes sense to book your airline ticket as soon as possible. The airlines offer lower rates 4 to 6 weeks ahead of a flight. Waiting until the week or the day before to buy your ticket can be expensive. If your client is paying the fare, you don't want to have to explain why your airplane ticket cost $2,400 and you sat in first class because it was the only seat left. That's a great way to *not* get booked again!

On the Road Again: Driving

Many acts, including magicians, comedians, and presumably ventriloquists, fit into a category called "40-milers." Others are called "100-milers." These acts only do performances within 40 or 100 miles of their home. They have no desire to fly across the country, regardless of the money. So they drive.

Packing for a drive is the same as packing for a flight. Driving entails a few differences: you need to factor in plenty of time to get to the job. If you have a nice club date 30 miles from your house on a summer Friday, and you know traffic will be nightmarish around rush hour, don't wait until 4:45 P.M. to leave! Go at 2:30 P.M. and be early! Remember that getting and keeping work in a competitive business is predicated on professionalism.

If you're driving long distances, give yourself plenty of time to rest. Pull over if you're tired. No need to ruin a great performance by totaling your car—or worse!—on the drive home.

Now, before you attempt anything dumb: for those of you living in major metropolitan areas that have high-occupancy vehicle (HOV) or carpool lanes, you really shouldn't put a hat and sunglasses on your figure, set him in the passenger seat, and have him pretend to dialogue with you as you drive with one hand on the steering wheel and one hand on the figure, making it look like two "people" are in the car!

Hotel and Rental Car

This is just basic stuff: the staff who clean and care for your room deserve to be tipped, even if it's just a couple dollars for a night. They work hard and deserve that, especially if you leave out your figure and scare them half to death when they open the door to your room and see it at first!

Request first-floor hotel rooms if you can. Lugging those bags can be a pain, even if the bigger ones do have wheels!

And if or when you rent a car, get a car large enough to handle all your cases!

The Least You Need to Know

- ◆ Don't expect too much from your first performance. Pick one thing you want to do perfectly, concentrate on that, have fun, and then move on!

- ◆ What is the key to your success? That's right—stage time! And there are simple things you can do to get yourself onstage regularly, besides being the brilliant performer you are!

- ◆ Finding those first few jobs might seem difficult, but once you're in the flow, you'll have more opportunity. You'll eventually have a chance to get some regular work. It's out there—go get it!

- ◆ You're probably going to end up traveling, at least somewhat, as a vent, whether you're a 40-miler who never goes farther than 40 miles from home, or you're flying around the world.

Chapter 21

Working Kid Shows

In This Chapter

- ◆ Working for children
- ◆ Tips for preparing for different age groups
- ◆ Niching your way into kid markets
- ◆ Tailoring your act for tots

The children's market is huge, and many entertainers work for kids because their acts are perfect and there's a need for good kids' entertainment. Children are an exceptional audience for ventriloquists. The kids' show market breaks down into different groups, though, and you need to know the difference between toddler shows, big-kid shows, and family shows.

There's a certain etiquette required in the children's market, and that bleeds into working for spiritually based venues like churches and temples. Obviously, profanity and vulgarity are prohibited, but there's more to it than that.

If one in five members of your audience is under age 13, you're doing a children's show, no matter the venue. Festivals, fairs, and libraries are similar in that the audiences are the same age. There are differences, of course—they don't serve beer at the library like they do at the festival, right? Writing your act, or adding material and jokes that pertain directly to the audience you're working for in schools or libraries, will make you a hit with the crowd and the staff.

Working for Kids of All Ages

There's a prevailing impression that working for children is somehow beneath most professional entertainers and should be reserved for second-rate novelty acts who can't make it in with the club/casino/theater crowd. Hogwash! This is a huge market, tailor-made for a ventriloquist who can deliver the goods and give children an exciting, expert 45-minute performance.

Who Are You Working For?

The first thing you need to do when you're booked for a children's show is find out who the children are. There are two very different subgroups within the group known as "kids": small children and bigger kids.

Small children are ages 2 to 6. Their base of reference is narrow because they've only been on the earth for a couple years. Comedy and music and performance have an entirely different meaning for them, and your show has to cater to the things they understand.

Big kids—the 7- to 12-year-old crowd—have built up a wealth of TV-watching time over the past couple years, and they've seen a lot of show business. You can perform regular routines and jokes for this group, and they'll get you.

A third but just as important group is the family show. When you're booked to do a family show, you're really doing a kid's show. Or better said, you're doing a kid's show for adults. Here's a good rule of thumb: if your audience is 20 percent or more children (1 in every 5 audience members under age 13), you're doing a children's show.

Hiccups

Sometimes as a children's entertainer, you will find yourself performing in front of four or five audiences in one. You'll have senior citizens, adults, young adults, children, and very small children in the crowd. In this instance, you have to play to the youngest people in the room; otherwise you'll lose their attention.

Kid shows are unlike all other shows. From the moment you walk into a venue for a kid's program, whether you're at a school or in someone's home, your approach will go a long way toward the success of your performance. Children pick up on everything, including whether the entertainer is nervous, considers the job "beneath" him, or has little interest in being there. If you have genuine respect for the folks in the audience and some energy to go with your production, you're halfway home, regardless of the material you present.

Encouraging Audience Participation

We live in an interactive society, where children *expect* to be part of any show (this used to be called "audience participation"). Thanks to computers, video games, etc., kids today have been brought up with the idea that they're not only observing entertainment, but they're also a part of the show! If you can work two or three short audience-participation bits into your routine, you'll be all the better for it.

Here are a couple audience participation ideas to get you started:

With all children's shows, but particularly the toddler shows, you should set some ground rules. Tell everyone you're happy and excited to be there. Tell them they'll have a good time. Tell them—and make this very explicit—that everyone has to listen. You can take this further and ask them to clap as loud as they can. Ask them to clap as softly as they can. Ask them to whisper "Hello." Then ask them to shout "Hello!" This sets you up as the authority for the show you're going to do, and it serves to get the kids' attention right away.

Hiccups

Don't start your act with an audience participation routine! You'll find that children who've seen some good kids' entertainment will sit right up front and beg you to pick them to be part of your show. You'll have to defuse this situation by doing some set material for at least a third of your program, a part of your show during which you can look around the audience and find children who are genuinely enjoying themselves but maybe don't expect to be called up onstage.

Don't just pick anyone (or the loudest child right down front) as a helper or an aid in your audience participation routine. Try to get someone representing every age group in the audience (it's okay to use adults!). Get someone from every part of the crowd, too—in the back, up front, and to the sides. If there are children, particularly older children, sitting right next to a teacher or authority figure, they're probably there for a reason, so maybe just skip over them for now.

If a child is seated by him- or herself, you might be inclined to think, *I feel bad for that kid—I'll get him or her up here and make them a star!* Bad move. If a child is seated alone, that's usually a sign he or she is uncomfortable or awkward and probably won't want to come onstage anyway. It's not your job to "save" the kids. Do your best to entertain them, and even *include* them (as you will everyone in your audience) with eye contact and a smile, but resist the urge to bring them up onstage.

Perhaps most important—and this goes for every person in every audience and every situation—don't use anyone as the brunt of your jokes or belittle any child in any way. Your helpers are not hecklers. You asked them to be a part of your show, so treat them well. If anything, the jokes should be directed at you.

It's always fun for an audience to help with your act. If your figure is despondent or frustrated that it can't move its arms, maybe someone in the audience can come up onstage and help it by moving its arms. Better yet, have your young audience member put their arms under the armpits of the figure, thereby becoming a pair of working arms and hands for the figure! You'll have great fun with this, as your audience member helps the figure smooth its hair, scratch an itch, scratch *you*, etc.

You can also get someone in on the act by having some props your figure needs—perhaps a new hat, or a shirt, or shoes. Have an audience member help dress the figure.

Kid Show Basics

Here is some basic children's show information, some of which applies to all audiences and all shows.

Be aware that your figures or puppets might scare children (and adults). This is a not-uncommon reaction these days. There are some movies and books out there that make puppets look pretty frightening. Soft figures are always a better choice with children, especially the toddler set. For the adults who are scared? Uh … no comment.

On occasion, you'll have an unruly child in your audience. He or she can be any age and any background, but they usually sit up front and want to be the center of attention. They'll say things out of turn, and they'll constantly disrupt your show (if you allow it). These children may not even know they're being unruly, having been raised in front of a computer or TV screen or in a situation in which they're encouraged to speak up. Handling this situation quickly and painlessly will go a long way toward establishing your confidence with children's programs. Your mental checklist in this situation is: don't panic, explain (again) in sincere tones that it's important for everyone to listen, and tell them, "I know you want to be a good audience member."

Sometimes, especially after a show, children will want to handle your figure. You can allow that if you want, but be aware the consequences might be severe—they might break or damage controls, break a string or an eyebrow, drop or harm the figure accidentally, etc. Of course, you can say, "No, I'm sorry," which is a disappointment to the kids. Another choice is to have a kid-friendly puppet or figure in your act that the children can play with after your show.

A good time-killer and fun way to introduce your figures to a children's audience is to beg applause. You can coax children to applaud and whoop and holler as you introduce your figure, who "will only come out if it thinks the audience really wants to see it." So you tell the children to applaud, but the figure won't come out. You have the kids applaud louder and holler, but the figure still isn't convinced. On the third try, the kids will make a *lot* of noise, and you'll bring out your figure. Three times is enough with this bit. Don't push for four.

Your Kid Show Breakdown

You can break down your children's show performance by time, and that might help you better prepare and plan your act. Your running order might look something like this:

Opening. Greet the audience and explain what you expect. Ask everyone for loud applause, for soft applause, to whisper hello, or to shout hello. This should take about 6 minutes.

First figure/first routine. Audience applauds for introduction of the figure, the figure comes out, and you do your first routine. Six minutes.

Audience participation. Invite an audience member to come up onstage and help the figure put on some clothes and sing a song. Six minutes.

First figure put away/second figure routine. You help your audience member helper go back to their seat and then put away the first figure. You get your second figure out and perform. Seven minutes.

Second audience participation. Another audience member is requested to come up onstage, and he or she is the arms for the figure. Eight minutes.

First and second figure together. You help the second audience member helper back to his or her seat, and ask for "encouragement" from the audience to get the first figure back. You do a short routine and song with both figures. Eight minutes.

Question/answer. This is a great way for the audience to interact with your figures and for you to learn what children like. In the beginning, you'll only want to do this for a couple minutes, but this will grow to the point that you'll be able to do an entire 30-minute set just answering children's questions! Five minutes.

Good-bye. When closing, you are in control and you'll tell the children to return to their rooms, meet their teachers, or whatever the booker/school/synagogue/parent wants. You can, however, offer to close out the program any way your client would like. For example: "You have been a wonderful audience! My friends and I want you to know how much we appreciate you. Now, it's time to go. Please listen to your teachers or staff, and go back to your classrooms quietly. If you had fun, let me hear you whisper 'YES!' Great! Now quietly, this group can leave first [as you point to the audience seated stage right, in the first five rows or so]."

Pull Strings

There are going to be occasions in which older kids—the 13- to 17-year-olds—are thrown in with the smaller ones. You can't help that. It's up to you, however, to make them feel as if they're part of the program and they're not being ignored. Teenagers are pop culture addicts. Part of your homework for your children's shows will be to update yourself on current pop stars, current hit TV shows, and major motion pictures—especially the horror and comedy movies written for teens—which will keep their attention from drifting too far away as you work.

Bits Sure to Get Laughs

There are some basic laugh-getting bits for children's shows, and you can use these, edit them to your own purpose, and change them any way you like.

It takes some practice, but the double-take—your figure gives you a look, looks away, and then spins its head back to stare at you, mouth open—can get a laugh.

You can also get laughs with your figure's head in a variety of ways. As you're giving a long talk, have your figure roll its head back to stare at the ceiling, shake itself, and look at you. As it does this, it slowly rolls its head back to look at the ceiling, shakes itself again, and finally dramatically rolls its head back one more time. You finally notice. "What are you doing?" you ask. No answer, just a snore. The figure went to sleep because you're so boring! Ha ha ha!

Funny sounds are a hit with the toddler set. Instead of your figure saying, "Huh?" as if it doesn't understand you, have that "Huh" drawn out, high-pitched, overexaggerated, and over the top: "*Huuuuuuuuh?!?*"

Instead of just saying "no," have the figure draw out "No" for a long time: "*Noooooooooooo ....*"

For whatever reason (this is well documented) the *K* sound is funny. So certain words, by themselves and by definition, are funny to kids. Try these in your routine, and you'll see what I mean:

- Kalamazoo (*Z* can be a funny sound, too)
- Rancho Cucamonga
- Kumquat
- Cork
- Hanky panky
- Cancun
- Kukaburra
- Can-can

Another ventriloquist classic is the look. While you're talking to the audience, the figure begins to imitate your head movements. When you shake your head "no," the figure shakes its head. When you nod your head "yes," the figure nods its head. You see and hear the children laughing. "What are you laughing at?" you ask them. The figure stares at you, you look at the figure, it looks away innocently …, you look back at the children in the audience, and the figure opens its mouth and laughs silently. The children laugh. You look at the figure again and it stops, starting again when you look back to the audience.

Finally, you look at the figure and catch it laughing at you. "Are you laughing at me?" The figure shakes its head "no." You say, "Good. You'd better not!" and look back to the audience, at which point the figure begins to laugh silently again for the benefit of the kids. You can use this up to three times during a 45-minute performance.

Schools as a Market

There are two kinds of school programs you'll be asked to do.

In-Classroom Workshop

This is the easiest one there is: you're asked to go into a classroom and perform for a few minutes—15 to 20 minutes maybe—and then answer questions and conduct a how-to workshop about ventriloquism and vent figures. This can be a lot of fun, you won't need to do much preparation, and you'll become comfortable working in front of children.

These classroom shows are a great place to use a sock puppet. You're up close and personal with the kids so everyone can see a sock puppet. You can show the students how to make it, manipulate it, synchronize words, and bring the puppet to life. You might bring in some extra props—yarn for hair, felt for eyes, duct tape to hold the props in place, and so on. If you're really ambitious, this can become a class-wide workshop. You show the children how to do it, answer their questions, and leave the sock puppet with the class. They can then spend a day or two making their own sock puppets and writing a script.

It's an easy sell: it works as a theatrical production, it works as a writing class, and it's a great time-killer. As a bonus: teachers like these kinds of projects that cross-reference more than one subject.

School Assemblies

This is a little tougher—okay, a lot tougher. You'll be asked to do the school assembly in a variety of venues: you might be in the school auditorium or theater, with ideal acoustics and a great sound system. You might be in a gymnasium with marginal acoustics and no sound system. Most of the time your setup will be something in between—in a cafeteria or all-purpose room that has some sort of stage and maybe some lighting.

First things first: you'll need a sound system. It's always best to have your own system, which you will come to know well the more you use it. You don't need giant Marshall amps and woofers and fireworks—this isn't a rock 'n' roll show (although that would get the kids' attention!). You need a portable public address (PA) system that fits in the back of your car or minivan, sets up quickly and easily, and fills a room that seats up to 300 people with good, clear sound. You'll need a good microphone, a microphone stand, and an amplifier. You'll also need the accompanying cords and speakers that complete the system. Many kinds of equipment fill the bill here, and you can find them at your local music store or online (see Appendix B for some sources).

Next comes the challenging part. The school assembly is a part of every school year in every district. Conferences are held where acts audition for teachers and principals, but just as many school assembly entertainers get work based on the quality of their presentations and the value they add to the class work and curriculum for grade schools across the country. Make no mistake: this is a lucrative market for a number of entertainers. To be successful here means you're working four or five times a week, maybe even twice a day.

To make yourself profitable while satisfying a need in schools, you need to write a show based on subjects and premises the teachers and staff believe to be important. There are two ways to go: you can write your act about one of the current buzzwords in public education, or you can find out what the school would like you to base your presentation on.

You're better off choosing a subject, writing a show centered around that subject, and marketing it to schools. By finding out what each individual school wants, you're opening yourself to a variety of problems, not the least of which is the fact that you can't please everyone. If the school gets the choice, there will be meetings and suggestions, and they might want you to cover three or four concepts for fear someone will feel left out. By taking control of the situation and giving the teachers your show outline, you take all the guesswork out of the process.

It's best to concentrate on one subject or premise, and write your show around it. Some of the buzzwords popular in public schools today include:

- ◆ *Bullying.* A presentation that shows how bullying is wrong, how bullying is cowardly, and how to stand up to bullies will be popular in the school market.

- ◆ *Self-esteem.* Children feel picked on and rejected in so many ways in schools today that a show based on self-esteem will resonate with students and staff alike.

- ◆ *Math/reading/art and music.* These are all courses of study that need reinforcement in school. By making math fun, reading exciting, and art or music come to life, you're helping the teachers do their job in a fun and exhilarating way.

As you work more and more as a school assembly performer, you will get firsthand information about the newest buzzwords, and you can change your act every year accordingly.

The best way to write your school assembly show is to nail down your premise. Let's pick mathematics as your subject. You'll want to make five or six points about math in your 45-minute set. Using your figure (a great word when math is the subject!), you can show children how they'll use math in real life at the

> **Suitcases**
>
> Don't choose history as one of your subjects in your show. History can be construed, and it can be a source of frustration for people. It's not worth losing jobs and angering anyone over. You can reference history, but don't make it the sole focus of your act for school assemblies.

bank or while keeping track of how many points their favorite team scores. There's a case to be made that math "makes you smart," but still, math can be fun. And whether you know it or not, you use math every day—telling time, buying candy or drinks, using the lock on your bike or at your locker—even though you don't realize it.

There will be lots of opportunity for humor in your script, and you'll no doubt be asked to return for a future engagement. And that's the whole point! You satisfied a need, and you earned a client—not to mention a paycheck!

Houses of Worship

Similar to school assemblies, but closely linked to family shows, the spiritual market is growing every year. If you're of the same Jewish or Catholic faith, you'll have a big leg up on other entertainers when trying to find work in those markets. Most other religious-based groups don't care so much if you're not a member of the faith. They're much more concerned with you inadvertently using a keyword or phrase insensitively. Mutter "Jesus!" when you stub your toe going onstage, and you insult the entire church congregation who came to see your act.

Every religion has certain faith-based ideals and doctrines that should not be broached from the stage. A routine about marriage and raising children might play well for you in the secular world, but in some religious faiths, those things are holy and not to be made fun of.

If you get booked for a program with a religious faith you don't know much about, your best bet is to do some research and ask some questions:

- Are there any subjects I shouldn't touch on?

- Is there a particular word or phrase the church/temple finds profane?

- Is there anything I should know before I perform?

You need to do your homework!

On the other hand, a growing number of acts work solely for their faith. The Christian entertainment industry is a multibillion-dollar business, with TV specials, hit recordings, and DVDs. A ventriloquist with working knowledge of the Bible can have a career doing nothing but college shows. There are (and always have been) Jewish comedians, and now there's an entire market for Jewish entertainment that plays to synagogues and the flock therein.

Many of these faith-based shows are come-one-come-all affairs, in which the audience is made up of everyone in the extended family: mom, dad, son, daughter, stepson, stepdaughter, grandmother, grandfather, the kooky cousin, and the close friends and

their kids. You're really playing to four or five different audiences: toddlers, big kids, teens, adults, and grandparents. Doing a 45-minute act for this crowd is a challenge without having to worry about insulting people by slipping up and saying something that goes against their faith or doctrine. It's up to you to be prepared. The payoff is good because there is money to be made. One bad mistake during a show, however, will set you back months.

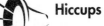

Hiccups

Certain denominations of the Christian Church believe an animal puppet that talks—known as anthropomorphism—is sacrilegious. Knowing that before you do your 20-minute talking-chimpanzee routine is probably a good thing.

Festivals and Library Shows

At first glance, these are two disparate and completely separate programs. But the similarities are so close they deserve their own section. For starters, the performance space for festivals and libraries is a real crapshoot. At a music festival, you might be asked to perform between superstar music acts, or you might be relegated to a tent in the back of the grounds, where face-painting and hay wagon rides are going on as you perform. The library show will be less frenetic, but the performance space might be extremely uncomfortable, in the basement or a corner that hasn't been used in some time.

The real joy of these shows is that the subject matter is up to you. Usually, audiences are made up of the younger set—small children and bigger kids in the 6- to 8-year-old range—so you're not doing lots of big routines. You're keeping things simple. Your set will consist of reactions and sounds as opposed to lots of punch lines. You're probably only going to do a 30-minute show, so that makes things pretty palatable, too.

Obviously a program about reading and the joy of books is going to be a hit with libraries, so you can kill two birds with one stone if you write a show about reading for your school assembly program.

The key to both festivals and libraries is to be flexible, be prepared for very young audience members, and keep your performance time tight and crisp. A 30-minute show—40 at the most—should suffice for this crowd. You probably won't be performing in the optimal performance space, and that's okay.

Pull Strings _____

Most libraries and schools will have a theme or a slogan for the year that will be displayed on a banner or sign out in front of the building as you drive up. Working this into your act, in even the most mundane way, will endear you to the client.

This also works for corporate clients when you do shows at their conventions and conferences. Finding out about this slogan before you arrive at the venue, and having a specific routine or song written for it, makes you a hit before you even utter a word onstage.

Kid-Proofing Your Act

So you've been asked to do a show at your nephew's school in a couple weeks, but you've never worked with children so you're not sure what to do. It's okay! You're going to do a great show, you'll be the hero of the family, and your nephew will think his aunt or uncle is the coolest.

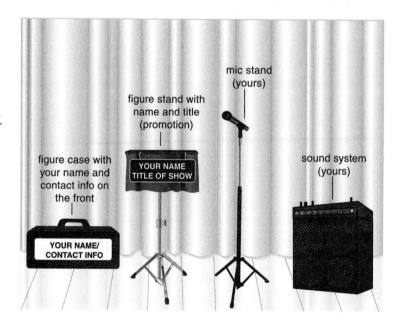

Here's the typical setup for a children's show performance. Bring your mic and sound system, use the figure stand and case as promotion pieces with your name and basic contact information displayed.

Obviously, if you've been working comedy clubs and casino lounges, you'll want to stay away from the profanity and the bedroom and bathroom jokes. But how else can you tailor your show to your nephew's age group? Call your nephew's teacher. What's the class or the school working on? What's the slogan in the media center? What's something the children are working on this year as a school? When you get that information, add it to your act.

What are you going to use for a figure when you do your children's performance? Animal puppets are big favorites with the little ones (big ones, too, really). Small animals always win the hearts of your audience. You can make this kind of figure a big hit in many ways, using audience participation (here's a great chance for a helper to come up onstage and help dress the animal puppet) and having the animal answer questions from the kids as a way to kill a few minutes.

Keeping the interest and attention of children under age 12 becomes more and more problematic as society shifts. One way to keep your act vital and keep your figures looking as if they're really alive is to keep them moving. Your figure should never be still for more than a moment or two. There should be nonstop action—the figure looks at you, it looks at the audience, it looks up at the ceiling, when it speaks it looks right at you (and you look right at it!) and then it does a double-take and looks back at the audience, it opens its mouth and does a silent laugh, it buries its head into your shoulder, and so on. You remove it with your off hand, and it burrows right back into your shoulder. The more animation and movement you get out of your figure, the more the children in your audience will buy the figure's character and personality.

You'll take whatever you can out of your club/casino/stage act and put it in the performance for your nephew, but chances are you're going to need some other stuff to fill time. You're working for children, remember, and they have energy to *burn*. Use it! If you're doing a 30-minute presentation, you'll probably want to use at least three different puppets for the show.

You can introduce them individually, asking for a round of applause for the first figure you bring out. You need a *lot* of applause for your second figure, the one that's shy and doesn't want to come out of the case. The first round of applause encourages this puppet, but it's not enough. The second round of applause is almost good enough, but the third round of applause finally brings it out!

You can soak this in for a couple minutes and then begin your routine. You'll ask for applause for figure number 3 as well, and after you put them all away, you'll want a round of applause for the figures and the audience members who helped you onstage during the audience participation bits.

Pull Strings

Want to earn some extra credit? Have the kids applaud the teacher or staff member who brought you in!

I cannot stress this enough: treat the children with a great deal of respect and dignity. If you're used to crass and ornery comedy club audiences, you'll need to reboot your system for the children. You're not going to be heckled by these kids! If they do shout out things during your performance, they're not aware they're doing anything wrong! No matter what happens, you cannot insult or disparage the kids in the crowd. Getting a laugh at a child's expense, no matter where you're working, isn't appropriate. You'll find that children will respect you if you give them respect as well.

With all audiences, but particularly with young ones, eye contact is very important. Try to sweep the audience with your eyes during your act, maintaining at least some relationship with them from the stage with a look and a nod or a smile. This is good stage etiquette, and it's going to make your performance better and more memorable for the kids.

When your set is over, hang around and talk to the kids. Seeing you up close gives them a chance to ask questions and tell you how much they enjoyed you. You might be surprised to know that even 10-year-olds have camera phones nowadays, and they love taking pictures. If you want to make a lasting impression, have pictures taken with you, your figures, and every kid who asks for a photo.

Parting Thoughts on Kid Shows

Don't underestimate the minds of kids. They're smart. They've seen a lot online, on TV, and in person. You can't just show up and expect they'll be amazed by someone with a ventriloquist figure on his or her arm. You're going to have to prepare for them the same way you put together a set for an adult show, a corporate event, or any other kind of audience. But you'll find children to be an amazing group to work for. They're thrilled by quality entertainment. Their laughter and energy is infectious.

You might enjoy the children's show as much as you like playing for adults. There's nothing wrong with that! You might end up becoming a children's entertainer and loving it. Better yet, you might find that you can work for any audience: adult, child, or family. Why limit your act in any way, especially when you're starting out? Adding the ability to entertain and educate and reinforce children can only make you a better act and a better ventriloquist. Plus, it gives you another market to work and another income stream.

One of the biggest advantages to playing for the children's/school/spiritual/family market is the great turnover of people. Every couple years, when you return to a school, library, or church to do a kid's program, you have an all-new audience! You don't have to worry about repeating material or doing the same program because the audience is brand new!

More than that, this is an unlimited market for a ventriloquist, with a never-ending upside and the opportunity for as much work as you can handle! The professional ventriloquist offers a show that combines fantasy (your figures and their stories) with real life (you, the vent) right in front of the audience, in real time. Children are as ideal an audience for your act as anyone!

> **Suitcases**
>
> The children's and family market goes beyond what this chapter has covered. Other organizations and kids settings include Boy and Girl Scouts (including annual conferences), Future Farmers of America, children's sports banquets, end-of-year awards banquets, business and corporation holiday shows, parent and teacher associations, education seminars and conferences of all kinds, library and bookstore shows, county fairs, state fairs, and street fairs—the list goes on. It's one of the biggest markets in show business!

One more note for the ventriloquist who goes into the kids and family show market: this isn't the glamorous career the vents you see on TV and in Las Vegas enjoy. This is completely different. Those acts depend on PR firms, high-powered booking agents, and bookers worried about ticket sales and the competition. Those acts have to come up with bigger, better, and more all the time. The competition is fierce, and the demands are sometimes overwhelming.

The ventriloquist who works in the children's market is independent, self-sufficient, and autonomous. He or she calls the shots and works when and as much as he or she likes. Agents don't play a big role here. Nobody makes a million dollars a year in the children's market, unless something very unexpected happens. You can make a million dollars, however, doing children's shows for all the markets mentioned in this chapter. And some people will be quite happy with a fulfilling career such as that.

The Least You Need to Know

- ◆ Three groups make up the kids' market: toddlers, big kids, and family shows. These are separate audiences, but you will sometimes play all three at once!

- ◆ Your approach to performances for kids is important because they pick up on everything. Your attitude and energy will help make your show successful.

- Children today are used to being part of the show. You're going to need some audience participation bits within your set.

- Soft and animal figures are big with kids. Be sure to keep them moving, animated, and "alive" during your set.

- In every show, you're in control from the start. Tell the children they need to listen and respect each other.

- When you're working for schools and libraries, include themes in your show that make your act marketable and needed. Reading, books, self-esteem, and bullying are perfect subjects for school shows.

Chapter 22

Enhancing Your Performance

In This Chapter

- ◆ Adding music to your act
- ◆ Bringing your other talents to the table
- ◆ The importance of staging
- ◆ Working in some improv
- ◆ A few thoughts on niching your show

Ventriloquism has been associated with two other art forms since it became an accepted entertainment skill hundreds of years ago. It is either used to make people laugh, or it is an inspiring example of music performance. You might be a great singer. You might be a decent singer. Or you might not be able to sing a lick. It doesn't matter because you're going to put music in your act and your audience will love it, no matter how good your pipes are!

Before you started this book, before you made the leap of faith to follow your dream and become an excellent ventriloquist, you did something else. Perhaps you were an accountant or a teacher. Or maybe you're a young person who loves sports. Whatever it is you have done and are doing, that's going to become part of your act in some way.

Comedy is an art form that goes beyond the nuts and bolts of writing jokes and editing them into a script. To make your performance as strong as it can possibly be, you need to stage your act, at least in your mind, as to how it will be presented and how the audience will see it. Your props need to be set, and you need to have space for audience participation bits. You'll need to go over cues for sound and lights with the tech staff.

This chapter also covers improvisation comedy, how you can use it, and how it will improve and enhance your act.

Finally, in the competitive entertainment world, what sets you apart and makes you a viable performer, one worth booking in the comedy club or at the college for the big bucks? Your show is different, it's funny, and it's the one everyone *needs* to see. Now you have to get out there, prove it, and niche yourself with every performance!

Making Beautiful Music

There's an unwritten rule to ventriloquism: you either have to be funny and deliver great punch lines, or you have to sing really well so the audience responds to not only your ventriloquism talent, but your music as well.

Work backward with me a moment. Let's say you're a very good singer, maybe a great singer who can read music, follow a lead line, and bring emotion and clarity to a song. Great! That will play into your act in ways that cannot be quantified! As a singer, you can do impressions with your figures, or have figures that look like the singers you're mimicking (if you can afford them). There are so many extra ways for a good singer to perform vent and create a memorable performance through music.

Song parodies are a natural comedy premise for the working vent. Pick a well-known classic song, maybe even something as easy as "Happy Birthday," and rewrite the lyrics. The trick is to make every other line a punch line (with punch words, the same way you learned in Chapter 13), and sing the song you're parodying really well. This works for the audience on so many levels it's overwhelming:

- You amaze them with your musical ability.

- The figure is singing, thanks to your ventriloquism skills, which amazes the audience.

- You've incorporated comedy into the process by writing funny lyrics to the song you're performing!

It's a win-win every time!

Another choice, of course, is to write and record your own comedy songs, download them to a disc or digital music player you bring with you to your shows, and either access the music via a player device onstage or have a tech person start the music on cue. You can even burn your own compositions to a CD or DVD you can sell as downloads online or as hard copy sales on-site.

The same thing goes if you're not all that great a singer. Let's say you're a marginally talented singer—you can carry a tune, but your voice isn't magnetic or majestic. It's too thin, too reedy, or too soft. No problem! You're not a music act; you're a comedian with a ventriloquist figure. You're still going to use music in your live performances, but the focus of your act is comedy. The great singer/ventriloquist will no doubt be using lots of songs and musical stuff in his or her act. You won't. You're more into the comedy, but the couple musical routines you do will be crowd pleasers. Frankly, if you rehearse and perfect the short musical bits you do in your show, people will still tell you you're a great singer and the music was their favorite part of the show!

> **Pull Strings**
>
> You'll probably have to start your vent career doing musical numbers a cappella. At most open-mic nights and in venues where anyone is allowed to go up and perform, a karaoke machine is not always available. Be prepared to sing without accompaniment.

Choosing Your Songs

First, you should start working on parody songs. Pick either very popular music everyone's heard, or pick songs your audience will know as soon as you start singing. For example, if you're doing a show at a college, performing a parody of a Barry Manilow song won't mean anything because the students won't know that song. However, any reference to popular hip-hop stars and/or alternative hit songs of the day will be immediately recognizable.

Parody lyrics don't have to be knock-down, drag-out funny. You're working within the song form, and you're also working at making people laugh. Ideally, the punch lines will come with every other line, or on the line that rhymes in the song. There are universal songs that everyone knows, of course: Christmas carols, "Happy Birthday," and Beatles songs, to name a few. Stick to these for general audiences. Write your parody by changing the song title to something that sounds similar but is funny or topical. One example might be Eric Clapton's "Cocaine." Change the title to "Propane," and change all the lyrics in the song to reflect cooking, barbecue-style, on a grill with a propane tank. Easy, right?

Your Singing Figure

As an average singer, you must make your figure sing in an over-the-top style so the audience can hear everything, but also sell the idea that the figure really can sing.

One way to make this idea work is to beg the figure to sing: "Come on! We want to hear you!" Then look to the audience, "Don't you want to hear [*insert figure's name*] sing?" The crowd will cheer for the figure, who can soak this in a little bit before saying, "Okay. I'll sing. But you have to help me!" You can act a little taken aback but agree to help out on the chorus or something.

To make this routine a winner, have the figure become more and more confident and cocky as the song goes on. Eventually, the figure is cutting you off and singing by itself, soloing, basking in the glory of its talent and musical skill.

If you're not a singer, or if you're embarrassed by the way your voice sounds, this is your lucky day! Your figure has no clue what a bad singer it is. So you can beg the figure, "No! Please, don't sing!" Your figure is nonplussed, of course, and might ask the audience if they would like to hear it sing. The crowd will, naturally, cheer for the figure. You roll your eyes as the figure jumps into a song parody or a real song and sounds terrible.

You can play this up with your figure: "That was terrible! That was some of the worst singing I've ever heard!" Your figure, of course, is clueless. "No way!" it says, "I know that was good. Better than _____," and you'll fill in the blank with a popular or not-so-popular singer of the day.

Adding Accompaniment

Eventually, you'll want to add accompaniment when you're doing a musical routine in your act. You have lots of choices here. You can burn music bits to a CD and bring it to the venue where a sound tech will have to learn the cues and press the button for the right song at the right time. Or you can have a digital music player hooked into the sound system, which you can start and stop by using your off hand. The music tech can also handle this if you do a rehearsal of what songs go where in your act so he or she gets the cue.

Some venues will have a live band or orchestra onstage when you work. You'll need some charts and sheet music so the director can learn the music and teach the musicians, and you'll need a couple rehearsals before you actually go onstage in front of an audience. Live music lends decorum to any act. If you're a good singer, this might be the best way to go.

Using Your Other Skills

What have you been doing to this point in your life? If you're a young person who just started ventriloquism, you must have been doing something else before you began reading this book and discovering your love for the art. Maybe you liked sports or chess or farming—it doesn't matter what you've been doing. You absolutely have to incorporate the knowledge and the love you have or had for that activity into your ventriloquist routines.

And if you're an adult, what was or is your job? What were your hobbies before you picked up ventriloquism? Try to work your life experience and outside knowledge into your show.

Let's say you're an accountant and you're tired of crunching numbers, so you've picked up this book. You've been practicing, and you've become pretty good at writing a joke, talking without moving your lips, and bringing your figure to life. Great! Now it's time to use all the accounting information and knowledge for your stage act. There must be inside jokes among accountants. There have to be funny experiences you've had at the office or you've heard about from other accountants. That is a subject that you should be using onstage in your live act. Talk about things you know, and find humor in the job you've had. You can share this with your figure, or you can make your figure an accounting "expert" who tries to help you or audience members with their finances and taxes.

Maybe you're too young to have had a job. You still have hobbies and things you like to do. Skateboarding? Computer games? Maybe you love art history or algebra class. Anything and everything you do for fun or even stuff you don't like but you do every day (school?) is a premise for you and your figure to discuss onstage. Your figure may want to skateboard in the Extreme Sports Olympics. There's an entire culture of skateboarding, and if you're a fan, you can use that as part of your performance— especially if you're going to be doing shows for your peers!

You can go as far as to make a figure from an object—not a person or an animal— say, a talking pencil for your routine about being an accountant. Or have your figure wear all the clothes a skater wears: helmet,

> **Pull Strings**
>
> Another way to grow as a performer and niche yourself as a ventriloquist is to force yourself to do some stand-up comedy. You'll gain some confidence, and by giving your audience a glimpse of your own persona, it will differentiate you from your figures and their personalities. In short, you'll become a stronger act.

kneepads, Vans skate shoes, tie-dye T-shirt, and so on. By making your act personal, you're sharing more than just some jokes with the audience. You're giving them a piece of yourself, whether they realize it or not.

You should be able to find a way to incorporate your day job or your other activities into your live act. Skilled in photography? You can take pictures of your audience with your figures at every performance and post them to your online social network page as a visual diary for fans to watch and keep up with. If you work as a cashier, you must have pet peeves and annoyances you want to share with folks. Now you have the perfect outlet. If you're a student, no matter what age group, you have a built-in comedy premise: school is hard, books are boring, math is impossible, and the cafeteria serves food that is inedible ("My Jell-O jumped off my tray onto the guy's behind me ... Jell-O should not have a brain!"). Whatever your background and whatever your "real life" is, make it part of your act.

Comedy and Staging

The way the audience sees you is as important as any other part of your show. You need to have a working concept of how you will set your stage—whatever stage it is, wherever it is—so everything is as easy for the audience to see and hear as possible. This includes making sure there's room for your case with the figure inside and your stool or stand for the figure, space for audience members to come onstage if you're doing an audience participation bit, and a place for the microphone stand. Make your staging a uniform procedure you go through for every show so things flow smoothly and you know what to expect before it happens.

In comedy clubs, the emcee will often ask you where you want the microphone—if you want a microphone—set on the stage. If you're using your own sound system, do a sound check and run a few lines of your act, just to be sure everything is in working order. If you're using a lapel or clip microphone, have the stage clear so you're not running into mic stands and cables on the stage floor.

If you walk onstage with your figure already on your arm, the emcee or a stage manager will have to set your stand or stool where you want it. If you're using your case as a prop during the show and retrieving your figure(s) from it during the performance, you need to be sure there's room enough for everything, including another audience member if you'll be doing an audience participation bit.

If you're using music and sound cues, rehearse with a tech at least a couple hours before your show starts, if not a number of rehearsals leading up to the show. It's a good idea to write out the cues and have them ready wherever you go. That way, even if you don't have time to rehearse, a tech can go over the cues with you just before the show, and you can outline the key points that will let them know what song to play or what lights need to be on and off as you're working.

The keys to a great vent performance include a sound system with a great mic so every word is clearly understood. The lighting should be bright enough that the audience can see that your lips don't move. If people are asked to come onstage for an audience participation bit, be sure there's enough light so they can see where they're going and not trip and fall.

No ventriloquist likes to work "in the round," where audience members are behind you, but this sometimes will be the case. If so, make that part of the show and have your figure say something to the effect of, "Will you people back here quit staring at my back! I can feel your eyeballs as if they're boring into me, like someone's hand has reached right into my back and is controlling every move I make. Now stop it!"

Off the Cuff: Improvisation and Ad-Libbing

A ventriloquist who can ad-lib a few minutes with an audience is a comedy goldmine. *Improvisation* isn't an easily acquired skill, but it is something you'll get better at with time. But improvising requires that same thing you learned a couple chapters ago: stage time. The only way to become a good improvisation act is to improvise at least 3 to 5 minutes every show.

There are some absolutes when it comes to improv. Always take the positive. If you use words like *no, never,* or *I can't* in your improv bits, you'll bring the bit to a close. Negatives can be funny, but you can only do that once and then you have to move on. Saying "No" successfully ends a conversation. Instead, find a way to say, "Okay." It's really the first rule of improv: say "Yes."

def•i•ni•tion

Improvisation is when an actor or performer creates a joke or a performance spontaneously, without rehearsal or forethought. The premises and subject matter are often introduced or suggested by audience members.

Easy Improv

One great way to get good at improvising humor with audiences is to ask questions. "Where are you from?" That might lead to "Where is that?" or "I like that city. Do you live right in town or in the suburbs?" Small towns are always worth a couple laughs. After someone answers with a town you've never heard of, you can ask, "What's your town famous for?" That answer will often lead to more laughter and funnier answers.

Another good question is, "What do you do?" Your response, no matter what it is, should excite you (at least from the audience perspective) and bring about another question. Pretend you're a talk show host interviewing someone. After you've done this a few times on your own, start having your figure "interview" the crowd. It says, "I want to get to know these folks! What is your name, sir?" Of course, the figure's comebacks to the answers from the audience can be more tactless and inane than anything you would ever say.

Your figure can get away with a lot more, too, and even might be "looking for a job" as a comedy premise. Start with questions like "What is your name?" "Where are you from?" and "What do you do?" Work with these for a start, trying not to repeat punch lines and punch words for the answers you give with each performance.

Improvisation requires a solid understanding of topical and current events, so you can throw these in every so often as you're talking with folks.

You'll come up with some stock lines, or answers that always get a laugh, after you've done a few shows in which you improvise with the audience. Of course, if you're using stock lines for your answers every night, you're not really improvising. Try not to rely on the same old thing, but always push yourself to come up with something new each time you go onstage.

Improv Games

There are some fun improvisation games you can use in your act to break that *fourth wall*, bringing the audience right onstage with you.

def•i•ni•tion

The **fourth wall** is the audience. If the stage has three walls— stage right, stage left, and upstage—there's no downstage wall because that's where the audience is. *Breaking down the fourth wall* means talking to the audience from the stage during your performance.

One such game is "Expert." In this improvisation, you announce to the crowd that your figure is an expert in nuclear science, or baking donuts, or anything that comes to mind. You can also ask the audience what your figure's expert field is. They'll shout out a bunch of ideas, and you just pick the one you have the most experience with. For example, you tell the audience, "My figure here is a world-renowned expert and government liaison in the business of … Oh, shoot, what is your expertise in? I forget." The figure looks at you as if you're crazy and says, "Huh?" You look to the audience. "Does anyone know what the figure's profession is?" You take the one that sounds funniest when the crowd shouts out ideas and work from there.

Another quick and easy improv game is "Emotion." You tell the audience that your figure's been going through a rough time and has repressed a lot of feelings. You're hoping the audience can act as a therapist by calling out emotions for the figure to exhibit. So people begin shouting out emotions: "Fear!" "Hate!" "Love!" "Frustration!" "Compassion!" The figure then tries to display those emotions with body and head movements. Of course, there are many ways to end this routine.

You, the director of the show, could just say, "I've never seen such emotion exhibited by one person before! The depth of your character and your understanding of expression is incredible! Show me love!" The figure strikes a pose. You say, "Amazing! Show me hate!" The figure strikes the same exact pose. You try a couple more, but it's become evident the figure has one emotion, and it's playing you!

Here's one more improvisation game that can be a lot of fun with a figure. You tell the audience that your figure has had an unbelievable experience recently, the kind of story that gets made into major motion pictures. In fact, this story is in the works at this moment to become a blockbuster film that will be out in a few months. Would the audience like to hear the story? The audience, naturally, wants to hear everything. You get your figure out and ask it to tell the whole story to the crowd. The figure balks at first, saying things like, "Will they be able to follow along? Do they know anything about the story yet?" Finally the figure agrees, and the story begins.

The figure says, looking at you and then the audience and then at you and then the audience, back and forth: "Well, I was driving into town. This town. I was driving into ... oh, I can't remember the name of this town ... this town is called ... oh, shoot ...." Someone shouts out "You're in St. Louis!" or wherever you're performing. The figure continues. "Yes! Of course! I'm sorry. I was driving into town ... into St. Louis ... and I realized I was hungry. I was starving I was so hungry. So I decided to get something to eat. And everybody knows where to eat in St. Louis ... I went to that restaurant ... you know, the one everyone likes ... the world-famous restaurant here in St. Louis ...."

Eventually the audience catches on: it's just a joke, and the figure is just making up a story as it goes along. The audience comes up with more and more outlandish ideas for the figure, as envoy from its country, until there is a death or resolve to the story.

Practice Makes Perfect

The one way to get good at improvising is to do it every time you go onstage. You can use your figure to do all the improvising punch lines if you like, or you can do it yourself. If you're getting booked in city showcase clubs to do spots, that's a good chance to take a minute and talk to one person in the crowd. If you're emceeing, you can spend your first 10 minutes and parts of the rest of your sets all night talking to the audience and asking questions. You can get good at this if you put your mind to it.

Many beginners and newbies to ventriloquism and comedy think they can get up onstage and "wing it" and the comedy will come to them as if by magic. This is rarely if ever true. Improvisation is a skill and a craft similar to ventriloquism. It has to be rehearsed and practiced. As with the techniques you've learned in vent, it's best to start with one idea or a minute out of one performance and work on your improv skills. Then go back to your set routine.

Niche Your Act

You can be a good ventriloquist on a number of different levels. You might be a great singer, and therefore you're a singing ventriloquist. Maybe you're a religious act and you're perfect for churches. Maybe you're doing school shows and that's your market. Whatever it is, you will reach the point where just being good at what you do isn't good enough. You need to niche yourself in the market. You have to find what it is about your show and your act that makes you viable and worth a client spending money on you.

When an advertiser places a product in a niche, he or she is defining the product's features that are aimed at satisfying particular needs or wants that consumers have. That's exactly what you want to do with your career. Your niche—the difference between you and everyone else—is a combination of all the skills you bring to the entertainment table.

Marketing Yourself

There are basic rules of thumb with any marketing campaign or public relations blitz. First of all, if at first you don't succeed, think of another marketing idea and try again. Nothing is ever static in show business, no matter what level you reach.

The first thing you're going to need is the video discussed in Chapter 17. However you can get some video done—preferably in front of a hot, live audience—you need to do it. You need to upload it onto the web. You need a basic website or social networking page because that's how established fans, new fans, prospective buyers, and agents will see you.

Today, your web presence is your TV show. Your website is your business card. As a matter of fact, all your business card should have on it is your name, e-mail address, website, and a phone number (and the phone number is optional). Your website needs pictures of you, a bio, the video, and some short information about your act. A contact phone number and business mailing address are helpful as well.

You need pictures. Have a shot of yourself with your figure, or the main figures you use in your act, and one of you by yourself. The shots should be exemplary of what you look like onstage. If you wear T-shirts and jeans onstage, don't wear a suit and tie in the solo picture of yourself or with the figures. Wear what you wear in performance, so the bookers can see what they'll get.

Having a slogan—something to place on your letterheads, contracts, business cards, and website—will make your act viable and easier to pitch and sell. TOM THE COMEDY VENTRILOQUIST is okay. It spells out the act in clear terminology: Tom is a ventriloquist and does comedy. Great. Another way is to niche yourself as a comedian and ventriloquist. For example: TOM. COMEDY. VENTRILOQUISM. LAWN WORK, with a big red line through LAWN WORK. This example gives the prospective buyer a little insight into what he or she is getting when hiring Tom. He's a ventriloquist, and he doesn't take himself seriously—in fact, his promo is kind of funny.

You cannot take the niche process too far. The more you sell your act to prospective buyers, the better. The first and best way, of course, is to have an exciting punch line–driven act that gets great audience response every time. Next, you need some feedback from people you've worked for. Thank you letters from pleased clients work well. Pleased clients who agree to write a reference letter on your behalf work well, too.

Selling Your Persona

Niching your act is more than just letters, nice pictures, and a website. To niche your act today, you need a persona as a ventriloquist. Why do you do what you do? Why do the figures act the way they do? Theatrically speaking, every time you go onstage you're doing a one-man show, whether it's for some children in a church basement or at Carnegie Hall in New York City. You have to sell that persona and that image every time you work, wherever it is you're working, for those who are in the audience at the time. This affects everything you do, including the way you write your script.

When you've reached the point where you're doing 60- and 90-minute shows, you need to go through your script line by line, joke by joke, and see exactly what you're saying to audiences. What do they take away from the program when they leave the venue? Is it style over substance? Have you taught something? Have you shared something of yourself, other than showing off your skill as a professional vent? This is the true niche of the ventriloquist—what the audience takes away from an evening of figures, comedy, music, and laughter.

Final Thoughts

Your career as a ventriloquist is not a wind sprint. It's a marathon. You'll have peaks and valleys, high points and low. Some of your ideas and comedy will fail; some will fly and earn you better jobs with more pay and more exposure.

The way you position yourself as an entertainer, as a ventriloquist, and as an artist will ultimately be the way you're perceived and booked for shows. Everything you say, everything your figures represent is your niche.

There's no authority on ventriloquism. *You* decide what you want to say, what kind of act you want to do, and how you want to be perceived. That will niche you, whether you follow any of the guidelines in this chapter, or do things your own way and without any guidance. That's fine.

If you combine everything I discussed in this book with some really well-written comedy, however, you're going to work a lot and a niche will come naturally over time. That's not such a bad way to spend a career.

Good luck!

The Least You Need to Know

♦ Music and singing should be part of your show, whether or not you are a singer.

♦ Whatever you were doing before you decided to become a ventriloquist, whether it was a professional job or hanging on the corner by the pool hall, find a way to work it into your ventriloquism stage act.

♦ Take the time to set up your show for comedy, no matter where you are or what the stage is—or isn't.

♦ Improvisation is a great tool and will make you a better act.

♦ Always view yourself as a creative business person, and find ways to market, or niche, what you do to audiences.

Glossary

agent   An individual who schedules acts at venues for his or her client. Generally, an agent collects 10 to 25 percent of a client's gross pay. Also known as a *booking agent* or *booker*.

bits of business   Specific actions or reactions a ventriloquist and his or her figure make during a performance that help define their relationship to each other or elicit laughter from the audience.

close   Another word for *finish* or *finale*, as in, "You will close the show."

diaphragm   The wide, muscular partition that separates the chest cavity from the abdominal cavity. The diaphragm is key to breathing and breath control.

figure   The preferred term a ventriloquist uses to describe the puppet or dummy he or she works with onstage.

fricative   Consonant speech sound, specifically the F and V sound for ventriloquists, made by forcing sound (breath) through a small opening between the lips.

gig   A live performance, particularly in a club or casino.

inflection   The act of altering the pitch, tone, and quality of one's voice.

manipulation   Movements, actions, and bits of business a ventriloquist uses to bring life to his or her figure.

material   Jokes, songs, dialogue, and routines a ventriloquist uses in his or her performance.

personal manager   An individual who handles a client's day-to-day activities with an eye on expanding the client's career. The personal manager is involved in everything from bookings to movie deals to travel arrangements to performance material. Also known as a *manager*.

polyphony   A musical term referring to sounds that occur melodically at the same time. Applied to ventriloquism, this term refers to replacing, imitating, or mimicking sound.

punch line and **punch word**   The words that complete a joke, almost always coming at the end of a sentence, that signal the listener to laugh.

register   The human vocal folds (cords) are capable of creating different tones—high, middle, and low—depending on the breath released from the diaphragm. This range of tones is the register.

taglines   For the joke writer, after every joke is written, an additional two or three jokes are written as "tags" to the first joke. These extend the same premise and thought—and, hopefully, the laughs!

technique   The combination of lip control and figure manipulation that makes up a ventriloquist act.

theory of three   A joke-writing and joke-telling concept that works something like this: funny joke, then funnier joke, then funniest joke.

voiceless   Sounds made without actually using the voice. Two examples are *P* and *K*, which are created when air is forced through the mouth to create friction with the lips or tongue.

Resources

There are countless books and videos on the market that attempt to teach ventriloquism. In this appendix, I have included some resource information for the best companies and people I have worked with who are part of this business, and who offer products and materials for everyone from beginners to seasoned professionals. This is not a comprehensive list, and you will no doubt add to it the more you work.

Books

Bergen, Edgar. *How to Become a Ventriloquist*. Mineola, NY: Dover Publishing, 2000.

Vox, Valentine. *I Can See Your Lips Moving*. Las Vegas: Plato Publishing, 1993.

Wade, Mark. *Kidshow Ventriloquism*. New York: S&S Books, 1996.

Ventriloquist Supplies

Axtell Puppets
2889 Bunsen Ave. Suite H
Ventura, CA 93003
805-642-7282
www.axtell.com

Steve Axtell has one of the most complete collections of ventriloquist supplies in the country. Books, videos, stands, and an amazing array of latex ventriloquist figures make his site a must-have for every ventriloquist address book.

Comedy Writer

pseaburn@compuserve.com

www.humorhandyman.com

Paul Seaburn, comedy writer, has a list of clientele a mile long. He has written for Jay Leno, David Letterman, and Conan O'Brien, just to name a few. His published work includes *A Wife's Little Instruction Book* and *50 Uses for Your Dog*, and he was the head writer for the children's TV show *Taylor's Attic*.

Maher Ventriloquist Studios

PO Box 420

Littleton, CO 80160

www.maherstudios.blogspot.com

Excellent source and information on ventriloquism, run by Clinton Detweiler.

MAT Puppets

www.matpuppets.com

Mary Ann Taylor runs this excellent soft-figure-making company.

One Way Street

PO Box 2398

Littleton, CO 80161

www.onewaystreet.com

One Way Street carries books, supplies, videos, instruction, figures, puppets, and all sorts of ventriloquist props and equipment.

Vent Haven Museum

33 West Maple Avenue

Fort Mitchell, KY 41011

859-341-0461

venthaven@insightbb.com

www.angelfire.com/ky3/venthaven/index.html

The most comprehensive museum and the yearly host for the only worldwide ventriloquist convention, the Vent Haven Museum is a great resource for ventriloquists and ventriloquism. The ConVENTion is the ideal place to meet people, get information, and learn more about the craft of ventriloquism. The 3- to 4-day event takes place every summer and includes classes, sessions, conferences, and lectures on everything from building a custom figure to building a solid comedy routine. The dealers' room is filled with suppliers for all things ventriloquism, and is open every day during the event.

Index